Also by Diane Wei Liang

The Eye of Jade
Paper Butterfly

Lake

with

No Name

Diane Wei Liang

Simon & Schuster Paperbacks
New York London Toronto Sydney

Simon & Schuster Paperbacks
A Division of Simon & Schuster, Inc.
1230 Avenue of the Americas
New York, NY 10020

First Simon & Schuster trade paperback edition June 2009

SIMON & SCHUSTER PAPERBACKS and colophon are registered
trademarks of Simon & Schuster, Inc.

For information about special discounts for bulk purchases,
please contact Simon & Schuster Special Sales at
1-800-456-6798 or business@simonandschuster.com.

The Simon & Schuster Speakers Bureau can bring authors
to your live event. For more information or to book an event,
contact the Simon & Schuster Speakers Bureau at
1-866-248-3049 or visit our website at www.simonspeakers.com.

Designed by Nancy Singer

Manufactured in the United States of America

10 9 8 7 6 5 4 3 2 1

Library of Congress Cataloging-in-Publication Data
Liang, Diane Wei.
 Lake with no name: a true story of love and conflict in modern China
/ Diane Wei Liang.—1st Simon & Schuster trade pbk. ed.
     p. cm—(Simon & Schuster non-fiction reprint trade)
  "Originally published in Great Britain in 2003 by Headline Book
Publishing"—T.p. verso.
 1. Liang, Diane Wei. China—History—Tiananmen Square Incident, 1989—
Biography. 3. College students—China—Beiing—Biography. 4. Couples—
China—Beijing—Biography. 5. Man-woman relationships—China—Beijing. 6.
Beijing (China)—Biography. I. Title
  DS779.32.L52 2009
  951.05'8—dc22   2009004371

ISBN: 978-1-4391-3686-7

For my mother

Contents

Author's Note

My mother found the name "Wei" in an old Chinese dictionary. It is a long-forgotten character meaning "sunshine."

In Chinese names, the surname comes first. Women do not take their husband's surname but keep their own. A prefix "Xiao" meaning "little" is often used for children, people in their twenties and thirties or someone younger than you. A prefix "Lao" meaning "old" is often used for people older than forty or to show respect. "X" is pronounced "sh", "Q" is "ch" and "Zh" is "ge" (a soft, not a hard "g").

The names of public figures including student leaders as well as those of my family, are real, spelled in the way of Chinese Pinyin as used in China. Other names are disguised.

All the characters in this book are based on real-life individuals. Details of their stories have been changed to protect them. Some of the conversations in the book are, of necessity, imaginary or reimagined; but they accurately reflect the mood of the times, the things we discussed, the way we felt and my memory of the events described. Other conversations are based on published reports.

Wherever possible, I have checked my recollections of the events in 1989 against published documents. Particularly valuable were two publications, which compiled collections of newspaper reports, television and radio broadcasts, speeches, minutes of meetings, press releases, transcripts of news conferences and internal Party communiqués: *Beijing Spring, 1989: Confrontation and Conflict*, M. Oskenberg, L.R. Sullivan and M. Lambert (eds.), M. E. Sharpe, Inc. (Armonk, New York, 1990); and *The Tienanmen Papers*, Zhang Liang, A. J. Nathan and P. Link (eds.), Little, Brown and Company (London, 2001).

Introduction

$\mathcal{T}$he party was in full swing when I left at 2:30 A.M. on the morning of 5 November 2008. I emerged from the crowded basement of entangled elbows and thighs, wine glasses and iPhones crackling with data-feed. The night was cool. I drove home, not entirely certain that I was sober, but aware of the moment and London unfolding in front of me like a dark blossom. I would have stayed, had my babysitter not needed to go home, and celebrated with friends when Barack Obama was elected the president of the United States.

The concept of "voting" was one I came to know at university. Nineteen years ago, in Beijing, I marched with my contemporaries wanting democracy for our country. At the time we thought we understood. In hindsight, it was a vague knowledge that we had acquired from books—we didn't know its true weight and shape. It was out of admiration for this blurred but desperately beautiful idea that we demonstrated and went on hunger strike. On certain days there were a million people protesting in Tiananmen Square. In the morning of 4 June 1989, the People's Liberation Army came with tanks and crushed the movement.

It was with the concerns of its aftermath and the friends that I had lost I began to think about writing a book. *Lake with No Name* was conceived in the summer of 2001 on a boat in Lake Lucent, my newborn baby next to me sleeping in a carrying cot. I was principally interested in the impact of history on the consequence of choices we made—i.e., to love or walk away, to go to the streets or stay home—choices that at a certain point in history became life changing.

Lake with No Name was written in eight months and published in the UK in 2003. After I finished the book, at the end of my nine-month maternity leave, I returned to my teaching post at the University of London. It took two years for me to realize that I missed writing. The Mei Wang Mysteries followed, which became a reasonable success and allowed me to write full time.

I had travelled to a number of countries to promote my novels. Whether I was in Sydney, Madrid or Seattle, people quizzed me about the Tiananmen events. The interest was such that Simon & Schuster decided to bring out this new edition of my first book. 2009 is the twentieth anniversary of the Tiananmen crackdown. This edition of *Lake with No Name* commemorates it.

China has changed a great deal since 1989. Rapid economic growth has elevated her into an emerging power, affirmed by the Beijing Olympic Games. China has become, in some ways more than what we had hoped for nineteen years ago, a modern and prosperous society.

Inevitably questions might be raised as to whether the deaths had been worthwhile. I suppose the same might be asked of any loss of human life in pursuit of an ideal—what would have been the correct price?

My mother came to London at the time of my daughter's birth and stayed for three months. Her presence helped to shape this book. After she left, I spoke to her about it on the phone, not least because she was a professor of Chinese literature. I was not surprised that she was against the project. She feared that the subject matter might prove unsafe. When I decided to act against her wish, she begged me to be careful of what I might write.

I made the decision to be truthful in my writing. But I was extremely aware that the book could put my family and friends in danger. This is the reason that readers will not find photographs among the texts. I took pains to disguise the identities of friends with whom I had shared Tiananmen Square, and for whom the book was written.

After *Lake with No Name* was published, my sister came to London for a short visit. I gave her a copy to bring back to my mother. In a lopsided way her not being able to read English came as a comfort to me—I didn't want my mother to worry. She had suffered immensely throughout her life—having had her job taken away in the Cultural Revolution and sent to labor camp, and at the end of her career to be made redundant because of her support for the students during the 1989 protests.

My mother was due to visit London at the end of 2004. A week before her scheduled departure she was diagnosed with lung cancer. She underwent chemotherapy. Three months later I brought my children to China for the first time. When we arrived in Beijing my mother was dying in the hospital. I was not prepared for the voracity of the disease or her decline. She died within days. Her last words to me were that she thought my daughter, whom she had only seen as a baby, was beautiful. But her heart remained with my son, whom she had looked after for the first year of his life, who stood by her deathbed a young boy.

I had wanted to dedicate *Lake with No Name* to my mother when it was first published but decided against it out of concern for her safety. Now with her having passed away, I am finally able to do so with this new edition.

Many people who inhabit *Lake with No Name* remain in my life. The memory of our youth and of that fateful night binds us, though the bond is being weakened by time and distance.

China changes every time I see her. More and more of her past are being erased to make space for the future. Lying at the southern tip of the Forbidden City, Tiananmen Square remains unchanged—a symbol of ancient wisdom.

My mother's ashes are stored in a locker in Babaoshan Revolutionary Cemetery. According to her ranking in the Communist Party, they could stay there for five years. Afterward we will have to find a place for her remains.

November 2008

Love you faithfully

Despite years passing

Youth aging

Love you

Deep in my heart

Forest flowers faded color

Too quickly

Life—always a river rushing east

Hope we will meet again

Same kind of day

Same kind of time

And the same kind of you

Sunshine and spring

Perhaps also the same kind of me—

Maybe

DIANE WEI LIANG

Beijing, 1989

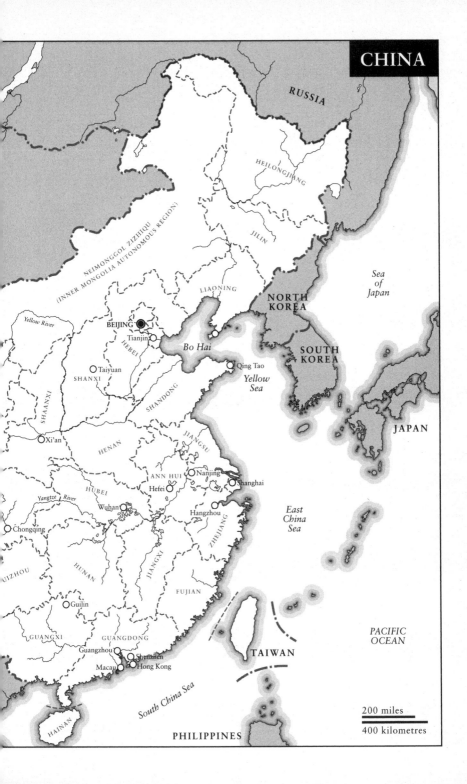

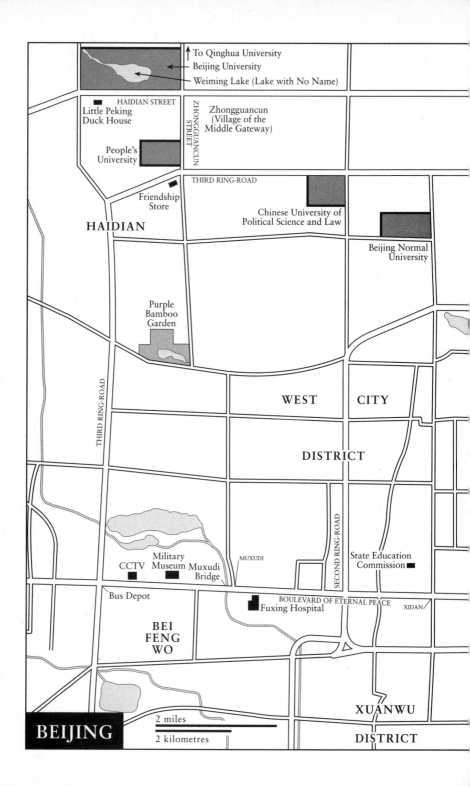

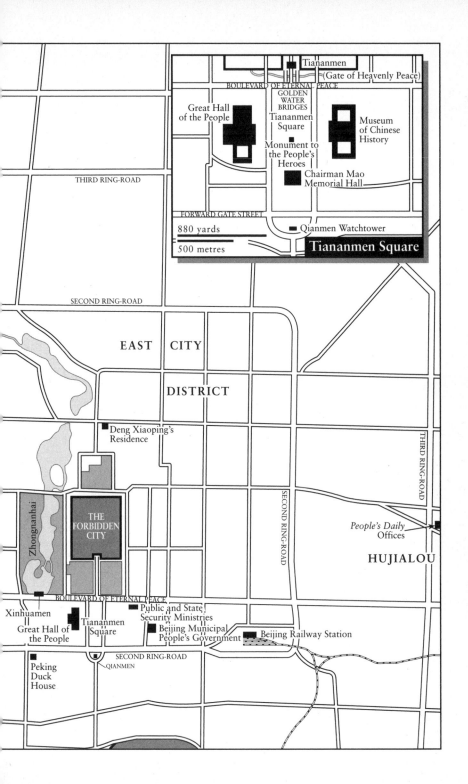

Tiananmen
(Gate of Heavenly Peace)
BOULEVARD OF ETERNAL PEACE
GOLDEN
WATER
BRIDGES
Great Hall
of the People
Tiananmen
Square
Museum
of Chinese
History
Monument to
the People's
Heroes
Chairman Mao
Memorial Hall
FORWARD GATE STREET
880 yards
500 metres
Qianmen Watchtower
Tiananmen Square

THIRD RING-ROAD

SECOND RING-ROAD

EAST   CITY

DISTRICT

Deng Xiaoping's
Residence

THIRD RING-ROAD

Zhongnanhai

THE
FORBIDDEN
CITY

SECOND RING-ROAD

People's Daily
Offices

HUJIALOU

Xinhuamen
BOULEVARD OF ETERNAL PEACE
Public and State
Security Ministries
Great Hall of
the People
Tiananmen
Square
Beijing Municipal
People's Government
Beijing Railway Station

Peking
Duck
House
SECOND RING-ROAD
QIANMEN

Lake

with

No Name

The Square, 1996

*I*t had taken me seven years to come home.

"Take a shower," my mother said to me. "You are sweating."

It was hot. In some places, the sun was softening the asphalt on the roads. But I was wrapped in my spring clothing; when I left Minneapolis, snow had just melted under the apple tree in the backyard. Beijing was suffering under a heat wave in the middle of May.

My mother, a thin woman barely five feet tall, buzzed around the small apartment like a tiny, joyful bee. Within seconds, she came to me with a bamboo fan. I drew the curtain, a piece of floral cloth on a wire, and took off my clothes. I wrapped a large towel around me and walked to the bathroom. The bathroom was too small to fit a shower curtain. An industrial size drain lay beneath my feet. When I stood on it, I stared down into the dark hole of the water pipe.

"Just remember, when you're done, you need to knock on the door so that I can turn off the water heater. Don't turn off the water until the heater is shut, otherwise it could overheat and explode."

When I heard my father shouting from the kitchen, "Heater is on!" I dropped the towel and turned on the shower. Warm water poured down.

I changed into a yellow linen dress and walked around my room. The concrete floor was cool, even on such a hot day. There was a single bed with floral bedding, and a plain wooden wardrobe against the wall. A thick layer of dust covered the desk. With a slight wave of my hand, the trace of my fingers showed the true color of the bare wood. I looked out of the window and saw people in the next building, a man in his underwear, two women cooking over their stoves. After years in America, the apartment seemed to me absurdly small, barely big enough for two people. Yet years before all four of us—my parents, my sister, Xiao Jie, and I—had lived in an apartment smaller than this one.

After I left China, my parents moved into this larger apartment fitted with a shower, allocated by the university when my mother was promoted to associate professor. No more twice-weekly trips to the public bathhouse. They had also acquired a microwave, a washing machine with a tumble dryer and a cable TV. My father had retired from his position as the head of personnel at the Beijing Bureau of Parks and Forests. Because most state enterprises were not making money, unemployment was very high. The government had thus lowered the retirement age to sixty for all state employees including civil servants, of which my father was one. My mother, who was three years younger, was thinking of retiring from her position as Professor in Journalism at her university.

After lunch, my parents stayed home for their afternoon nap. My younger sister, Xiao Jie, and I took a taxi to the city center. The taxi seemed to take me to places I'd never been, then I was told the names and realized that I had failed to recognize what used to be familiar areas. Freeways had replaced old buildings and markets. New high-rises dwarfed landmarks that used to be large and significant. Streets seemed to have moved blocks. Old-style courtyards gave way to elevated highways that offered me new angles on the city. Countless life-size statues of Mao Zedong had disappeared. In their place were gardens, boutiques and supermarkets.

At street crossings, our taxi slowed and I had a glimpse of the China I used to know. Travelers, now in cars rather than on bicycles, paid no attention to the traffic lights, despite blaring horns and people bellowing from open windows. No one was willing to give in. Drivers cursed each other at close range when their cars scraped by each other. Yellow dust, blown in from the Mongolian Desert to the west, clouded over everything. Cyclists escaped from tiny gaps wreathed in triumphant smiles. Traffic lights turned from red to green and back again like Christmas lights.

My sister and I shopped at Le Lafayette in Wangfujing, the main shopping district of Beijing and had coffee at the American Donut Shop.

On street corners, rickshaw drivers were trying to lure passersby.

"Little sisters, it is too hot to walk with your shopping bags. Where do you want to go? Let me take you there. It is cool in the rickshaw."

He had a point. The heat had turned from hot to unbearable.

"How much would it be to Tiananmen Square?" I asked him.

"For one hundred yuan I will drive you around the Square."

Naturally we haggled. A minute later, we gave the driver eighty yuan and got into his rickshaw.

"Why do you girls want to go to Tiananmen? There is nothing to see now. But go there in the evening. A lot of people go to see the ceremony of flag lowering."

We left the narrow and crowded side streets and turned onto the wide, leafy Boulevard of Eternal Peace.

Tiananmen Square slowly opened up in front of our eyes, like an old book of fairy tales. To the north, the magnificent Tiananmen—the Gate of Heavenly Peace—towered over the Square in glorious red and gold. It was at this Gate, forty-seven years before, that Mao Zedong had proclaimed the founding of the People's Republic. Now his portrait gazed south into the Square of Heavenly Peace. On either side of the portrait hung a large billboard that read, "Long Live the People's Republic" and "People of the World Unite." During the 1950s, Mao had had the Square enlarged to forty-nine hectares, three times its original size, so that people could gather in their millions for rallies. Since then, Red Guards had paraded in the Square, the public mourning of premier Zhou Enlai took place here and, of course, so did the mass demonstrations of the Student Democracy Movement of 1989.

Our rickshaw driver pedaled furiously; from time to time he wiped his face with a towel. Traffic was heavy but floated patiently around the Square. Large oak leaves bending over from their branches gave us shade.

Sitting in the rickshaw, I was so overwhelmed that I did not say anything all the way around the Square, which looked serene under the quiet afternoon sun. There must have been many thousands of people there; but to me Tiananmen Square looked empty. This was not what I had remembered—Tiananmen was a battlefield in the summer seven years before, crowded with people, the young people of China wearing their blood on their sleeves, hairbands and in their eyes. Flags leaped in the wind. Where have they all gone, those eighteen-year-old boys and girls, where are they now?

My sister and I got off the rickshaw in front of Tiananmen. The Golden Water Bridges were crowded with people, either entering the Square or crossing over to the Forbidden City. Armed policemen stood on the bridges, stone faced.

I had not set foot on this sacred ground since the last night I came as a student guard on 2 June 1989. Every step I took brought back memories and long-forgotten emotions of comradeship, tension and fear. I walked farther inside, climbing the monument to the People's Heroes, the obelisk at the center of the Square. To its south, long lines were waiting to enter the Mao Mausoleum. I was told that the line outside the mausoleum had become longer in recent years; not just veterans of the communist revolution but also young people wanted to file respectfully past the yellowing, embalmed body in its glass coffin. People came to seek comfort from the past, the time of certainty and order. Vendors zigzagged through those lines, hawking Mao badges illegally from their shoulder bags, while watching carefully for police patrols. During the Cultural Revolution, everyone in China had been required to wear these badges to show their loyalty and devotion to Chairman Mao and the Chinese Communist Party. I remembered wearing Mao badges and walking especially proudly with my parents during public celebrations of National Days and International Labor Days. Back then Mao badges were also used as rewards or holiday presents by people's work units. Today, these outdated badges were popular tourist souvenirs of a bygone era; some had even become collectors' items.

Around the base of the Monument were stone carvings of scenes from Chinese history—the Boxer Uprising, the Opium War, the Anti-Japanese Invasion and the Civil War. The Monument was built in 1958 to symbolize the resistance of ordinary people to feudal powers and foreign colonialism. In 1989 the students of Beijing found it particularly fitting to set up their command center here. The power of ordinary people was, as Mao used to say, "the force behind history." Walking around the monument, I could not help but think also of the heavy cost and suffering the ordinary Chinese have endured throughout our turbulent history.

I had finally returned to the place where my friends and comrades had marched, sung, fought and died. On this ground below me, thousands of hunger strikers had refused food for days. They could feel the life of twenty years slowly leaving them. Happiness was on their minds—happiness for the ordinary people, their children growing up. They had to close their eyes. They had no strength to look at the sky or clouds anymore.

I could see Chai Ling, rebellious even when we roomed together while studying psychology at Beijing University, soft spoken, acerbic and determined. She grew fragile, thin and exhausted by the self-imposed starvation, yet she still rose to the challenge she had given herself, to organize the vast body of discontent, to turn a million discordant voices into a single cry for freedom.

I saw Dong Yi, among the thousands of students who had come to care for the hunger strikers, kneeling over, a bottle of water poised to offer to the injured, his face filled with sorrow. Suddenly he shouted, "Quickly, another one's passed out. Stretcher!" His voice echoed across the Square, like rolling thunder. Medical students in white coats dashed over. Ambulance sirens screeched, tearing open the sky.

It was the best time. And it was a terrible time. We were young and full of hope; we were passionate about our cause. We were ready to pay the dearest price for a more democratic and free China, because we never doubted that we would win and that our sacrifice would be worthwhile.

But how our faith was crushed! One night, tanks rolled down the Boulevard of Eternal Peace, troops opened fire at unarmed students and citizens and blood flowed. Overnight, I lost the innocence of my youth—and the love of my life.

The images of my last days in China came back, each one clearer than the last. I felt that I was going to crumple under the pounding waves of emotion, each stronger than the one before.

Standing on the base of the monument, I could clearly see the Square, occupied only by strolling tourists, snapping photos. I had returned, but so had my turbulent memories, and there seemed to be no place for them in the peaceful scene I saw in front of me.

One

Labor Camp

Plum blossom enjoys roaring snow; it should not be
surprised to find a few flies frozen to death.

—*Mao Zedong, 1962*

In my memory, my childhood landscape is one of paddy
fields and green mountains stretching to the end of the
sky, beyond clouds; air filled with the sweet scent of
wildflowers, rivers meandering below, teeming with life and bamboo
rafts punted by strong Miao boys sliding in and out of sight on the
winding waterway. When night fell and the moon was high, love
songs echoed across the river.

But my childhood was not supposed to have looked like this. All my
friends, the children of my mother's colleagues, grew up on a labor camp
on the east coast of China. I used to ask my parents, "Why did we go to
Sichuan instead of Shandong?" Eventually, one day, they told me.

"Because that was where your father went and we decided that the
family should stay together," said my mother.

"But why couldn't Baba come with you to your labor camp? My
friends told me that they did not starve there and that you could do a
lot of fishing too."

My mother sighed. When my parents had met, my father was a
People's Liberation Army officer stationed in Beijing and my mother
a college student. In those days, people had to live where their resi-

dence permit, or *Hukou,* was registered. Then my father retired from
the army and was sent back to his hometown, Shanghai. My mother
felt lucky to be allowed to stay in Beijing. Once they were married, my
father was permitted to visit her in Beijing twice a year, and she was
able to visit Shanghai twice a year as well. They tried very hard to gain
permission to move my mother's *Hukou* to Shanghai, but it turned out
to be more difficult than they thought. Then events overtook them.

I was born in 1966, the year of the Cultural Revolution. My parents were caught up in the chaos that swept through the country: factories stopped production; homes of Party officials and intellectuals
were searched and destroyed; *pidouhui,* or public beatings, were con-
ducted daily across the country. Middle school and high school students, now called the send-down youth, were transported to People's
Collectives around the country to live and work with peasants. Then,
in 1970, intellectuals (a term reserved for those, like my parents, who
had been educated at college) began to be sent to labor camps to work
"with their hands" and so to rehabilitate themselves and fulfill Mao's
vision of a peasant-based society.

My mother's work unit, which was connected to the Department
of Foreign Affairs, had set up their labor camp in a rather lovely part
of the countryside in Shandong province, near the Yellow Sea. My
father's labor camp was very different. It was in a remote mountain
region in the southwest, looked down upon because it was populated
with the Miao minority and had no modern living facilities. There the
intellectuals were assigned hard labor, building secret military facilities
against a nuclear attack from the West.

"Your mother and I had a choice," my father told me. "Either
we could go to separate labor camps or your mother could exchange
her place in the 'better' camp with someone from my work unit. Your
mother chose to go to Sichuan with me." At this, he looked at her and
smiled. They exchanged glances as naturally and effortlessly as they
had exchanged their lives. It seemed that it was the simplest thing that
one could do—to be together as a family.

So the earliest memories of my childhood began in one of the
most beautiful and magical regions of China. The labor camp was in
the deep mountains of Nanchuan County, a region bordering Sichuan
province and Yunnan province in the southwest of China. The mountains were giant, green and endless. When the rainy season came,

shades of green would all smudge together into yet another nameless shade and spill over the edges, like paints dissolving on a canvas.

The Miao—a mountain tribe who settled in China's southwest in the ninth century—are a people of song, dance and crafts. Miao women wear long dresses over wide, flowing trousers. Hand-embroidered trims of flowers, birds and beautiful shapes in bright colors breathe life into their costumes, and many of them wear matching headpieces. In the morning, returning from the market, usually in small groups, carrying their goods in baskets on top of their heads, they'd travel up the mountain trails singing. I'd hear their songs long before I'd catch sight of them.

When night fell and the moon was high, young men and women would gather on hilltops on either side of the river, declaring their love and admiration for each other. Singing is the way of courting for Miao people; it was said that the way to a Miao girl's heart was through song. With love songs echoing over the mountains, it seemed to me that life would always be full of romantic tunes.

Unfortunately for my parents life in the labor camp was nothing to romanticize about. The living quarters had been built up on the top of a mountain while the building site was down in the valley. Every morning, my parents would get up early to drop me off at the kindergarten and then walk down the mountain trail to work. The intellectuals either transported bricks from storage sites to the building site or simply laid bricks, day in and day out. The construction site was guarded by the People's Liberation Army (PLA) and workers were supervised by army engineers.

After working on the construction site for most of the day, my parents had to attend group study sessions, during which they read and discussed editorials from the *People's Daily* or passages from Mao's little red book. Like everyone else in these reeducation sessions, my parents had to do self-criticism and pledge their loyalty to the Party and Chairman Mao. Any hesitation or questioning about what they had to read meant severe punishments such as public beatings and prison terms.

As innocent children, my friends and I had no idea of the political oppression that our parents lived under. While our parents labored away on the building site in the valley, we attended kindergarten. My favorite teacher was Mrs. Cai, a soft-spoken, kind lady in her fifties.

One day she told us about her homeland, the beautiful island in the South China Sea called Taiwan, and taught us a folk song that her mother used to sing to her when she was our age. I loved the song and could not wait to sing it for my parents that evening. But I was disappointed. My parents were not overjoyed, as they usually were when I showed them something new I had learned from kindergarten.

"Who taught you this?" Mama asked. She immediately said to me, "Don't sing it again. You don't know who might be listening."

I could not understand why my parents were so afraid of my singing the new song. After all, Mrs. Cai had also taught us many revolutionary songs. The next evening, a few parents came to our apartment, all with the same worries. "We are their parents, what they sing or talk about reflects on us," said one of them. "We simply have to do something about it before they cause trouble."

"Life is tough enough without their singing counterrevolutionary songs and talking about Taiwan," joined in another.

Thus the parents decided to report Mrs. Cai to the authorities. A couple of days later, our teacher vanished. No one, including the parents, knew what happened to her. Many years later, my parents still talked about Mrs. Cai and felt guilty for what might have happened to her. But back then they believed that they had no other choice. They needed to protect their family. Such was the extent of fear in the labor camp, as elsewhere in China during that time.

Life in the camp was difficult. Because the living quarters were high up in the mountains, water had to be carried from the river below. It was then poured straight into a large tank in the open air for every family to use. Many people became sick after drinking the water. Food was shared out weekly, allocated by my father's work unit. Meat was scarce: although each family was supposed to have two kilograms of meat a month, some months we only received half that. We had a small coal-burning stove outside the door. Every evening, as soon as my parents came back from the building site, tired, sweaty and thirsty, my mother cooked dinner with the little we were given. At dinnertime, the stairway was always filled with the smell of cooking oil and smoke from the small stoves, while wives and mothers chatted loudly up and down the stairs.

For my parents, the possibility of living together in Shanghai after the camp gave them strength to endure the hardship. Certain promises were given to my mother before she came to the camp that if she could show the Party her willingness to "swallow bitterness and endure hard work," she might be able to gain the necessary approval and be allowed to move to Shanghai. Coming to the camp, however, had been particularly hard for my mother. A few months earlier, on 3 September 1969, my little sister, Xiao Jie, was born. Guessing the probable conditions at the camp, my parents decided that it would be better to leave my sister in Shanghai with my paralyzed grandmother and a nanny.

The situation was made worse for my mother by the fact that she was not allowed to go to Shanghai to see her child. There were two reasons. First, my sister's *Hukou* was not in Shanghai although she was born there. Her *Hukou* had to be with my mother's, which was in Beijing. Second, because my father had now "moved away" from Shanghai, mother had no official connection with the city any longer.

Mother missed Xiao Jie terribly. In the night, after a long day's hard work moving and laying bricks, Mother would lie on the bed, talking to my father of her second daughter, counting the months since her birth, wondering whether she had cut new teeth and imagining how she might look now. As the rain beat down on summer leaves outside, she would weep while remembering the day she last saw her newborn child.

A few months after my parents and I arrived at the labor camp, my father made his first trip to Shanghai to visit his mother and more important to check on my sister. He took a long-distance bus for two days to Chongqing, a city at the other end of Sichuan province and a port on the Yangtze River. There, he caught a messenger boat going down the majestic Yangtze to Shanghai. The boat journey took another four days. When he came back, he brought with him the most beautiful things I had ever seen: candies in colorful wrapping paper, and cookies with a heavenly smell.

"Listen now, Wei, these candies and cookies need to last for a long time . . . until the next time I go to Shanghai. Every week you will get your share, but no more." Baba put the candies and cookies in two aluminium tins and locked them up in the cabinet beneath the desk drawer.

For the next weeks, my biggest joy was to receive candies and cookies from my parents, until one day when I made an amazing discovery. I found that if I took out the drawer on top of the locked cabinet, I could reach down for the tins. I ate as much and as quickly as I could. My parents finally discovered what I'd been up to when they found the tins empty. I still remember the way my mother and father looked at me, sighing. I realized then that I'd made them sad, because they were not able to give me more for many months to come.

When winter came again, Baba made another trip to Shanghai. My parents and I walked down the mountain trail, on a clear and fresh morning, to send Baba to the bus stop. Like local Miao children, I carried my tiny backpack-style basket on my shoulders. I had saved up four tangerines, allocated by the work unit, for my father to take on his journey. My heart was filled with expectation and anticipation of what he might bring back this time.

One day, what felt like months after Baba had left for Shanghai, I returned home from kindergarten to find the rooms we lived in crowded with people. There were loud voices and laughter. I walked into the crowd rather curious and was happy to see my father standing in the center of the room. It turned out that he had just come back from Shanghai.

"Come over, Wei," a loud and large neighbor said, almost in my face. "Come and see your little sister."

Although I knew I had a sister, I searched hard through my memory but could not remember anything about her. Only later on in the evening, after much prompting from my parents, did I vaguely remember leaning out of a window and seeing my mother come home with a new baby.

But there was my father in the center of the room, holding up a rather skinny little creature with short hair growing in every direction. It seemed that she had just woken up from her sleep. She looked dazed for a while and then turned to the loud neighbor and said, "Ma-Ma."

"No, *this* is your Mama." The woman was embarrassed and pulled my mother forward from the crowd.

Everyone in the room laughed out loud.

Though we had more glass-papered candies as promised, I was disappointed. Suddenly everyone's attention was on Xiao Jie, my little sister. My parents did not even spend time to tell me how my candies should be regulated. Baba, however, did bring yet another novelty—egg noodles. The noodles looked so beautiful compared with the black mixed-grain noodles I was used to, and had a wonderful smell as well.

Unfortunately they were only for my sister as she was still too young and needed the extra nutrition they provided. But my resentment of my little sister did not last long. Soon enough, Xiao Jie started walking steadily and I could not wait to play the big sister.

Spring was the most beautiful season in Nanchuan, as endless azaleas blossomed from mountain to mountain. For many weeks, the green mountains would be completely covered with a red carpet, thick and heavy. It was through the fields of azaleas that I learned to love my little sister. Childhood for me will live forever in the touch of Xiao Jie's tiny hands, the sound of my parents' laughter and the sweet scent of azaleas.

The climate of southwestern China is extremely humid. To cope with the humidity, the locals rely on a very spicy diet—the famous Sichuan cuisine—to help stimulate internal circulation and sweat. Summer in Sichuan is usually very hot, so hot that the people in the labor camp could only work in the mornings. In the late afternoons, when the effect of what the locals called the "poisonous sun" died down to a more tolerable degree, Mama and Baba would take us swimming.

The river running at the bottom of our mountain was our salvation in the summer. The part of the river we always went to was not terribly wide, though the current in the middle could be strong at times. There were huge rocks scattered in the water, making swimming a dangerous adventure if one was not careful; so our parents never allowed us to go too far into the river. Xiao Jie and I, not able to swim much anyway, usually had a wonderful time playing on the shallow riverbanks. Occasionally I would search for wildflowers in the mountains surrounding us. Sometimes brave boys would dive from the giant rock in the middle of the river into the white current, emerging triumphantly somewhere downstream, and I would clap my hands with delight. To me, the river was cool, clear and beautiful; every now and then, I also wondered what was upriver from us.

"I don't really know, Wei," said Mother. "I suppose some cities or villages."

Unfortunately, we soon discovered what was up there. In September 1971, the regular rainy season came early, as soon as summer ended. It poured for many days and many nights. Together with the rain came a hepatitis epidemic. Many in the labor camp believed that it was caused by a chemical factory upriver dumping chemical waste into what was also the source of our drinking water. Though the authorities never confirmed this theory, the factory was closed down a couple of years later.

We had a small clinic in the labor camp and one doctor. The nearest hospital was "many mountains away." Families were first asked to treat the sick at home. Soon, the spread of the disease became too alarming to leave the isolation and medical care of infected individuals to their families. A sick camp consisting of several large military tents was set up by the army engineers.

Xiao Jie was the first in my family to fall ill. One evening she started to run a very high fever and exhibit symptoms of the disease. Immediately, my parents realized the danger; Xiao Jie was only two years old at the time. Mama put on her raincoat and ran out to find the doctor. Baba stayed with Xiao Jie and nursed her fever by putting a hot towel on her forehead. But she showed no sign of improving. She was crying and turning in pain.

"Wei, go back to your room and don't come out here again," Baba yelled at me loudly. "Do you want to catch the disease too? Go back right now!"

I went back to the room that I shared with Xiao Jie but left the door open slightly so that I could hear and watch what was happening in my parents' room.

Mama came back some time later, soaked from the rain.

"What did the doctor say?" Baba asked.

Mama cuddled Xiao Jie tightly in her arms. My sister had started to lose her voice from constant crying. Tears streamed down my mother's face.

"The only doctor is on duty at the sick camp. He does not have time to come to see Xiao Jie, nor does his assistant. They are swamped by the number of patients in the camp."

"What about medicine? Is there anything we can give to Xiao Jie to get the fever down?"

"They have penicillin, but only for patients at the camp. The disease has spread out into the whole region and medicine is running out. The camp can take Xiao Jie tomorrow morning but not tonight. The barefoot doctors from nearby villages have gone home to rest."

The barefoot doctors were peasants who had been given some

basic medical training so that they could take care of health problems in remote regions and villages.

I don't think that any of us slept much that night. My parents could do nothing but put hot towels on Xiao Jie's forehead in the hope that the fever would ease through sweat. As the night went on, Xiao Jie became silent. She had completely lost her voice and her face was burning red. Mama and Baba spent the whole night holding her in turn. In the morning, when my mother took Xiao Jie to the sick camp, her eyes were bloodshot from her own tears.

For the next couple of days, Mama did not sleep much. Because Xiao Jie was seriously ill, the doctor put her in the isolation unit and would not allow anyone to visit. Mama stayed up almost every night, walking the floor in the apartment, wondering about the condition of my sister, hoping and praying. She was also prepared to go to the sick camp at a moment's notice if the worst should happen to my sister, and be at her bedside as soon as possible. My father stayed up with her during those nights, comforting her whenever she burst into tears. On those nights, I lay on my bed listening to the endless rain beating on the window; staring into the dark I hoped that I would see my sister soon.

On the third day of my sister's admission to the sick camp, my parents were given the good news that Xiao Jie had come out of the critical period of the illness and my parents could now visit her at the camp. After they came back, they were deliriously happy and could not stop talking about how well she looked.

"When can I see her?" I asked them as soon as they came in from the rain.

"We don't know. It could be a while. The doctor said that she had to stay in the isolation unit for some time before she could be allowed to mix with others."

"Can I go with you to visit her?"

"No," Mother said sternly, "we don't want you to get sick."

That evening, despite my parents' attempts to keep it from me, I also came down with hepatitis. Maybe because I was older than Xiao Jie, or maybe because living in the mountains had made me stronger, I was not nearly as sick as she was. Though I had to be admitted into the sick camp, I did not need to go to the isolation unit. When I arrived at the children's unit with Mama, I found all my friends from the kindergarten were there. Many of them looked yellow and swollen.

By the end of the month, most people at the labor camp had the disease and had to move to the sick camp. Lack of doctors, nurses and medicine had seriously delayed the recovery of many patients. Most of the time, the doctors could only focus on reducing casualties. It was said that the epidemic had swept through the entire province that year and that the central government had organized the delivery of emergency medicines to aid the fight of hepatitis. Unfortunately, since Nanchuan was very remote from the major cities in the province, medicines took time to reach us.

By the second month, all the women who had not yet contracted hepatitis were needed to nurse the sick. My mother volunteered, partly to be close to her family as, by then, my father had also come down with the disease. The sick camp lasted for almost three months. Eventually the medicine arrived and most of us recovered. When I was discharged from the sick camp, I actually felt sad. All play and no school ended. Life went back to normal, except that now kindergarten felt boring.

At the end of 1971, the news of Lin Biao's death reached the labor camp. Lin Biao was the defense minister and the vice president of China. He was also Mao's right-hand man and chosen successor. My earliest childhood memories included a vision of Vice President Lin waving the little red book. I was told that no one loved Chairman Mao more than Vice President Lin.

The official version was that Lin Biao had been plotting to assassinate Mao. When this attempt failed, he tried to flee to the USSR and died when his plane, also carrying his son, crashed in Mongolia. The death of Lin Biao came as a surprise to many, including my parents. I remember neighbors and friends coming to our home after receiving the news.

"Who would have thought that Lin Biao would plot to overthrow Chairman Mao?" said our loud and large neighbor. "I actually believed that he was Mao's most loyal follower."

"See, this is why his deception was very good and why Chairman Mao was wise to be alert. Chairman Mao always said that 'we need to be aware of those who have honey in their mouths and a knife in their hands,'" said another. "Lin Biao was the most dangerous kind. He managed to deceive the entire country with his 'never let the [Mao's] little red book leave hands,' nor 'long live Chairman Mao' leave lips.'"

As we learned after Mao's death many years later, the Lin Biao crisis created a vacuum in Mao's power system. In those years he had come to rely a great deal on Lin and his friends. With Lin's death, and almost all the marshals denounced for speaking out against the Cultural Revolution, Mao was faced with the prospect of losing control of the most powerful force in Chinese politics: the military. Mao had to compromise by bringing back those disgraced officials who still had a lot of influence in the army. Deng Xiaoping would "come out of the mountains" not long after.

When the spring came to Nanchuan, our lives changed again. The secret military facility was finally complete—only to find that there was no use for it. By then, the effect of the Cultural Revolution had taken a huge toll on the country's economy. Living standards for the Chinese people had dropped even further. Mao also realized that unless people saw improvements in their lives, resentment and even rebellion might flare up. In a complete reversal of his previous policy, Mao ordered intellectuals to go back to cities and perform their normal duties. The labor camp was closed down.

Mother had hoped that by having spent almost three years at the labor camp, she would have earned the right to move to Shanghai with my father. However, despite previous promises she did not get permission.

"Labor movement is completely controlled by the central government, unfortunately," they told her coldly. Mother was very upset and angry. Now she had to go back to her old work unit in Beijing. So it was decided that my sister and I would go to Beijing with my mother, and attend school there. My father would report back to his work unit in Shanghai and try somehow to move to Beijing later.

Spring went by quickly as all the families prepared for long journeys home. A few people who decided to give up their city *Hukou* to stay in Nanchuan were invited to good-bye dinners by those who were leaving. One of them was a handsome young army soldier, Xiao Li, who had married a Miao woman; he'd been a good friend to my father in the past two years. In our home, we had mostly basic furniture that was distributed to us by the work unit. This furniture was not of good quality and considered not worth taking with us to Beijing. My parents gave our furniture to this young man to set up his home. He was very grateful.

Ten years later, Xiao Li traveled to Beijing and visited us. I waited with great anticipation for his arrival. I still remembered the handsome young man with soft white skin. Once again my thoughts went back to the mountains of red azaleas and white-water rivers. When he finally came, I could not believe my eyes. His face was dark and rough. Although he was about fifteen years younger, he looked my father's age.

Xiao Li told my father how thankful he still was for my family's kindness. He took out beautiful handmade insoles in typical Miao patterns, traditional Miao gifts to make your shoes more comfortable.

"My wife made these herself. One for big sister," he turned to my mother, who was bringing in tea, "and one for you, Old Liang.

"These are for the children. I hope they fit, because she sized them by guessing."

He took the tea. We were all sitting around the table, looking at him. We each had different thoughts going through our minds, thoughts that stretched back ten long years. I searched my memory for the young man who often came to our apartment for meals, and to whom I loved to show off my reading skills.

"Good tea." He nodded at my father gratefully. He told us that he wanted to move his family back to Shanghai so that his son would be able to go to a decent school and thus have a future.

"I talked to so many people, in Nanchuan, Chengdu (the capital of Sichuan province) and Shanghai, but no one wanted to help. They said that I had given up my Shanghai *Hukou* and there is nothing they can do now." He sipped more tea and continued. "They said that my son was born in Nanchuan and our family *Hukou* was there, so it was in Nanchuan that we need to stay for the rest of our lives. But if we stay, my son will have no future; with the kind of schooling there, he would not even have a chance to go to high school."

After Xiao Li had left and the tea was cold, my parents talked at length about the labor camp years, the young man and the fate of others we'd known.

"He should never have given up his Shanghai *Hukou*," said my mother as soon as Xiao Li left. "It's worth its weight in gold." Then she turned to my father who was putting away the teapot and cups. "Remember how difficult it was for me to try to move to Shanghai? And I was a highly qualified university graduate! Twelve years we had to live apart."

"In the end, I had to exchange my Shanghai *Hukou* with someone in Beijing before I could move here," echoed my father. "A Shanghai *Hukou* is worth more than the weight of it in gold."

"But it was not his fault," Baba continued, now angrily. "No one knew where events would turn next. First, it was the 'Great Leap Forward': everyone sent out to make steel. Then it was 'Let A Thousand Flowers Bloom,' when you were supposed to criticize the shortcomings of the Party."

"Had you done so, you would have been put in prison in the 'Anti-Rightist Movement,'" said Mama.

"Then there was 'Up the Mountains and Down to the Countryside,'" I added, remembering the older brothers and sisters of my friends, many of whom had gone to work in remote People's Collective Communes in the Cultural Revolution.

"One moment you were red, another moment you were black. One year we were sent to the labor camp, three years later we came back. It was revolution—reorganizing the whole society," said Baba. "Like all of us, Xiao Li just wanted to live a life. He did the best he could."

Red was the good communist color. Black was bad, shorthand for capitalists. In the Cultural Revolution, people were categorized into either red or black depending on their birth. Reds included peasants, workers, revolutionary officers and their children. There were nine black categories that included landlords, capitalists, "stinky intellectuals" and their descendants. Another of the black categories was "spy," which, broadly speaking, included anyone with overseas connections. People in the black categories became the targets of the Cultural Revolution. Many were stripped of their jobs and positions, sent to labor camps, imprisoned or even killed.

There was always great sadness when my parents recalled how the Cultural Revolution had destroyed the lives of many of their friends and colleagues. They wondered about their own lives and how it might have been if the Cultural Revolution had not happened. So many what-ifs came to mind.

At last summer came to Nanchuan, and the day of our departure. A number of my parents' friends, including Xiao Li, came to help.

We chose to leave in the early morning so that we could avoid the time when the sun was brutally hot. In fact, we left so early that there was still fog lingering around the mountaintops. Two strong young men pushed wooden carts loaded with our belongings, while five other people carried smaller pieces of luggage. My mother carried Xiao Jie in her arms, while Baba had a carton of crockery in one hand and me in the other. I had to leave my beloved basket behind since there would not be any use for it in Beijing.

As we moved slowly down the mountain, we could hear the sound of the river in the valley. Looking around, there was endless green for as far as the eye could see. Wildflowers peeked out here and there. As we walked down, the labor camp where we had lived for the past three years faded from view. Soon, we could see the road at the bottom of the mountain. We had walked the trail for the last time.

After the luggage had been loaded on top of the bus, we waved good-bye to those who had helped. The bus started to move. I turned around and looked out from the back window . . . and I saw a little girl walking down the mountain trail with a tiny basket on her back, alone, surrounded by endless burning-red azaleas.

Two

Little White Face

Magnificent fortresses and a lengthy road hard as steel,
today we start our journey from the very beginning.

—*Mao Zedong, 1935*

When we returned to Beijing, my mother found out that both her job and housing had been taken away.

While the intellectuals were in the labor camp, a new movement called "Aid-the-Left" had swept through the cities. Army personnel moved into government premises and universities to support rebellious Red Guards, who had taken over the running of the country. So, from the summer of 1972 to the spring of 1973, intellectuals returned with great hope to the cities only to find that they and their families had no place to live. Furthermore, despite their return, China as a nation was still busy making revolution. Most desk jobs had been eliminated. Factories were running, but only under the command of Red Guards or youth Communist Party leaders.

We were forced to stay in temporary accommodation for many months, and in the end this uncertainty made my mother decide to send my sister to her parents in Taiyuan for a year. For the second time, she had to give up her younger daughter.

It was many months later when my mother was finally given a job as an administrator of a reeducation program, housed at an abandoned university campus at the edge of the university district in West Beijing.

Prior to the Cultural Revolution the university had educated the many diplomats of China. After the Cultural Revolution started, universities across the country were shut down. Instead, the youth of China were sent to the countryside to work in the fields for People's Collectives and to be educated by revolutionary peasants.

While the youth were reeducated in the countryside, the rehabilitation of the intellectuals continued in the city. Many reeducation programs called *Xuexiban,* or learning classes, were set up, with the aim of teaching returned intellectuals Marxism, Leninism and Mao's own thoughts. "Thought reform is a long march of ten thousand kilometers," said Mao. After the labor camp, these classes seemed pointless, but not too harsh, to my mother.

While my mother took up her new duties, I went to Dayouzhuang primary school. In Chinese, Dayouzhuang means "the village that has a lot." But nothing could be further from the truth, as, in reality, Dayouzhuang had very little. The main street of the village was a dirt path and had only two shops: a small mixed-goods store selling everything from cooking sauce, spices and soap, to towels and pillows. Opposite the store a grocer sold fruit and vegetables, and meat on odd days. Most of the time, the meat counter was empty.

My primary school was located at the west end of the village, in a traditional Chinese courtyard house, which, prior to 1949, belonged to the village landlord. Almost all the students at the Dayouzhuang primary school were peasants' children from surrounding villages. The school had a terrible academic standing in the district and a reputation for crime and disorder. Unfortunately for me, my mother's work unit fell within its jurisdiction.

Our classrooms had no heating. When winter got brutally cold, between December and February, a small stove was distributed to each classroom. All the students stayed after school to make coal balls for these heating stoves; we had to roll the coal into pellets small enough to feed the classroom fires. Our hands and faces cracked in the howling Mongolian wind as we sat on the steps of the school courtyard trying to roll perfectly round coal balls. When it got too dark to work in the school yard, my classmates and I would leave school with blackened hands and go home to see what kind of magic our mothers had cooked up with the only thing we ate for the entire winter—cabbage.

As it was, most of my classmates, the peasants' children, did not have enough cabbage. Only government employees had the privilege of four kilograms (which was to last them the whole winter) of cabbage for each person in the household. Because my father lived in Shanghai, the day for picking up my mother's allocation of cabbage was always a big event for her. She had to start organizing the wooden cart and her coworkers' help a few days ahead, in order to be able to carry the cabbages back. In those days, the longest line in Beijing was the one outside the cabbage distribution station. I remember having to wait for half a day to hand in our cabbage coupon and then another half a day to bring the cabbages back. My mother and I then packed them in baskets and stored these outside our windows. My mother would then spend the following days making pickled cabbage, while I counted the "ice flowers" formed on the window. Our living room–kitchen, one of the two rooms allocated to my mother, would be filled with clay jars and pickled cabbage throughout the winter. The smell was terrible, and, every day, when I returned from school, I had to stop at the door to let my nose get used to it. To make sure that the pickled cabbage would take us through the winter, my mother made pickled cabbage soup for nearly every meal. For many years afterward, whenever winter came, or when there was even a touch of cold in the air, I was sure I could smell boiled pickled cabbage.

Yet I liked winter. Winter was the time that the ground was frozen and peasants huddled around coal-burning stoves. In winter, *Xue Nong,* or "Learning from peasants," a reeducation program for schoolchildren, was halted. Here in the north, where the climate was harsh and fields less fertile than those in the south, most People's Collective Communes produced wheat or corn. Wheat was planted as soon as there was no danger of frost and then harvested in August. Because of the long winters, there was not much the peasants could do with the fields after the harvest and this meant that prosperity and living standards in the north were always lower than in the south.

Xue Nong usually kicked into high gear in the summer and ended after harvest. It was always a big event for the school as it weighed heavily on the standing of the school in the eyes of the Party and the district committees. Before the pupils were marched out to the fields, there was always a "pumping up session" during which our teachers laid out the goals and rules as well as reiterating Mao's teachings on learning from peasants.

"Our great leader Chairman Mao says 'the essential issue facing the Chinese Communist Party is not the worker problem but the peasant problem.' Peasants are the foundation of revolution," said our class teacher. "This is why Chairman Mao has called on the youth of the country to reeducate themselves by going 'up the mountains and down to the countryside.' Millions of Chinese youth have answered the call of our great leader and enthusiastically gone to work on People's Collective Communes. You also need to go back to the roots of revolutionary values because, as our beloved Chairman Mao has said, 'learning from peasants is a reeducation that should start early in life.' Tomorrow we will go to the number fourteen People's Collective Commune to help our peasant uncles and aunts collect wheat."

Our teacher, Miss Chen, continued, "Most of you are from peasant families. You should therefore shine at *Xue Nong*. This is the time that you can demonstrate to your elders that you are continuing the red traditions that you have inherited. For the few who have not had the good fortune of coming from such revolutionary backgrounds, this is the time for you to learn from peasant uncles and aunts and develop communist spirit. In either case, I want you to work hard on the fields tomorrow—don't bring shame to yourselves or our school! Last year, we came third in our district's *Xue Nong* performance table. This year, we want to do better—catch up and overtake last year's champion, the North Palace Gate primary school!"

Wearing my straw hat and plastic open-toe shoes, arms swinging high and breathing deeply the smell of human waste and animal manure used to fertilize the fields, I was ever eager to sing revolutionary songs at the top of my lungs. We marched through the village; a little girl carrying a baby on her back sat on a high wooden doorstep, looking at us with her dark face and long eyes. We marched on yellow dirt paths across fields. Women working in the fields sometimes stretched up and rubbed their backs as we passed. Young peasants sitting lazily on horse-carts gave us few glances as they tossed roasted sunflower seeds into their mouths. The driver waved his whip loudly and yelled "Jia, Jia." Horses pissed and dropped manure as they passed us.

The sun was very hot by midday and I would be sweating before we arrived at the wheat fields. Yet I did not wipe away my sweat. I wanted so much to be a model student in the fields. *Xue Nong* was a challenge for me. A few days before, we had gone to another People's

Collective Commune to help cut wheat. I could not wield the giant *Lian Dao,* the curved cutting knife, let alone actually cut anything with it. The peasants working there did not want me around, saying that I only got in their way. My classmates laughed at me while swinging the *Lian Dao* skilfully in front of me.

Today, we had come to a field where the wheat had already been harvested. Our job was to pick up bits and pieces of wheat that had been dropped by peasants. The teacher spread the pupils out to cover a two-meter radius each. Then the line moved forward together. I picked as fast as I could, my eyes wide open for fear of missing a single piece. At the end of the day, my eyes dry as a desert, I was still the last. While my classmates had already reached the end of the field, I was still picking under the burning sun. My mother sighed when she nursed my bloody hands and arms, pricked by sharp wheat ends. For the next three years, I was always the last in my *Xue Nong* classes. My teachers marked me down and warned me of a tendency for being a "Capitalistic Smelly Princess."

Another part of "learning from peasants," *Kang Shuang* or fighting frost, was much more physical than even some of the peasants' children could handle. Autumn is short in Beijing. Winter and therefore frost could come quickly and without warning. Frost was especially damaging to cabbages if they were left in the fields. Thus, *Kang Shuang* became everyone's job and priority. When the first frost came, office workers and schoolchildren were quickly gathered to help collect and move the cabbages into storage.

A frosty morning in Beijing could be very cold and dark. By the time we got to the cabbage fields, many people would already be busy. Oil lamps were lit and placed on high columns in the fields. Supervising peasants waved their oil lamps and screamed at people to move faster. On one of these days, my classmates and I lined up to receive cabbages in our arms and then carry them to be stored under plastic.

"Can you really carry three?" the peasant asked me.

"Yes," I insisted. I wanted so much to show that I was as good as any peasant's boy.

"Two is enough. You don't even have gloves," he said, stacking two large cabbages onto my extended arms.

They were ice cold. Once I started walking, I could immediately feel my hands losing all sensation. That morning, my mother had forgotten to give me my winter gloves—though they would not have helped anyway because they were not waterproof. Soon the bottom leaves defrosted and water soaked up my sleeves. Behind me, my teacher shouted: "Get running. Time is gold."

Peasants waving oil lamps were also shouting: "Run, run," and "Faster, faster."

I ran as fast as I could, while trying not to fall in the dark. In the distance, the flames of oil lamps flared, like tired eyes trying to keep awake. Peasants were stacking cabbages into big piles and then latching plastic covers around them. The dampness of the air soon penetrated my padded coat. I could feel my trousers sticking to me more and more. My hair was damp and probably frozen. I could no longer feel my hands. Once I dropped off the cabbages, I wiped my running nose with my sleeves. The tip of my nose was softened by my breath and soon became red and sore.

The next day, I was running a high temperature. Many of my classmates were also sick. As I lay in bed nursing my illness, the radio broadcast heroic stories of *Kang Shuang* and the wonderful results that had been achieved. Thousands of *jin* (half kilograms) of cabbages were saved at such-and-such People's Collective Communes; and so our wintry diet was preserved.

Because I was not born a peasant's daughter, my classmates called me "little white face," an image borrowed from traditional Chinese opera that meant the cunning and clever sneak who sponged off the red peasant class. It did not make any difference to my schoolmates that my parents were both members of the Communist Party. After all they were only ten-year-olds; they learned to hate because they were told to—my parents were intellectuals and thus my blood was not as red as theirs. It took me years to forgive them and to accept that they were only innocent children trying to play an adult's game. Unfortunately innocence can sometimes be deadly too.

It started one winter morning, when I arrived for my class. I saw a few boys already sitting in their seats; they seemed to be in an upbeat mood. As usual, I kept my head low and sat down at my desk quietly. I took out all the books from my bag and started to put them in the desk. But they would not go in. I looked inside and saw my desk was stuffed with ashes. The boys sitting behind me laughed with joy.

I did not turn around and still kept my head low. Though my mind told me to ignore their whispers and laughter, my ears strained to hear every word they were saying. More and more of my classmates arrived. There was more whispering and more laughter.

"She deserves it." A girl's voice.

"Now, let's see what she is going to do." Followed by joyful laughs.

Not knowing what to do, I put my books on my lap.

The bell rang and our science teacher, a muscular young man in his twenties, came in. Immediately the class representative screamed "Stand up!"

But I could not get up, not with all the books on my lap.

"Why don't you stand up?" The teacher stepped close to me and stared down at my face.

All the tears and sorrow that I had tried so hard to hold back rushed out at once. Big teardrops wet my neatly stacked-up books.

"What's the matter?" He came closer and asked me in a soft tone.

I could not talk for the tears that were choking me. I looked at my desk and more tears fell.

"Does someone want to tell me what is going on?" The teacher spoke sternly to the class.

Only my sobbing was heard in the classroom.

After what seemed an age, a tiny voice that was almost not there said: "Someone put coal in her desk."

The teacher came around and saw for himself the desk full of burned coal.

"Who did this?" he shouted. "Who?" His face was turning red. "You little bastards. You'd better confess. If I find out who did this you will pay. You will pay dearly. Don't you bet that I won't find out . . . you will be sorry once I do. If you think that you can do something like this on my watch, you are mistaken!" His shouting became screaming, his face redder. "Now, which one of you will come and help me clean up the desk?"

A solidly built peasant boy came forward. The two of them carried my desk outside and dumped the coal in the courtyard. While they were out, I felt all my classmates staring at my back, and heard soft whispering. I knew that many of them were enjoying it. I sat in my chair feeling humiliated. But I hated only myself. I wished that I were stronger, strong enough to stand up for myself. A loud voice in my head, in the tone of my mother, told me to stop crying. I bit my lips and squeezed my hands hard to make the tears stop, without success.

From that day on, I was moved to the front row, where I sat for the next three years. But the ash did not stop appearing in my desk; only I stopped crying or telling the teachers about it. One day when I walked into the classroom and found more ash in my desk, I simply flipped the desk over and dumped it out at the front of the classroom. When the geology teacher asked what was happening, I looked straight ahead and did not say a word.

And then the ashes stopped. Perhaps once I stopped showing how much I minded, the fun for the perpetrators no longer existed. But the battlefield moved outside the school, where more serious suffering could be inflicted on me.

I had always participated in after-class activities at school. For some time, I was particularly active in the school dance group that went on to win awards in competitions around Beijing. I even had a small role in a propaganda movie. Rehearsals for the dance group were usually long-winded and demanding. Two professional dancers from the Cultural Group for Singing and Dancing came periodically to give lessons.

After the rehearsals I walked through the village main street, sometimes picking up some spices for Mama, my school bag hanging over my shoulder. The narrow dirt path was lined with long mud walls and mud houses on either side.

"Little white face, where are you going?" A face appeared from the top of a mud house.

I was startled. As I looked up, I saw a gang of children, most of them teenagers, sitting on the edge of the mud walls. I recognized two younger boys who were from my school.

I turned around, not saying a word, and started walking away faster.

"You think you are better than us, don't you?" the oldest boy shouted. "Ah, look at you, your white shirt and white hands . . . Capitalist Little White Face." I walked on. Suddenly something hard landed on my back and I stumbled forward. As I turned around to see what had happened, another stone flew at me, hitting my left arm. I felt a sharp sensation and saw blood coming out of my elbow.

I started running. Stones kept coming at me, followed by loud laughs.

My mother was close to tears when she cleaned my wounds. I

sat on my little stool while my mother knelt down next to me with a warm, wet towel. On the floor, the now-bloodstained white shirt was floating in a bucket of water, and the blood started to dissolve slowly.

"How did it happen? Who were these bad boys?" Mama asked.

"I don't know. I've seen the oldest boy around the village, but I don't know who he is. He is not a student at the school."

Mama put some iodine on my wound and said: "It's going to hurt. But it is good for you. Your wound will start healing very soon. And tomorrow, I will go and talk to your principal and find out who these bad boys are."

While my mother and the school were trying to identify those involved, the attacks continued. No matter how late I left the school, the gang seemed to be always waiting for me on the low mud wall. The location of bruises and cuts changed depending upon where the stones landed. Sometimes, just when the scab had formed on an old wound, a new stone would break it open again. As the weather got hotter and flies and mosquitoes multiplied, my wounds started to get infected. Underneath the new scab, thick, yellow pus would come out and then form a crust. So at times I would have this rather fat elbow that I could not bend or cover up with my shirt.

My sister returned from my grandparents' to live with us and, the following January, at five, was old enough to enter the same primary school. It soon became obvious that she was my sister, and she too began to be harassed. I could have endured more abuse from my schoolmates, but I could not watch my little sister being pushed into the stream on her way home, or being called names simply because she was my sister. Sometimes they even came into our home to bully her.

One day, I was in my room doing homework when I heard my sister's cry for help. I leaned out of the window, and saw a group of thugs from school pushing her around in the courtyard. The thugs were a head taller, and twice the size of my little sister. They shoved her from one to the other, and then shouted at her, "Are you trying to hit me?" Before she could balance herself, they pushed her back again. She landed on the dirt, crying harder each time she fell. Blood rose to my face. I picked up a large watermelon knife and started racing downstairs. I hardly knew what I was doing. All I knew was that I hated what was happening to my sister and I wanted to stop it. A neighbor heard my scream and came out. He stopped me on the stairs when he saw the knife and asked what I was going to do with it. When I eventually came out, yelling, screaming and crying, accompanied by the neighbor, the thugs were already gone. My bruised little sister was left alone standing next to her jump rope, crying.

My mother finally tracked down the gang leader, a middleschool dropout who lived with his grandfather on the outskirts of the village. Because he was not a student at the primary school, there was nothing the teachers could do. The Party Committee of the People's Collective Commune to which his grandfather belonged did not want to do anything. Because the boy had a long history of violence, they told my mother to go the police rather than deal with him themselves. "We have tried, believe me, Comrade Kang," they said to Mama. "He is a tiger that has grown too big for this mountain."

The police laughed at my mother when she went to see them. "What do you want us to do? Has anyone died? Every day we are so busy, catching counterrevolutionaries, and you are asking us to look into school bullying?"

School bullying may be a small crime to the police, but it is a big knife in a mother's heart. In desperation my mother took me to see the boy's grandfather, hoping that a parent-to-parent talk could stop him from hurting me and my sister.

On a cloudy afternoon my mother and I walked along the muddy path to the end of the village. Here low-built peasants' sheds seemed to be in danger of falling down at any time. Bare-bottomed toddlers played with the dirt and each other. Elderly women squatting in front of the sheds tossed roasted sunflower seeds into their mouths, cracking them open loudly and then spitting out the shells with a twist of their tongues.

There was a shed leaning next to the field that smelled of manure and human waste. My mother knocked on the barely standing door. A soft, old voice answered. Mother pushed the door open slowly and, as the door opened, the light of late afternoon rushed into the dark room.

Holding my mother's hand, I saw before me the oldest man I had ever seen. He sat in the dark corner; underneath him, the dried cornstalks that were his bed. The inside of the shed smelled just the same as the filth outside. The old man squeezed his eyelids together, trying to make out who had come into his home.

My mother walked closer to the old man, and, seeing no other furniture around, stood in front of the old man and explained the purpose of her visit.

"That useless bastard. What shame he has brought upon the family. The evil of our ancestors, it must be. We are paying for the sins of our ancestors. His poor dead mother, he sent her to her grave. Do you know that he sent her to her grave?" The old man nodded his head as if to show that he was convinced of it.

"He was never a good student, had to re-sit two years in primary school. Then he was expelled from middle school for fighting. Fourteen years old, no place to go and no one wants him. What did our ancestors do? His poor dead mother." The old man sighed.

"Old Grandpa, can you please tell him to stop attacking my daughter? She has not done anything to hurt anyone," begged my mother.

"I am half blind, not much use for the People's Collective Commune or anything else. At least my grandson brings home water and helps me out when he is around. He does not listen to me anymore, if he ever did. His poor dead mother, she broke her tongue trying to straighten out the boy. Comrade, what am I to do? The sins of our ancestors . . . his poor dead mother . . ." the old man kept repeating.

My mother took my hand and we left. The clouds had thickened and it looked as if it were going to rain.

For years I hated school. I hated every single day that I had to spend there, and more, I hated going home. Before the end of the day, I would quietly pack up all my books. I was like a soldier waiting for a command, or a sprinter waiting for the starting gun. As soon as the bell rang, I would jump out of my chair and run from the classroom. I ran the way a bird flies. I was fighting to be free. I ran as fast as I could, in pouring rain, howling wind and thick snow. This was the only way that I could escape the attacks—getting out of Dayouzhuang before the thugs had had time to get ready for me. Later on, in high school and university, my coaches were deeply impressed by my long-distance running ability. My high school coach said, on watching me run competitively for the first time, "You have such a talent. You are a natural gold medalist." Sadly it was not my talent but my desire to escape that

made me a good athlete. There were two other daughters of intellectuals in my school who suffered similar, though not as appalling, abuse
from the gang. I think I may have been singled out by them because
there was no father or brother at home to protect me.

Home was always warm. Every day when I returned after school, I
would light the stove, put on the porridge pot and then sit down at the
desk to do my homework. It would be another two hours before my
mother could come home. Outside the window, I could see children
playing in the courtyard. But I never joined them. The world was cold
out there.

I hated my teachers, for as much as they sympathized with me,
they did not help. I hated my mother, who seemed too weak to protect
me; and most of all I hated my father. If it were not for the photos
in the album, I would have forgotten how he looked. Every year he
appeared for a few days and then left me to stand alone against the
entire world. When I needed him, to walk back with me from school,
to help take on the evils I faced, to reassure me and to give me hope
and faith that somewhere, someday, the sun would shine on me, he
was not there. I felt that I faced the world alone and, to an extent, that
feeling has always remained with me.

When my father was finally granted permission to move to Beijing, in 1976, the walls were painted, curtains cleaned and furniture
moved about. When we went out, neighbors, friends and acquaintances alike asked my mother about the news they had heard.

"Lao Liang is coming soon?"

"Yes, in July," my mother replied with such a glow.

"Wonderful. You will have someone to depend on," they said, as
if my mother had not managed to bring up two children and have a
career all on her own for nearly ten years. Twelve years earlier, just
graduated from college, wearing two pigtails, she was called *Xiao Kang,*
Little Kang. Now, middleaged, with two children, bags under her eyes,
people respectfully greeted her as *Lao Kang,* Old Kang.

But Mother did not care. She was simply happy and looking forward to the reunion of her family. I was happy for her, and happy for
me because now I thought there was someone who would stop the
bullying.

The night of my father's arrival was magical, but it was overshad-
owed by what happened the next morning. I woke up and saw him

screaming over my head: "Wake up! Wake up!" As soon as I opened my eyes, my father pulled me out of the bed and carried me, running, from the room.

The ceiling above us was shaking, paint and chalk falling down, lightbulbs cracked, broken glass everywhere. Loud crashes of bowls and pots falling down and being kicked by people on their way out, running toward the stairs, echoed in the hall. Everywhere people were screaming with fear, "Earthquake! Earthquake!"

Outside, some fifty feet away, stood many of our neighbors and my mother, with my sister in her arms. "Wei!" Mother waved her right hand madly when she saw us coming out of the building. Immediately I ran to her. She put down my sister, gave me a tight hug as if she would never let me go again.

The sky continued to rotate and the ground to shake. Loud cracking sounds coming from the center of the earth brought fear to everyone standing in the courtyard. The courtyard was surrounded on all sides by three-story buildings that might collapse at any time. Some windows were shattered. Every now and then, bright lights flashed at the edge of the sky, people gathered closer together and wondered where the fire was burning.

When the aftershocks slowed, people went back inside and brought chairs and blankets out. On 18 July 1976, the reunion of my family began as we sat in our chairs and huddled underneath blankets. Together, we welcomed the dawn of the new day.

The earthquake, which measured 7.8 on the Richter scale, happened at 3:42 A.M. It rocked Beijing and brought chaos to the city, but was centered on Tangshan, a city 200 kilometers to the east of Beijing, famous for its china and coal. It completely leveled the city of Tangshan and within minutes buried a quarter of a million of its residents under the rubble.

As soon as the day broke, the sky clouded over and it started to rain. The rain then poured without end. The fear of aftershocks kept everyone outside. Like the others, my parents tied a large piece of plastic on top of four bamboo sticks and made a roof for us. They also put up our foldable travel bed underneath the plastic so that my sister and I could get some sleep. But as the rain got heavier, our little tent became rather unstable. Soon rain started to come in through the cracks around the edges, the ground got muddier and our blankets wetter.

We lived outside for another month. During that time my parents took out our savings to buy larger and heavier plastic, and our tent grew bigger. As soon as the rain subsided, the sun came out and burned nonstop for two weeks. During the day the temperature inside our plastic tent could be as high as 40°C. Then at night, mosquitoes came in through every little hole, in their hundreds.

In the middle of all the chaos and madness, I heard that a good friend, Tong Nian, had lost both of her parents in the quake. Her parents were colleagues of my mother's who had been working in Tangshan the year before. They were due to leave for home and were already in a hotel when the quake hit. A few days after the quake, eleven-year-old Dong Nian and her fifteen-year-old sister were told that the hotel where their parents had been staying had been leveled and there was no chance that they could have survived. Overnight, Dong Nian and her sister were orphaned. Their parents' bodies were never recovered. For years, every time I saw her, I could not help thinking about the day when I heard the news, and I often thought about how her life must have changed at that moment. But I never dared to mention her parents to her. Twenty years later I saw her playing with her son in the sunshine. She seemed happy and content and yet, in her smile, I thought I detected the same shadow that had been there for the last twenty years.

School resumed. But nothing was normal again. Because the structure of the old schoolhouse had sustained damage during the quake, we spent more than two weeks having our lessons outside. Finally, in September, came our return to the reinforced schoolhouse and the event that changed China, and our lives, forever.

On the morning of 9 September 1976, all three radio stations (Central One, Central Two and Beijing) kept broadcasting that there would be an important announcement at 4:00 P.M. Everyone wondered what it could be. We were assembled in our classroom to listen to the broadcast.

First, funereal music came on all three radio stations again and again. Then, right on the hour, the news announced: "The chairman of the Chinese Communist Party Central Committee, the founder and the leader of the People's Republic of China, Mao Zedong, passed away at ten minutes past zero on the morning of 9 September 1976."

Mao had not been well for some time and had already suffered from a couple of heart attacks that year. Finally on 2 September, another massive heart attack proved to be too much for the eighty-three-year-old. The ruler of a quarter of the world's population, and a country that was larger than the whole of Europe, died seven days later.

On my way home I thought about what our teacher had said. She told us that Chairman Mao had loved us and we should feel sad and mourn his passing. I told myself that I should cry for such a great man and the leader who had rescued China from humiliation by foreign powers. Mournful music echoed from every corner, and yet for all the love that we were taught to hold for the great Chairman Mao, I did not cry.

The mood among my parents and their colleagues was subdued. The work units had organized massive ceremonies to mourn the death of Mao. But the level of emotion was not the same as for the passing of a loved one. With Mao's death, people felt as if a support had been taken away, someone that they had depended on for the past twenty-seven years was lost and so was certainty. Throughout their lives, Mao had dictated their fortune and the fate of China. Now, with Mao gone, people wondered and worried about the future of China and how they might be affected personally.

For the next two weeks, the entire country was in mourning. Organized visits to say one last good-bye brought endless lines of people to the Great Hall of the People where Mao's body lay underneath a Communist Party flag. Funeral ceremonies were held in every work unit around the country to commemorate and give thanks for the great deeds of a great man. Newspaper articles listed over and over again the great achievements of Mao, such as China becoming a permanent member of the UN Security Council and a nuclear power.

I was then considered a model pupil in the school, so I was made newsreader for our public address system. Thus it was my job to reread the memorial speech at Mao's funeral service on 18 September. Before going on air, I had practiced with my mother, and by myself a great many times, so that I could read it as properly and professionally as possible. Confident and in a sober mood, I started my broadcast that day.

Somewhere into the broadcast I started to laugh. It may have been the contrast between my seriousness and the mindlessness of the others in the room, or my constant practicing that had made me too weary of my own voice. But I could not stop laughing. The supervisor was terrified and pulled me out of the broadcasting room right away. "What's the matter with you?" he bellowed.

I kept on laughing, tears poured from my eyes and I could hardly keep my back straight.

"Go back to your classroom!" He pushed me out of the room.

To this day I cannot explain why I did that. It was just one of those freaky things. Luckily I was not punished for having counterrevolutionary tendencies. I was simply fired.

Less than a month after Mao's death came the news of the arrest of the "Gang of Four." The country was told that after Mao Zedong died, Madam Mao and three of her allies had been plotting to overthrow the Party Central Committee and Hua Guofeng, the premier of China and Mao's chosen heir. First, three of Madam Mao's allies, Wang Hongwen, Zhang Chunqiao and Yao Wenyuan, were arrested in the Great Hall of the People. Then, an hour later, Madam Mao was arrested at her residence in Zhongnanhai.

Mass demonstrations immediately took place in Tiananmen Square to celebrate the news. The rest of the country then followed suit. My parents took part in the celebrations with joy. "From now on everything will be fine. Better days are coming!" they said. The Gang of Four, who had been responsible for many atrocities during the Cultural Revolution, were later put on trial and sentenced to fifteen years in prison. In 1995, Madam Mao committed suicide in her cell.

The Cultural Revolution, which had ruined the lives of millions of Chinese for the past ten years, had finally ended.

Three

Love

Look for him a thousand times, turn around, he is
standing alone below the hazy light.

—*Xi Qi Yi, ninth century*

Dramatic changes took place immediately after Mao's death. Deng Xiaoping came back to power in early 1977. Hua Guofeng, Mao's chosen successor, was quickly relegated to a lower position in the Party hierarchy. The old guard, who had suffered greatly in the Cultural Revolution, resurfaced. Traditional educational systems were reestablished, and universities reopened. Millions of send-down youth, now older, married with children, with their dreams shattered and their backs bent, returned home desperately looking for jobs.

Part of the effort to restore normality in the country included the reopening of four elite boarding schools in Beijing in 1978. These four schools took in the top 800 of the 300,000 primary school graduates. I scored one of the highest marks in the entrance exam and became one of the first boarders at the Number 174 Middle School (later renamed the Middle School of the People's University). In the same year the U.S. and China established a diplomatic relationship. China opened itself up to the rest of the world after thirty years of isolation.

Like the rest of the country, I was given a new outlook on life. While the generation before me spent most of their school years mak-

ing revolution, and the best years of their adulthood in the People's
Collective Communes, I was allowed, at school, to study, and to learn
foreign languages, and when I graduated from high school, to go to
university.

Ten years passed swiftly after the end of the Cultural Revolution. By
the time I was about to turn twenty, I was slim, bright-eyed, with long
black hair and a few light freckles on my face. And I was in my second
year at Beijing University, studying psychology. The year was 1986.
Top Gun was the top movie in America, the Chernobyl nuclear reactor
exploded in Ukraine. I met Dong Yi.

I had split up with my boyfriend from the first year, Yang Tao.
Yang Tao was politically ambitious, someone on the fast track who
had, before his year abroad, risen to become president of the govern-
ment-sponsored University Student Association in Beijing. Back then
I was cowed by his dominating temperament and was only too happy
that he went overseas for his final year at university. I ended our relationship soon after he left China.

I was carefree, wrapped up in my studies and with no expectation of meeting anyone else at that time. I spent much of my free
time reading and writing alone at Weiming Lake—the Lake with No
Name—at the center of Beijing University's campus. The name of the
lake comes from an anonymous poem: "Though yet to be named / for
tomorrow is eternal / for the day shall come." The lake was surrounded
by green hills, traditional butterfly-roof buildings, weeping willows and
a forty-meter-high traditional Chinese tower—the pagoda. The lake
was especially beautiful in the evenings, when the moonlight danced
on the water, lovers strolled down the stone paths around the lake and
nightingales sang in the scented woods. Many poets had declared it to
be one of the most romantic places in the city.

I fell in love with the lake when I came to visit the campus at seventeen. Beijing University was the best in China (like Harvard or Yale
in the U.S., or Oxford or Cambridge in the UK) and naturally the first
choice for all confident high school graduates. Unfortunately I was not
confident then. But once I saw the lake I knew where my destiny lay.
During the four years I spent at Beijing University, I often went there

with my books. Sitting beside it, I was always the person I wanted to be, a writer and a lover.

On the evening that was to change my life, I was cycling back from the lake to my dormitory. The night was filled with the fragrant scent of spring flowers. A gentle breeze lifted my long, flowing hair. As I passed the library, I saw a crowd gathered outside the eastern entrance, at the foot of the two-story-high statue of Mao Zedong. The library had only recently been completed, but the Mao statue had been standing there since before I was born. Here our larger-than-life leader was middle-aged, wearing his signature jacket and a People's Liberation Army cap. His left arm rose up as if to wave at everyone passing. He looked down on us with his fatherly smile, enough to give anyone a chill. It was so real, and yet Mao had died, an eighty-three-year-old man, ten years earlier.

Every Wednesday evening, an English Corner convened at the foot of the statue. Chinese students and Westerners came here to speak to each other in English. The English Corner was a phenomenon that began when a couple of years earlier, at a corner of the Purple Bamboo Garden, one of the parks in Beijing, a few young Chinese students started meeting Westerners every Sunday to practice English. At the time, China had a six-day workweek and Sunday was the only day in a weekend. The informal gathering gradually grew. Hundreds of people came to the English Corner, many from miles away. When the Corner became too crowded, people started their own English Corners in other parts of the city, in whatever space they could find—community parks or under the old city walls. Every university in Beijing soon had its own English Corner.

I had passed this one on campus many times before. I had not participated because my English was poor. But that evening I felt braver than usual and impulsively decided to stop. I parked my bicycle against the lawn fence and drifted into a few ongoing conversations. I floated for half an hour from one conversation to another, without understanding what was being discussed and wondering whether I should just leave. Then a young man with square shoulders and a pair of large eyes set deep into his face asked me, in fluent English, to join his group. When he realized that my English was really not up to scratch, he made an effort to slow down, repeating his words again and again, waiting patiently for my response. Others got impatient and left.

"Would you be more comfortable speaking Chinese?" he asked kindly, when there were only the two of us left. I nodded. We moved farther away from the crowd.

"This is the first time you've come to the English Corner, isn't it?"

"Is it so obvious?" I said.

"No." He smiled. "I come here every week. I have never seen you before. No, your English is not terrible. You just need a little more practice. Then you will feel more confident."

His English was very good and I told him so and asked how he managed to become so advanced.

"It is mostly practice. Besides, I need to improve my English if I want to score well on TOFFLE and GRE."

I knew TOFFLE was a test on English as a second language that was required by every university in America for non-English-speaking applicants. But I had never heard of the GRE, which he told me was an entrance exam for graduate schools in the United States. "I am applying for PhD programs in quantum physics, my specialty."

That was how I met Ning, a graduate student in physics and one of the first I had come across of the increasingly large number of students who were preparing to leave China to study and make their lives abroad. Ning was intelligent (he registered a worldwide patent at the age of twenty-three) and kind. His generosity would one day help me in my hour of need. After we met, he visited me almost every day. He read the books I was reading and brought me poetry. As we met more often, I noticed a kind of restlessness about him, always a wave of the hand or a tapping foot as he spoke. He seemed unable to tolerate silence and always needed to be on the move. Soon Ning told me that he was in love with me. I might have fallen in love with him, but love is a funny thing. Fate sometimes intervenes and dictates who we love and when.

About three weeks after I first met Ning, I went to visit him in his dormitory. His roommate opened the door and said that Ning was not in, but might be on his way back, and if I wanted, I could wait for him there.

"By the way," he said, smiling at me, "I am one of Ning's roommates, everyone calls me Dong Yi."

Dormitory rooms at Beijing University (as a matter of fact, at almost every university in China) were too small to accommodate chairs. I lived with seven other girls in one room; we had four bunk beds and a table in the middle. The living standards in graduate-student housing were much better. There were three single beds in Ning's room, but still no chairs. So Dong Yi and I sat down, as was customary, on the two beds on either side of the table.

"This guy will be going to America soon, he is rarely here anymore." Dong Yi pointed at the third bed. He seemed sweet and shy. "You are the girl from Psychology. Ning has spoken a lot about you."

"I hope all good things," I said.

"Oh, yes. Absolutely fantastic things."

His voice was gentle and yet assured. It had the same effect as a smile, understanding you just as you want to be understood, flattering you as much as you think you deserve and casting a judgement on you forever in your favor.

"But he never mentioned you. I thought I had, by now, met everyone who was anyone in his life." Suddenly I was annoyed with Ning.

Dong Yi laughed. "Roommates are not usually important. Would you like some water? I am going to have some myself," he asked.

"Sure, if it's not too much trouble."

Unlike we undergraduates, who had to pile books on our beds, graduate students were given space for a shared bookshelf. Dong Yi took out two mugs from his part of the bookshelf; a homemade curtain concealed neatly lined books, papers and mementos. When he got up to bring the Thermos, I looked over to his bed. In comparison with the messy beds that were all too common for male students, Dong Yi kept his clean and neat. Two books were stacked up next to his pillow. A reading lamp clipped onto the headboard lit up a large wall calendar; May's portrait was of an up-and-coming young actress.

"The water is hot. I just brought it back from the boiler house." Dong Yi poured two cups of water from his Thermos—Beijing water had to be boiled before it was drunk. I took the cup and my heart raced as our fingers touched.

Dong Yi was beautiful. He had a face that seemed to come straight from a marble sculpture of the perfect Chinese man, combining the high cheekbones of the south and the symmetrical composition of the north. His lips were full and, as with his eyes, capable of speaking the deepest intimacy.

"Are you reading Tolstoy?" I asked him, knowing perfectly well what his answer would be.

Dong Yi picked up the book next to his pillow. "Yes. Someone gave it to me. Have you read it?" He looked at me with his tender smile and curious eyes.

He passed *Anna Karenina* to me. I opened to the page where the bookmark was. Anna was on the train going back to St. Petersburg.

"Yes. But I like *War and Peace* better. Although it is bloodier and Prince Andrei dies at the end, the love story is less sad than that of *Anna Karenina*. It is a hopeful, rather than a doomed love story," I said.

"Thanks for telling me the ending."

"You must have known how *Anna Karenina* ends. This is the most popular book of the moment." I laughed. *Anna Karenina* was then the in book for intelligent Chinese. People seemed to have found parallels between nineteenth-century Russia and twentieth-century China. In fact the social norms were more severe in China in the twentieth century than they had been in Russia in the nineteenth century. Being able to love freely was still a distant dream for many Chinese; eloping for love could still bring death to both lovers. Society punished cruelly those who did not conform.

"No, I mean the ending of *War and Peace*," said Dong Yi teasingly. "Perhaps I should read it sometime. Ning says that you are also a writer, is that so?"

That afternoon Ning did not return until quite late, so Dong Yi and I had plenty of time to get to know each other. Dong Yi told me his story.

At twenty-five, he was five years older than me and came from my mother's hometown of Taiyuan, the capital of Shanxi province. Shanxi is a coal-producing province in the Yellow Highlands near Inner Mongolia. The province has few other resources; the land is largely unfertile and the province suffers from extremes of weather, bitterly cold in the winter and then baking hot in summer. In the 1950s, in answer to Mao's call to rebuild the poverty-stricken inlands of China, Dong Yi's father moved from Guangdong province near Hong Kong to Shanxi. He was a high school math teacher when the Cultural Revolution began in 1966. Overnight, his students began to call themselves Red Guards, self-appointed guardians of Mao Zedong's thoughts, and foot soldiers in the battle to smash the Four Olds (old thought, old culture, old customs and old practices). They burned books and tortured their teachers.

In cities all over China, books were looted from libraries, bookshops and private homes, piled in main squares, and set on fire. Teachers were forced to attend *pidouhui*—people-beating meetings—where they were tortured in public. Within a few months, thousands of people were killed in Beijing alone, and many of them were teachers. They were beaten to death, shot in public or buried alive.

After the initial killing phase of the Cultural Revolution, which eventually included gun battles between different factions of the Red Guards themselves, Mao Zedong decided that it was best to end the near-civil-war chaos, and he sent the Red Guards to the countryside to work on People's Collective Communes. Schools were closed down. Dong Yi's father survived but was forced, for the next seven years, to work as a street cleaner.

Dong Yi and I sat across the table from each other and drank hot boiled water. I told him about my mother, who studied journalism in college, before the Cultural Revolution. In those ten revolutionary years she did not write a single report. Instead she spent the first part of the decade in a labor camp and the second part running "Mao Zedong thoughts learning classes" for jobless intellectuals.

That afternoon I told Dong Yi much about my family and childhood, some of which I had never told anyone else. Somehow I felt a mysterious connection between us. Dong Yi was different from anyone I had ever met; he spoke of responsibilities, as a son to his parents, and as a citizen to his country. Unlike Yang Tao, he was not interested in gaining political power. He simply wanted to give back and to make people happy.

"What do you think about Taiyuan?" Dong Yi asked, while pouring me another cup of water.

The first time I had gone there I was only twelve years old. Taiyuan struck me as a very poor city. The shops were nearly empty, even during Chinese New Year. My grandfather had bought me candies that were black and tasted terrible. My aunts and uncles wore old padded Mao coats. When I needed to go to the toilet, one of the grown-ups had to get up in the middle of the night and go with me to a row of holes dug in the ground outside. The stink from them was so suffocating that I could not breathe. "Mind you, my grandfather was a highly ranked Party member of the Shanxi provisional government—my sister and I were picked up at the train station by his driver for goodness' sake. When I left, I swore never to go back there." I laughed at the memory.

I had kept my promise until the year before, when my parents asked me to accompany my sister there again. This time I could see that life had improved. My grandparents had moved into a new two-story villa built specially for high-ranking officials, with more than one bathroom. But outside the provincial government compound, ordinary living still seemed backward. When I left, I renewed my conviction never to return.

"I hope that I have not offended you," I said to Dong Yi, suddenly sorry that I'd had so few nice things to say about his hometown. "But somehow I feel that I can tell you exactly what I think."

"No, no," Dong Yi was quick to reply. "I am glad that you are so honest. If I have a chance, I won't want to go back either. It has also become clear to me, the more I am away, just how narrow-minded and repressed people in Taiyuan are."

The bright afternoon light dimmed and turned soft. Birds called to each other from the aspen trees, like the two hearts inside, echoing each other in harmony. Ning returned. Dong Yi said warmly, "Where have you been? Wei has been waiting for you for hours."

"Waiting for you outside your dorm." Ning stared at me and spoke angrily. He then threw his books on his bed without looking at either of us. "What have you guys been talking about? Me?"

"I am afraid not. Dong Yi has been telling me about his family and childhood. You won't believe how much we have in common!"

"Really? Good for you." Ning still sounded angry. "But if you don't mind, I'd like to rest now."

I picked up my bag and left. I didn't mind a bit. That afternoon I had fallen in love.

All my life, I had led a lonely existence, rejected by society, my peers and, I thought, my father. I knew that it was not fair to blame my father for not being there when I grew up, but nonetheless I resented having to fend for myself, when he wasn't there to protect me, from the bullies at school and the dark years of the Cultural Revolution. During those years, sisters turned in brothers, wives denounced husbands and lovers and friends betrayed each other. People did so to escape death and imprisonment, or to protect their children who otherwise would have been punished by association. Living through such times and trying to make sense of them was difficult for any child, especially one without a father. I learned to protect myself and to keep my feelings inside; and I trusted no one.

Now that I had met Dong Yi, I felt suddenly connected with the world. I felt part of a family outing on a warm, sunny day, on a corner of a green lawn where children played and giggled. I felt, that day, that I could travel with him to eternity and back, and repeat it again and again until I died. In Dong Yi I had found the true meaning of love—to trust oneself in someone else's hands, to believe in and thus to have faith in humanity. I knew then as I know now that I could always depend on him, no matter how time or space separated us. I did not know then, as I discovered later, what such faith would mean for us both in the years to come.

The next day Ning came to apologize. "I am sorry, Wei. I behaved like a fool yesterday, I know. I do hope that you will forgive me. I don't have the right to be jealous; but I was hurt. Of course it was not your fault, but when it comes to you I am selfish. Sorry, you know what I mean. I can't compete with Dong Yi. Everyone likes Dong Yi. He is good-looking, nice and mature. Please don't stay mad at me. I could have pretended to be noble and said that I was worried about you being hurt. After all, he has a girlfriend."

"Don't worry. I am not in love with him." I brushed off Ning's comments as casually as I could, while his words pressed down on me. Why did we have to meet, and I fall in love with him? Why in such a vast world couldn't I meet someone else, someone who was free to love me back?

Yet I could not stop thinking of Dong Yi, nor stop going to see him. He was to me as light is to a moth, too beautiful to resist. I wanted to be within his reach, to be near him, to hear his voice, to entrust my life to him. Somehow I was convinced—or perhaps rather I hoped—that there would come a time when he would accept my trust and treasure my heart, as his eyes seemed to assure me every time I saw him.

My twentieth birthday was at the end of June, two weeks before the summer recess. Ning and Dong Yi were supposed to come at 8:00

P.M. to celebrate with me. All my roommates had gone to study. I sat on my bed, staring at the cake box. It was already past 8:30 P.M. Where had they got to?

The evening was quiet. Outside my window, over the aspen trees, twinkled the silent stars. I heard my heart beating, my breathing, the diminishing anticipation and the all too familiar loneliness of being shut out from the world. I felt sad. Everything I saw was in black and white. Perhaps this was going to be the truth about my life; perhaps I was going to be separated from the rest, the Technicolor movie playing somewhere beyond me, outside me.

And then, suddenly, the door opened and Ning and Dong Yi fell inside, holding a brown paper packet.

"Sorry, sorry we are late," Dong Yi was shouting.

I smiled, happiness rising in me like bubbles in champagne.

"All his fault." Ning sank onto the bed across the table, catching his breath. "Dong Yi insisted on buying you a roast chicken. We looked all over the place, but only found it over at Yellow Village."

Yellow Village was half an hour away.

"You really didn't have to. So much trouble."

"I told him that. But he said it's got be special." Ning pointed at Dong Yi, waving his hand as if to dismiss what he had said.

I looked at Dong Yi who was holding the packet of chicken, smiling. His face was lit up with the joy of having gone to the end of the world to bring happiness, just for me. At that moment, I thought he loved me.

"Let's go to the lake. The stars are out," said Dong Yi, reaching out his other hand for the cake box.

An hour later, we had consumed the roasted chicken, the cake and *Chi Sui*—"Gas Water"—that we had bought from the university store. The night grew darker, the stars brighter. We lay on the grass on the bank. The Big Dipper hung elegantly across the sky, where a few thin clouds were drifting toward each other. I followed it to the North Star that was radiating in the sky. This was the star that could lead lost travelers to safety, but where was my North Star? Who was going to guide me? What should I do? Should I tell him that I loved him?

"From this angle, the world looks so big and we so small and helpless," said Dong Yi.

I turned to look at him; his face was serene in the starlight. If I told him how I felt, what would be his answer? I wanted so much to know what his feelings were for me. I did not dare to ask, for I was afraid that the slightest whisper would make him disappear from my world.

"I like being small. You know what I mean? When you become as small as a little dot, all your troubles are gone too," I told him. We were only one arm's length apart, but it seemed that all we could share was the vast sky above and the memory of this night. I wanted to cry, but had lost my voice.

I stayed for summer school while Dong Yi and Ning went home. I took a course on the history of Islam, another on the art of moviemaking (the only way to access Western movies). At the weekend, I went back to my parents' apartment, and sometimes I went shopping with my sister.

On the streets of Beijing, those who "got rich first" began to stand out from the crowd, cruising on Yamaha motorbikes. In 1978, special policies and economic zones were instituted by Deng Xiaoping to "allow some people to get rich first." But, for the majority of Chinese, life floated slowly by on bicycles, with little variation from one day to another. Fathers and mothers went home with groceries in the baskets hanging from their handlebars, young men and women returned to the apartments of their parents and grandparents. They looked tired and unenthusiastic, riding slowly among thousands of bicycles, without any conviction of getting anywhere.

But still, it was summer and I liked the summer. Everything seemed easier. I did not have to worry about doing well in exams because summer school courses were not part of my degree. I did not have to struggle too much with my feelings for Dong Yi, since I knew I wasn't going to see him for two months. The days were lazier and greener in summer and I had more time to read. I went to the lake a lot and sat under the weeping willows, and read Dickens, the Brontës, Hugo and Dostoevsky.

As much as I liked the summer, though, I was ready to go back to school as soon as the first autumn wind blurred the lake's perfect reflections. The separation of the summer seemed to have bonded Ning, Dong Yi and me closer; as soon as the new term began, the three of us became inseparable. We started to go to student canteens for meals together, we went out to restaurants, and went running in the afternoons and, of course, together we attended the democracy salons that sprang up on campus.

In 1986 China went through a relatively liberal period. Students were allowed to demonstrate on the streets for freedom of speech and democracy. Inside universities, democracy salons became the new fashion, where people sipped instant coffee (another new fashion in China; the Chinese do not traditionally drink coffee) and debated the merits of various political solutions. It wasn't thought to be dangerous. After all, Mao himself had attended them in the 1920s. Most of the democracy salons were housed in unheated, dark rooms with no decoration. Desks and chairs were grouped in circles. Topics changed every week, and were different at each salon as well. Despite political tolerance for these debates they always had a dangerous edge, I felt, which was tinged with elitism and nostalgia. As the evenings wore on, the room would fill up with the smell of coffee, thick cigarette smoke and red-eyed students.

The first time the three of us attended a democracy salon, Dong Yi kept quiet most of the time. I was rather disappointed and did not say much as we walked out of the salon. On the other hand, Ning was still excited about the debate and continued with his thoughts. "I am all for the Asian Model—economically free, politically centrally controlled. Why not? Just look at Singapore and Taiwan, two of the Little Dragons: there is your evidence of stability as well as economic prosperity."

"I'd be careful with the so-called Asian Model," said Dong Yi. "The problem is that you assume economic prosperity can be achieved without democracy or accountability."

"Yes, I do. Because China is too big a country to be set running freely—it will be like a runaway train, out of control," retorted Ning.

"What about corruption? What do you do when the leader of the government is not the 'unselfish wise man'? What then?" asked Dong Yi.

"We will come up with a system by which we can hold government officials accountable," answered Ning.

"How can you make the government more accountable if there is no democracy? Those government officials will answer to no one. The Asian Model depends too much on the 'quality or character' of the leaders. It is dangerous. China relied on a charismatic leader called

Mao Zedong once, and look at it now." Dong Yi's reply seemed, to me, assured.

At that moment, I felt extremely attracted to Dong Yi. Though he was not aggressive in his arguments, I saw clearly his conviction in what he believed to be true. I saw the intelligence and knowledge beneath his quiet manner, and was bowled over by it. In the following months, as we attended more democracy salons and more debates about the future of China, my respect for Dong Yi grew. I became more attracted to him and gradually my own views became affected by his.

But, in all this time, I never forgot about the girlfriend Ning had mentioned. I neither asked, nor did Dong Yi volunteer anything about her. Only Ning's words of her intruded into the spaces between classes and studies and, on sleepless nights, I would have long and disturbing thoughts about her, of who she was, what she was like and how much Dong Yi loved her.

I did not go to the democracy salons only with Ning and Dong Yi. Sometimes I went alone, to listen to the debates, and sometimes I went with other friends, among them a first-year graduate student in economics called Chen Li. I had met Chen Li during one of the student demonstrations.

The year 1986 was an exciting one for China. Hu Yaobang was still the Party General Secretary, and the political atmosphere was more tolerant than it had ever been. Elite groups of students and intellectuals were looking to the West for alternative ideologies and political systems; scholars such as professor Fang Lizhi wrote about human rights abuses and the lack of democracy in China. At Beijing University, students debated in the Triangle, the gathering place at the center of the campus, and put up wall posters calling for more freedom and democracy in China.

Since the first emperor of the Qin dynasty united *Zhong Gou*, the Middle Kingdom (the Chinese name for their country), in 221 BC, China had come under strict, centrally controlled rule. Over the next 2,000 years, wall posters became an important—and often the only—means for the ordinary Chinese to voice their opinions. Wall posters were still the preferred choice of student protesters in communist

China because almost all other communication channels were control-led by the Party and so were not available to ordinary citizens.

The economic reforms that had taken place since 1978 brought tre-mendous changes to China. Free market economy experiments, in the special economic zones instituted by Deng Xiaoping, had proved huge successes. Average living standards for the Chinese people had greatly improved. However, by 1986, reform seemed to have ground to a halt. Inflation was running higher and higher, corruption was rampant. At all levels, government officials and Party leaders abused their power and "got rich" first. Many intellectuals had thus questioned whether Communism could coexist with the free market economy—the fun-damental policy of Deng Xiaoping—and called for political reforms as well. University students took to the streets in various demonstrations demanding free speech, open elections and democracy.

It was on one of those nights, amid a traditional Beijing University show of celebration and support—lit papers and strips of cloth falling from dormitory windows like sparks raining down from heaven—that I met Chen Li. He lived in the graduate student dormitory across the road, and like me, was outside his dorm building cheering the student demonstrators marching by. Some twenty minutes later, we marched together with our friends to the Triangle and then out onto the streets.

Chen Li took me to many debates at the democracy salons, per-fecting his argument at each one he went to. Chen Li always said that being a political economist meant that he preferred to look at politics from an economic point of view—no politics was good politics if it did not lead to economic advances, and vice versa.

"This should be the case for China particularly, because China is among the poorest countries in the world and the majority of Chinese are undereducated," explained Chen Li.

Many in the salons disagreed with him. Students of Chinese his-tory understood that politics had nothing to do with economics. In China, "thought struggles," as Mao had put it, had always taken prec-edence over the well-being of its population, from ancient dynasties to the communist state. It was with the mind, not the body, that the rulers were concerned.

When autumn gave way to winter, Weiming Lake froze over. The ice rink opened. Students in thick padded coats filled up the place, girls looking especially colorful in their home-knit wool hats and long scarves. Dong Yi asked me to teach him how to skate. I tried, but he kept on falling—into me, into other skaters or simply onto the ice.

"This is hopeless, I give up." He held on to me while I dragged him to the railing.

"Don't give up. It is still early. We could do a few more rounds. Only practice can help you."

"Not today. It's Liu Gang's birthday. Did I tell you that we're giving him a party? His girlfriend has come up from Hangzhou for it. I need to get things ready." He sat down to untie his skates and then said almost as an afterthought, "Why don't you come to the party with me?"

Liu Gang lived in the room a few doors down from Dong Yi, and I'd first met him when he'd put his head in Dong Yi's door, one evening, to say hello.

So I went with Dong Yi to his friend's birthday party. Liu Gang's room had been transformed for the occasion. Beds had been pulled to the side, three tables pushed together, "Happy Birthday" pasted onto the wall. Guests brought meals purchased from student canteens, Coca-Cola and roasted peanuts. Dong Yi and I brought Qing Tao beer.

"Welcome, Dong Yi. How are you, Wei?" Liu Gang was in a happy mood. He was a young man with a serious face. When I first met him, I didn't like him, because he never seemed to smile. After I'd met him a couple more times, he was still cold and unfriendly, and I told Dong Yi that, probably, he didn't like me. But Dong Yi assured me that it was not the case, Liu Gang was simply the kind of person who was only comfortable with close friends. That evening, I understood why.

"Nice to see you, Mai Li." Dong Yi smiled at a slender woman with a husky voice who turned out to be Liu Gang's girlfriend. "When did you get in? It's very cold here, isn't it?"

"I came in last night and will stay for a few days," replied Mai Li. "It's a busy time for me. Liu Gang is busy himself too, with the classes as well as the magazine."

Presently Mai Li and Dong Yi lowered their voices and began to move to the corner of the room. I looked around, wondering whether I should leave. Dong Yi noticed my discomfort. He took my hand and whispered in my ear, "Liu Gang is the editor of *Free Talk*."

I knew that *Free Talk* was an underground political magazine devoted to democracy, freedom and political reforms in China. It had been circulated quietly, with much excitement, during the mass student demonstrations in 1986, though I had never read an issue myself.

Mai Li asked Dong Yi if he thought Liu Gang was in any kind of danger.

"Honestly I don't know for sure. *Free Talk* has definitely got the government's attention. So far, Hu Yaobang has been tolerant about student protests and political debates. Yet, for we all know, the political mood at the top could change at any moment." Dong Yi paused for a second and then asked Mai Li, "What have you heard? Something's concerning you."

"Heard of what?" Liu Gang came up from behind and put his arms around Mai Li's waist.

"Political changes," said Dong Yi softly.

Liu Gang looked around, the other guests were busy chatting, drinking beer and tossing roasted peanuts into their mouths.

He whispered to us that he'd been told, by a reliable source, that there was soon to be a major shift in the government's policy toward the students, and that the government would soon ban all public gatherings and student demonstrations.

"What do you think of that?" he turned to me and asked me suddenly. His eyes locked onto mine, waiting. But my mind seemed to have frozen.

"We . . . we, of course, will not give up. We won't be frightened," I muttered and my face turned red. I felt as if I were being quizzed by my professor in front of people whose opinions mattered a great deal to me.

"When we have young people like this, we don't ever need to be afraid. We will be fine." Liu Gang smiled at me for the first time. I felt immediately at ease. He looked at his girlfriend and smiled, as if to soothe any worries she may have had.

Later on, especially in the 1989 Student Democracy Movement, I realized the significance of Liu Gang's role in the Democracy Movement in China. He was a pioneer, someone who, unlike most of the student leaders who emerged on the front line of politics in the spring of 1989, had chosen the life of a dissident early on.

"Let's go have some dinner," said Liu Gang.

We moved toward the center of the room. Mai Li quickly moved on to talk about other things. Suddenly she asked Dong Yi about his girlfriend, whom she called Lan. "Will she come to see you soon?" she asked.

Dong Yi kept smiling at Mai Li, but I noticed a momentary discomfort, which he managed to cover up almost immediately. At that moment I moved away. I had finally heard her name. Her existence had been confirmed.

We sat down at the enlarged table. Tea was made and passed around, cigarettes lit, beer bottles opened, lids came off steamed rice, double-cooked pork and Sichuan chicken. The party moved into full swing.

"Try some of the Thousand-year-old Eggs. Mai Li brought them especially from Hangzhou." Liu Gang cut one open. The egg white was brown and translucent, the yolk solid black. "They call this black gold. I know that none of you have had Thousand-year-old Eggs as good as these," he urged.

A man approached Dong Yi as we were sitting together. "Dong Yi, how are you?" he said. "Remember me, Liu Gang's *Lou Xiang*?" *Lou Xiang* is a Chinese word that has no direct English translation, meaning someone from the same province or hometown, who can thus claim a relationship as close as a relative.

"This must be your girlfriend. She has come up from Shanxi too?" said the *Lou Xiang*.

"No. This is Wei," said Dong Yi abruptly. "She is an undergraduate student in psychology.'

"Did you break up with your old girl? A lot of people move on when they come to a big city like Beijing. But you work pretty fast."

"Wei is just a friend," Dong Yi insisted.

"Oh." The *Lou Xiang* dumped almost half a bottle of beer into his mouth in one go. He gave Dong Yi a big pat on the back.

I sat there in the heat and smoke and wondered who I was to Dong Yi. I was angry. Was I just a friend or his girl in the city? Did the time we spent together, all the tenderness I showed toward him, mean anything to him?

Dong Yi was embarrassed only for a short while before he eased into his circle of friends. I tried my best to chat with strangers about what I was discovering about Freud and other famous psychologists in my degree studies, about music or even the weather, but none of these things interested me that evening. Every now and then I looked over at Dong Yi, hoping to catch a glance and to be reassured that he was still there with me. But he was busy, being happy, being with friends and drinking.

When the party ended, Dong Yi walked me back to my dorm. The night had turned bitterly cold. It was getting close to—10ºC. The wind roared. It hurt when I breathed.

"I am sorry, Wei. I thought you would enjoy the party." Steam and the smell of beer came out of Dong Yi's mouth as he spoke.

"It is all right. I enjoyed it," I lied. My head hurt so much that it seemed better to just let it crack open.

"I did not expect all that talk of Lan. I am really sorry."

"Not to worry, really, I am fine," I lied again. The alcohol and insipid conversations had tired me out. I had a headache, my mind was fuzzy and I wanted to go to sleep.

But I could not sleep. I tossed and turned, thinking of Lan. Did she come up to Beijing often? Perhaps Dong Yi hid her visits from me. Did he hide the fact that he spent most of his free time with me from her? Oh, how my head hurt! What was going on between them, and between us?

I don't know how I finally fell asleep. When I woke up, I had already missed breakfast and my morning class. I went to Yanchun Garden, a restaurant on campus that served breakfast until 11:00 A.M. I bought a bowl of rice porridge and two meat-and-vegetable steamed buns just before the breakfast window was shut. Afterward, my head felt better. I counted the money left in my wallet, gave it all to the man with an oily face behind the counter and bought a bottle of Chinese champagne.

When I knocked on Dong Yi's door, he was still sleeping. After a few minutes, he opened the door, looking dazed. His hair was all messed up, sticking out in all directions.

"What time is it?" he asked as he let me in.

"Almost twelve noon." I put the champagne on the table.

"What's this? Something to celebrate?"

"No. I just had enough money left for it. Did you have a class this morning? No? Well, I missed mine. I thought we might as well continue drinking."

So we drank champagne out of tea mugs. Dong Yi did not have breakfast. After half a bottle of champagne, he was rather drunk.

"When I started to date Lan, I was nineteen, like you," Dong Yi said, after I'd told him about Yang Tao. "We were classmates in high school. I helped her to prepare for college entrance exams. I got in but she didn't."

They had been together for six years.

"Yes, six years is a long time. You'd think you'd know one another after that long, but I seem to know less about Lan now. We never discuss the things you and I talk about. Nothing, not philosophy, politics or literature."

"Has she always been this way?"

"Don't think so. We used to get on so well. We could really talk, for hours. Things seemed to have changed since I came to Beijing."

He then explained that Lan was a fragile person, likely to get sick as soon as someone else did. She had come to depend on him because she had had a lot of problems with her parents, particularly her father. They were not educated. Her mother worked at a textile factory and her father was a miner. They had told her that her happiness depended on marrying well.

"Are you going to get married?" I asked, fearing the answer. This would be a very good marriage for her—a husband with an MSc in high physics from Beijing University.

Dong Yi smiled, embarrassed, and did not answer my question.

"Do you know that I have given up a chance to study overseas?" he asked instead. "My old university wanted to send me to America for graduate school, under the condition that I would come back and teach there. I said no. You know why? Because I wanted to leave Taiyuan!"

"Well, you've made it. You are in Beijing now."

"But I can't stay. Lan can't move her *Hukou*." Dong Yi looked sad. I had never seen him looking sad. "Sometimes you wonder why we live such a life. What's the point?" he sighed.

Champagne is supposed to warm you up, but instead it made me shiver. No, it was not the champagne, but the sight of my love's sorrow. I couldn't stand it. I couldn't watch him suffer.

"Don't despair. There might be things you can do to bring Lan here. I don't know what they could be, but moving a *Hukou* is possible. My father moved to Beijing."

"Yes, from Shanghai. It's always easier to go from high water to low, but impossible in the other direction."

"What are you saying?"

"I've no other choice but to give up my career and go back to Lan after I graduate."

I couldn't believe what I'd just heard. How could a young man destroy his own hard-earned future? Dong Yi was taking on too much responsibility. He was too noble, too self-sacrificing. I couldn't let him do it.

In his voice, I heard the cry of longing to escape. Come to me, my love, I thought. Give me your hand. We have come so far. We're so close now!

Suddenly Ning returned, interrupting our conversation. The day had passed us by. The afternoon was already ending, the champagne bottle long empty.

In the China I grew up in, it was simply not acceptable for an unmarried couple to live together or have sex. In the countryside, where arranged marriages were common, the bride and groom would have met, got married and had a child within a year. Even in cities like Beijing, matchmaking was still the main avenue for young people to find a spouse. That was how my parents met. Once two people had been introduced, they would normally spend a little time getting to know each other, and then be married within a year (sometimes within a few months). So, a relationship of six years was at least uncommon, if not a sign of problems and unhappiness.

That evening, I sat down and wrote to Dong Yi. I decided that it was time to tell him how I had felt since the day I met him and ask him to take my life into his hands.

> Dearest Dong Yi,
>
> I hope that I am not upsetting you by writing this letter. I don't want you to presume that you had in any way encouraged me to do so and I shall take your decision at face value whichever it may turn out to be. But I have to tell you about my feelings because if I don't I am afraid that my heart will break. It is too full and heavy for me

to endure any longer. I have been in love with you from the moment we met.

You probably have known for some time how I feel, because I am not a very good liar when it comes to emotions. I know that it may be unfair for me to say so, but I do believe that no one could love you more than I do. I understand you. I understand your thoughts and dreams. I love your mind and spirit as much as I love the gentle touch of your glance and the warmth of your hands.

A long time ago I started a journey to search for love and beauty, a journey that would last a lifetime. Would you come with me on this journey and be my North Star?

Shyly, I slipped the letter under Dong Yi's door. A few days passed; he did not come to see me. So I went to see him. Perhaps he did not get the letter, I thought.

"Yes, I got it and read it many times." He held the letter in his hand. My heart pounded in my chest with anticipation.

"I am sorry," he said.

Though I had prepared myself for all possibilities, still my tears fell.

"Please don't cry. I don't mean to hurt you, especially not you, my dear Wei. This is what I am afraid of—of hurting the people I care about."

"Clearly you do not care enough about me," I sobbed.

"No, that's not true. Please listen to me, Wei. If I said the same thing to Lan, trust me, she would not survive it," said Dong Yi, staring into my eyes. What was he looking for, signs of strength or pain? I stared back and saw so much grief.

"She told me that if I ever left her, she would just die. I don't know whether she meant it. But in my mind, I see just such a horrific picture. I am all she's got. I have been the whole of her life for the past six years. I can't take the risk." Dong Yi continued, in a gentler voice, "You are hurt now, but you will survive. You are strong. You will find someone to love again."

"But I don't want to love *someone,* I want to love you," I cried, despite his asking me not to. "Do you love her?"

Dong Yi did not answer immediately. He looked away. When his eyes looked back into mine, he said, "Yes." He paused for a few seconds and then continued, "But it is complicated. Lan and I have been together for a very long time. Our families are now practically one. Lan regularly checks on my parents and looks after my little sister, who is fourteen. Her parents have been pressuring us to get married for years. If I broke up with Lan I would be condemned by all her friends and everyone she knows, and so would my family by everyone they know."

"What about happiness and love? If you don't care so much for yourself, doesn't she deserve them?"

"You should see how happy she is when I go home. I am grateful for her, particularly now that I am away. She has been good to me and to my family for so many years . . . I don't know, Wei. You are young. You think the world is black and white. It is actually not that simple, in love or happiness. Can we live a happy life isolated from society and family?"

Dong Yi took out *Anna Karenina* from underneath his pillow and opened it. He tucked my letter carefully inside. "Could I please keep the letter?"

"What for, so that you can think ill of me?"

"No, just to think of you."

The more Dong Yi tried to ease my pain, the more I cried. No matter how much I wanted to be strong, I could not stop crying. His words had cut into my heart and made it bleed. The pain paralyzed my body. After leaving his room, I collapsed on the cold stone steps of the building's entrance. I could not make sense of it. Why did I have to chance upon him and his sorrowful smile? Why did I have to meet him, just so that he could break my heart over and over again? He was a star, only he was not shining for me.

Wind lashed the campus with snow and bitter cold. The lake that had brought me hope, desire and dreams had now brought me despair. My soul mate had said "there isn't much hope for us." He had come and gone, disappearing again into the hazy light, leaving my heart marked forever with his name.

Four

Marriage

It can't be helped, the flowers have all faded away . . .
all I can do now is to wander through the scented
garden alone.

—Ann Zhu, ninth century

A year had passed since I first met Ning and Dong Yi. I had more or less reconciled myself to the fact that if I wanted to see Dong Yi at all, I must bury my true feelings and think of myself as nothing more than a good friend of his. So I often saw Ning and Dong Yi together and, for our last trip before the summer break, we three had decided to go boating. We went to the Purple Bamboo Garden, a park in central Beijing famous for its interlocking lakes. The day was gray and humid; we debated whether to go because rain was forecast. In the end we decided to go because we might not see each other again for the entire summer break. Dong Yi was, as expected, going back to Taiyuan. I thought about traveling to Mount Huangshan, in the Yellow Mountains in the south. Located in the southern part of Ann Hui province, the Yellow Mountains have long symbolized magnificence, beauty and mystery. Li Bai (701–762), the great Tang dynasty poet, wrote the following lines:

Thousands of feet high tower the Yellow Mountains
With their thirty-two magnificent peaks

Blooming like golden lotus flowers
Amid red crags and rock columns

The Yellow Mountains are the highest peaks in the Yangtze lowlands, and are famous as a place for watching the sunrise. Thus, like many Chinese, one of my dreams had long been to climb to the top of the mountains and watch the sun rising up from the plains of central China. Ning was, however, very secretive about his plans, and insisted that he would tell us when we were in the boat.

There were not many people renting boats that day. We picked a white boat with red trims, its new paint still shining. Further off in the distance, white boats were dotted along the horizon. The lake was calm, yet the dark water seemed to us to conceal secrets. A group of high school kids rowed by, singing to each other across the four boats.

Waves followed our oars
Sky blue and clouds white
A bright tomorrow
Our hearts beat for a bright tomorrow

We laughed. I remembered that I used to sing the same song when I was their age. What excitement and hope we had when we were ready to enter university! In our own ways, we envied them, their carefree youth, full of hope and expectation of the life to come.

Suddenly Ning turned to us and said, out of the blue, "I received a letter from the University of New Mexico last week. Apparently someone has dropped out and my name was pulled forward from the waiting list. I have been given a scholarship to study in their PhD program. I did not want to say anything until we are all together. Guys, I have accepted the offer and will be going to America in September!"

He looked at us with shining eyes, waiting.

"This is great! Congratulations!" Dong Yi suddenly moved forward with his hands stretched out. The boat jolted, he fell forward into Ning, almost knocking him out of the boat. I congratulated Ning too, remembering what he had said to me when we first met. I was terribly happy to see such a wonderful outcome for a person as kind, generous and intelligent as him. It was also such a thrill for me to witness the happiness of my dear friend, the happiness of a dream come true.

Yet, at the same time, I felt a profound sense of loss. I could not believe that Ning would be leaving us so soon for a country on the other side of the globe, which in reality we knew very little about. When would I see him again? Maybe never. My thoughts also turned to Dong Yi. Without Ning, how would my relationship with Dong Yi change?

"Let's go ashore and get ice cream and roasted peanuts. This deserves a big celebration," Dong Yi said, smiling.

Over the next few days, the three of us stayed together and ate more and more in the name of the celebration. One evening, we had wonton soup at a small stand in a street nearby. Another night, we ate *Tian Ji Gou Zi*—fried breadsticks in spicy sauce and egg pancakes. Finally, on a terribly hot day, we had cold Korean noodles at a small restaurant.

It was dark when we finished eating, and emerged into an evening bright and fresh, with stars twinkling in the sky like diamonds. I could smell the scent of jasmine coming from behind the walls of the university. We discussed going together to the lake as we'd done so many times before.

"Sorry," Ning said. "I can't go to the lake with you. I have to go back to the lab to finish up an experiment."

"Couldn't you finish your experiment tomorrow? What a shame, it really is a beautiful night," I gently pleaded with him.

"No. I promised my adviser. He is waiting for the result," Ning said, shifting from side to side.

So Dong Yi and I said good-bye to Ning and made our way inside the south gate and down to Weiming Lake.

A full moon hung over the pagoda, as if someone had hung up a giant white paper lantern. The night was gentle, with scarcely any wind, though once in a while, soft waves surfaced from nowhere, blurring the reflection of the perfect moon. Deep inside the woods, crickets sang loudly. A few streetlamps were dotted around the lake.

We wandered from the main path down to the lake, looking for somewhere to sit. Most benches at the lake were tucked under overhanging weeping willows or behind waist-high bushes, which, under the cover of darkness, were the most private spots on campus.

"I am afraid that all the benches are taken tonight," Dong Yi whispered as we passed young lovers deep in each other's arms. They had no other place to go but to the benches around the lake.

We stopped on the stone bridge. The moon had also stopped here, in the water below us. Dong Yi leaned back against the bridge columns carved with lions in various poses. Next to him, feeling my skin touching his, I stood facing the water and the moon.

"Have you thought about going to America yourself?" he asked.

"Never before. But now that Ning is going, maybe I should also think about it."

At that time, many students wanted to go to America, some neglecting their studies in order to focus on the entrance exams for U.S. universities. But I was not one of them, though I had occasionally wondered about the world outside China and thought that it would be nice to see it for myself one day. But until Ning left, that distant, unknown world was one I was not prepared to explore.

"What about you?" I turned around to look at Dong Yi. What I saw was his shadow in the moonlight.

"You know my view—we can do more for our country by staying." Dong Yi was firm. I had known and always respected his desire to give back to our society and to work for a better tomorrow for China.

"It's a pity that so many bright and well-educated people are leaving China," Dong Yi sighed. "But then who can blame them? Everything is banned—wall posters, demonstrations and political debates."

Going to America had become popular since the beginning of 1987, after the Government banned student demonstrations. As the political environment turned increasingly repressive, the younger generation of Chinese lost hope. More and more of them were leaving, primarily to study, as graduate students, in America.

"Many people from my class are leaving for America this year, which made me think twice about my own choices. Liu Gang was surprised to hear my saying so. I don't think I have changed. It's just so difficult to keep the hope alive," Dong Yi went on.

"If you were to go, you would be even further from Lan," I said.

Dong Yi turned around and also leaned over the bridge. The moon underneath us seemed more real than the one in the sky.

"I suppose so," he said quietly.

We both turned to look at each other at the same time. Our faces were so close I could feel Dong Yi's breath. The moon lit up his face. There was something in his eyes that made me feel sure that the yearning in me—for him to lean forward, to hold me, to whisper words of love, perhaps even to kiss me—burned as deeply in him as it did in me.

Then he took a step back. A light breeze disturbed the reflection of the moon, and we walked on. I started to feel the weight of my schoolbag and shifted it to the other shoulder.

"Have you written any new poems lately?" Dong Yi asked.

"Yes. As a matter of fact, I just finished one yesterday."

"Do you have it with you, can I read it?"

"Well . . . I am not sure . . . you may hate it."

"Don't be silly. I love your poems. I think you should seriously consider publishing them. Perhaps submitting some to a magazine? I don't know much about poetry, but I think you've got a talent for words."

"Well, my spectrum is pretty narrow. All I write about is love and loss. Sometimes I wonder if anyone would be interested in them."

"Everyone. What more is there in life than love, happiness, loss and sorrow? Not much, I think. Come on, show it to me please."

I handed over the piece of paper where I had written my latest poem. We stood underneath a streetlamp so that he could read it. I followed his eyes going down the page and waited nervously for his reaction. I wondered whether he knew that I was writing about him.

Passing a southerly window
Sun sprinkles countless shadows
Beside your bed—
Wind-scented lime tree blossom—
Does it make you think of me?
As I could not help thinking of you?

"Wei, it is very good. Send it in to the writing competition, I am sure you will win," Dong Yi spoke enthusiastically.

Someone started to play a guitar on the stone boat next to the little island in the middle of the lake. A nightingale echoed from the opposite hill.

The moon had climbed above the pagoda. The night was soft and warm, like Dong Yi's hands. I wished that we were not walking along the lake but among those hiding in the dark, somewhere up the hill, on the benches under the aspen trees. I wished he had read the poem, not as a critic or a friend, but as a lover. I wished . . .

Suddenly, a bright light lit up the darkness of the woods. A young woman turned her face toward the light like a deer in headlights. She was lying on the lap of her lover. The woman immediately sat up and tried to hide her face from the beam.

"What are you doing up there?" shouted the security guard, still pointing his flashlight at the couple. "What are your names? Which department?"

The young couple sat there like statues and did not answer.

"Please let them be. They are just kids trying to be together," said Dong Yi.

The guard pointed the light at Dong Yi. He put up his hand and turned away.

"This is a campus, not a dirty whorehouse. We have a duty to keep our university clean." The guard moved his flashlight back to the woods. The bench was now empty.

He walked closer to us and continued, "You don't know how many criminal activities we uncover here at the lake. Just the other day we caught a couple up there doing, well, you know what. You will see their names announced on posters soon. They both got official warnings for indecency. This will stay in their files forever. Well deserved. People should be more like the two of you—walking around, talking and getting to know each other, nothing more." He walked on, flashing his flashlight here and there, keeping the campus clean.

We lost interest in searching for a bench and left the lake right away, keeping a distance between us as we walked.

Dong Yi went back to Taiyuan and, as planned, I went on my trip to the Yellow Mountains with my girlfriend Qing, who was then studying at the Beijing Agriculture University.

Both Qing and I loved traveling. At that time tourism had not yet developed in China and backpacking was unusual, still more so for two young girls like us. Having little money, we took slow trains that stopped at every small village on the line, and changed trains frequently. Sometimes we slept on hard wooden seats on the trains, using our backpacks as pillows (and to prevent them from being stolen), while at other times we curled up in empty public bathhouses. One night, in a public bathhouse, I was woken up by loud banging. Some time later, when the noise eventually stopped, I was still shaky with imagined fears. I could no longer sleep. Shadows of showerheads, the dank smell—everything around us seemed to be filled with danger. At one point I had to wake up Qing.

"Go back to sleep. There is no one else here but us. You are just scaring yourself." Then she fell right back to sleep.

But I did not dare to close my eyes for the rest of that night.

Finally, when the train tracks ended, at the last town before the mountains, we boarded a bus. For a few hours, we seemed to be lost in endless bamboo forests. Then the road started to widen as it went up. Other buses, mostly run by tour operators catering to foreign tourists, joined us on the winding road up to the foot of Mount Huangshan. In the distance, we began to see misty peaks, which frequently changed shape and color as clouds and mist drifted past.

We arrived at the bottom of the Yellow Mountains in the late afternoon. Qing and I stayed the night in a small hotel there. The next morning, we began to climb the highest peak, which rose some 1,800 meters. The climbing was slow and at times difficult. At many points in our climb, the path went right to the side of the cliffs, with a sheer drop on one side and vertical rock on the other. The only safety measures were iron chains nailed across the rocks. The climb was particularly challenging for me because of my fear of heights. Yet Qing and I could not contain our excitement as we climbed higher and higher as, at every turn, we were presented with breathtaking views through occasional gaps in the mist; all the while enjoying the clear, cleansing air, the peaks and the ancient pine trees thriving on bare rocks, looking as if they might leap from their precarious ledges and touch the sky.

On the first night, we rented padded winter coats and tried to sleep on the mountaintop. But it was freezing cold, and we could not sleep. We spent the whole night talking, dozing off and talking again.

Qing and I met when we were twelve years old, on the first day of our boarding school. She was one of my seven roommates.

"You would not guess who I ran into two weeks ago at Wangfu-jing—our old roommate Min Fangfang, 'Minnie Mouse.' It was so funny; we were both buying lipstick at the new department store. I did not recognize her at first. The flower had blossomed. How two years of university in Shanghai can change someone! Remember the first night at boarding school? There was a huge thunderstorm and she fell off her bed?"

"And cried." We both laughed.

The night was long and cold. After exhausting all possible conversation about the past, we talked about the future. However, the next morning we were so tired that we remembered little of our discussions. At dawn, it started to drizzle. We still made our way to the viewing platform—a group of giant rocks—hoping the weather would clear up before sunrise. But we were unlucky and so we decided to stay another night on the mountaintop, hoping to see the sunrise the next day.

That night we parted with fifteen yuan (about $1.50) for a bed inside one of the tents. We finally saw the sunrise the following morning, in all its glory, rising from the plains of China. On the horizon, the rich land of my ancestors fused into the sky, in golden rays of light, and I could see no border or limit. So this is China, my motherland. Over there, to the east, lay the low plains of *Zhong Gou* where life had existed for thousands of years. Further to the west, the Yangtze river flowed peacefully across the land, glittering in the morning light like a silver belt. As the sun rose above the horizon, light exploded, radiating hundreds of thousands of rays to the earth, penetrating air, clouds, rocks, beings, everything seemed suddenly transparent. "Dong Yi!" I said, silently, to myself. "Can you see what I see and feel what I feel?"

During that summer, Yang Tao, my ex-boyfriend from my first year at Beijing University, came back from a year overseas. When he left to go abroad, I had broken off the relationship, but when he returned, he simply picked up where he had left off and resumed the role of boyfriend. He showered me with gifts that he had bought in the West and told me in great detail about his new job at the Department of Foreign Affairs, his political ambitions and future plans for us. Yang Tao was about to become the youngest diplomat in China.

I did not know what to do, with Dong Yi back home and Ning getting ready to go to America. Although I'd not yet seriously considered going to America myself, like many young Chinese girls at the time, I was captivated by the glamour of faraway lands, the association with anything foreign and most of all by people who had worked overseas. I liked the fashionable clothing Yang Tao brought back for me from Paris, Rome and Cairo. Makeup had just arrived in China, and foreign brands were scarce and very expensive. Fashionable girls would sometimes starve themselves so that they could buy foundation and eye makeup. Yang Tao not only brought me large makeup boxes containing everything from eye shadow and blushers to lipsticks, but also brought spares for my roommates. They were naturally very grateful and extremely impressed.

"How lucky to have such a handsome and rich boyfriend," they said to me. Their envy boosted my ego, though I knew it was all superficial. But perhaps it was what I needed after Dong Yi's rejection. So for such silly and materialistic reasons, I did not refuse Yang Tao: that was my error.

We spent most of the last week of the summer holiday together, shopping at Western designer boutiques, and dining at fancy restaurants like Maximilian, the French restaurant owned by the designer Pierre Cardin. And one Saturday afternoon, Yang Tao took me to his dormitory room to show me more photos of his time overseas. Yang Tao was about to start working for the Department of Foreign Affairs in the autumn; until then, he was finishing his final degree requirements for the Beijing Foreign Language University.

The university was quiet, being the last weekend before the end of the summer recess. Yang Tao's dormitory was empty, and we did not see or hear anyone on our way up to his room on the first floor. Although it was sunny and bright outside, Yang Tao's room, which had only one window that faced north and was completely shaded by a large oak tree, was dark. The room was small and cramped with three bunk beds, and Yang Tao's bed was the lower left one near the door.

We sat side by side on Yang Tao's bed looking through his photo albums, Yang Tao explaining to me where so-and-so was and what was going on. Then he pushed the photo album onto the floor and lay me down on his bed. Slowly he began to kiss me.

"Don't worry. The first time will be painful, but I will be very gentle," he whispered, lifting up my skirt and taking off my panties.

Although I was twenty years old, I had never had any sexual experience. Of course I knew biologically what went on—but I did not know how I should react or what I should do. I lay motionless.

Afterwards, Yang Tao watched me putting my clothes back on. I felt awful, the pain between my legs was bad but the way he reacted took me by surprise. He panicked, suddenly saying, "I don't suppose you are on birth control. We need to get you some morning-after pills. You don't want to get pregnant."

At that moment, fear set in—pregnancy. What would I do if it happened? How would I face my parents? My life would be ruined. I would be expelled from the university . . . the idea of a child, or an abortion, chilled my bones. And Yang Tao might lose his job at the Department of Foreign Affairs if he was to get an underage girl pregnant. Twenty-three was the minimum age requirement for marriage and therefore sex. I knew that Yang Tao was equally worried as he decided that we should go right away to the main street in Haidian, to get some contraception.

The largest store on the main street was the Chinese herbalist-cum-pharmacy. A large billboard opposite the store showed a painting of a revolutionary couple and a smiling child, captioned "Marry late, control birth." The maiin street was crowded with weekend shoppers, but luckily for us few people were in the pharmacy.

We hesitated at the door. Yang Tao said, "We need to act naturally. We will say we are married and just had an accident and need morning-after pills."

We walked in, my hands shaking. The store was wide, rather than long, with waist-high glass display cases all the way around. Wall-to-wall, behind the cases, stood imposing tall wooden Chinese medicine cabinets, with hundreds of tiny drawers and shiny metal handles. When I was little, I thought going to the herbalist was something like going to a temple; wisdom was stored in those tiny drawers, stacked right up to the ceiling.

As soon as we stepped inside, we were swamped by the smell of dried, bitter roots, marinated animal intestines and crushed herbs. A middle-aged woman wearing a white coat sat behind the counter reading a popular novel about the send-down youth. After hearing Yang Tao's story, she looked at us, studying our faces. I was sure that I was done for. "She knows that we are lying. She will call the police. The police will come and take me back to Beijing University . . ." I was still quite confused from everything that had happened to me in the past hour. It had not taken long; it was all over in minutes. But how much pain it had cost me, and now it threatened to ruin the rest of my life—and I had so much to look forward to!

"Over there in those boxes, help yourself," said the woman eventually, burying her head in her book again.

Because of China's overpopulation, birth control was greatly encouraged. The government had made birth control pills and condoms free to all, as well as legislating that one couple could have only one child. Though I knew about the free birth control pills, I was surprised at how easy it was to get them. All kinds of pills and contraceptive devices were left in plastic trays scattered around the store.

We took one pack of each kind of pill and left quickly. I read the instructions behind a small fruit stall. They said to take one tablet right away and one the next day.

We then went back to Beijing University.

Ning's departure date was fast approaching. I went to see him one day. We both felt sad that he was leaving very soon. We were talking about the past year and the times we'd had together, when suddenly Yang Tao burst into the room. Without speaking a word, he jumped on Ning and punched him. My first instinct was to help Ning. But I immediately realized that that would only make things worse. Yang Tao had mistakenly assumed that Ning and I were lovers. Instead, screaming and crying, I pulled and pushed Yang Tao outside.

I later found out that one of my roommates had told Yang Tao that I had gone to see my friend in the Physics Department. Yang Tao then searched my bag and found Ning's address. Though Yang Tao apologized to me repeatedly over the next few days, I was deeply shaken by the incident.

Autumn came. The leaves on the maple trees were red, like blood. The sky looked higher now without the hazy sunshine of summer, and the air was fresh and crystal clear.

Ning left China.

It was just before dinner, my roommates had gone to the canteen, and I was doing my makeup for the evening. Yang Tao was going to take me out to celebrate my scholarship to graduate school.

Beijing University awarded a scholarship and a place in the graduate school to one or two top-ranked students in each department every year. I had been told that morning, our first week back, that I had the best grades of my class and thus had won the scholarship. I was not only given a place in the graduate school, but also the choice of studying with any professor in the department, a great privilege as it is usually the professor who does the choosing.

I called Yang Tao with the news. "Wonderful. We will go to the Russian Tea House for dinner. Wear the white dress I bought for you in Paris. I will pick you up at seven o'clock."

This was very exciting. The Russian Tea House was a restaurant frequented until recently only by the senior Party members, and I'd never been. I didn't even know someone who had. I had just finished making myself up when I heard someone knocking on my door. I immediately assumed that it was Yang Tao.

"You are early." I opened the door.

"I am?" I was surprised to see Dong Yi standing in front of me. I'd been preparing myself to go and see him but I wasn't ready at that moment. He stared at me for a few seconds and smiled, "Hello, Wei. Long time no see. How beautiful you look tonight!"

"How wonderful to see you. Please come in." I felt a surge of happiness at seeing him; I wanted to hug him and hold his hands and share my good news with him. But I didn't because, in China, physical contact is reserved only for lovers.

"When did you come back? How was your summer?" As soon as I said it, I thought of Lan and the entire summer that they had spent together. Right away I wished I hadn't asked.

"Fine. It is good to be back. Did you like your trip to the Yellow Mountains?"

I told Dong Yi about my trip and said that he should one day meet Qing. "She is a load of fun, very edgy and very rebellious. Sometimes I find it strange that she should be such a daredevil given her background—her parents are both officers in the PLA."

But Dong Yi interrupted my account of the trip, not something he'd normally do, and changed the subject. "In fact I have come specially to tell you something."

"I have something to tell you too. I am so excited—I have been given the scholarship to graduate school!"

"Congratulations! This is wonderful, Wei."

Then I heard someone knocking on the door. "Wait a minute, let me see who is at the door."

I opened the door. It was the boyfriend of one of my roommates. I told him that his girlfriend had gone to dinner at the number four canteen. Just when I was about to close the door, my diplomat appeared.

"Congratulations, my darling! I am so proud of you. I brought this. Open it." He came in holding his motorbike helmet in one hand and, in the other, a small red box.

"You really shouldn't have. This is my friend Dong Yi. He is just leaving." I felt embarrassed. I had not yet had time to tell Dong Yi about this new development in my life. I also felt concerned, remembering the episode with Ning, and wanted to get Dong Yi out of there as soon as possible.

"Hey," he said, nodding half-heartedly at Dong Yi. Then he turned back to me and said again, "Open it."

I opened the box. Inside was a golden necklace with a heart-shaped locket.

"Put it on. This was the first thing I bought for you when I was overseas. It suits you well." He helped me to put on the necklace and then kissed me on the cheek.

I could have died. I looked at Dong Yi who was clearly embarrassed, and words failed me.

"Are you ready to go? We don't want to be late for our reservation." He continued to ignore Dong Yi.

"I'd better go. Have a nice dinner." Dong Yi stood up to leave, clearly hurt.

"I will come to see you, maybe tomorrow? You wanted to tell me something . . ."

"No. It was nothing. Don't worry about it." Dong Yi hurried away.

The Russian Tea House was the only Western restaurant to survive the Cultural Revolution; apparently Party leaders liked the food. Maybe it reminded the senior Party members of the good times when the People's Republic was just founded, and the junior members of the years they had spent in the Soviet Union as young and promising Party youth. Set in a garden, the restaurant was in the grand Russian style, with high roofs and large columns. It had been a "Party leaders only" restaurant until 1984, when it opened to the public. But the diners were still mostly Party leaders, their families and friends. More recently it had also become a fashionable place for bosses of state-run enterprises to dine on company expenses, even though most of them could not use the forks and knives that were placed on the table instead of chopsticks. Unlike traditional Chinese establishments, the waiters wore white shirts and black trousers and attended customers with care. We had a big meal at the Russian Tea House that night. Yang Tao ordered caviar and champagne. As he corrected the way I used my knives and forks, I thought of Dong Yi. I wondered how he must be feeling, and what it was that he wanted to tell me. And I thought about what I had not told him.

I did not go to see Dong Yi the next day. I felt bad that he had found out about Yang Tao the way he did. A few days later I met him in the canteen. I could feel that he had put distance between us. When I asked him what he wanted to tell me that evening, he insisted that it was nothing.

I suspected that Dong Yi had not been telling me the truth. But I did not do anything about it. Nor did I tell him what had happened between Yang Tao and me. Instead, I turned my mind to other things. With a place in the graduate school guaranteed, the pressure of studying lessened and I spent more and more time away from campus. Armed with the American dollars that he had earned while being posted overseas, Yang Tao took me shopping in the newly opened designer boutiques. We went to expensive restaurants and hotel bars—Beijing's nightlife was just beginning, but only for the few who could afford it. Soon, I became one of the best-dressed students on campus. I think the reason that I never objected to these gifts was because although, from time to time, I still saw Dong Yi, our relationship had cooled considerably. Yet deep down I knew that I still loved him, and so, to avoid facing how I felt, I buried myself in the world of instant gratification created for me by Yang Tao: money, jewelry, designer clothes, alcohol and sex.

One evening, Yang Tao came and told me that he had asked the Beijing University representative of the University Student Association to keep an eye on me. He told me that there were some people trying to rekindle "the so-called democracy debate" and stir up antigovernment feelings on campus. He didn't want me to go near them, because he warned me that both the Student Association and the

Youth League were closely monitoring the situation and knew specific names and departments. "If these students do not stop, someone will get hurt soon."

He told me that I should be careful for myself as the future wife of an important diplomat. Soon I began to feel like a bird locked in a golden cage. Sometimes when I went to Weiming Lake by myself, I could feel the emptiness inside me. Sometimes I dreamed of the wonderful days I had spent with Dong Yi and Ning. And when I woke up, my heart would overflow with sadness and loss. I thought of Ning: nothing had been the same since he left; he seemed to be to blame for my now-pointless life.

And my life became more and more aimless as the term went by. I took no pleasure from it, hated it in fact, but I could not escape. I became depressed. My grades dropped and I withdrew from my friends. My relationship with Yang Tao also turned stormy, as he began to insist I give him an account of my every movement away from him and I became increasingly frustrated. Though many of my girlfriends envied my lifestyle, I desperately wanted to end it. I missed Dong Yi and Ning and the happy times we'd had together.

Three days before I was to report for graduate school, I suddenly realized the route I had to take to escape my situation. For three nights, I lay awake in my bed thinking about my life. I decided that instead of going on to graduate school at Beijing University, I would go and study in America, even if it meant that I would have to take extra English lessons. The golden land of freedom and prosperity became the solution that I was looking for.

So when the enrolment day came, I did not turn up to register. My department sent letters, and my classmates, to look for me. When I told my professors that I had decided to give up my place in the graduate school, they could not believe it. My parents freaked out. "How can you throw away such an opportunity? What will you do if you don't succeed in going to America? It's not as easy as you think!" Mama cried out to me. But my mind was made up. No one was going to talk me into changing it.

I was free; the bird had flown her golden cage. I had no regrets, just an irrepressible desire to fly into the open sky above.

On campus, I became an instant celebrity. Over the next year, whenever I visited my friends who went on to graduate school, people would come to their dorm rooms to see me. They would tell me that they had heard about me for so long and that they wanted to see what I looked like. I supposed that most of them were like my parents and thought that I was mad.

When I decided to drop out of graduate school and go to America, I was also able to end my relationship with Yang Tao. Luckily by then Yang Tao was again assigned abroad, so I wrote to him and ended our relationship. And then, one evening, I arranged to have dinner with Dong Yi.

The number three student canteen was full that evening. Hundreds of people crowded inside. They shouted out the menu to their friends, which was written on blackboards hanging at every window. They fought for places in the line. They greeted old friends and new acquaintances with the enthusiasm of a new school year.

Dong Yi and I tried our best to catch up amid the loud noise of spoons scraping on aluminium bowls and conversations carried out at full volume. I told Dong Yi about what I had decided to do with my life. He didn't seem surprised.

"How did your parents react?"

"They are furious. They think I've thrown away something certain for something as unreliable as going to America. They think I'm out of my mind. Of course I know that it is entirely possible that I won't get into any school in the U.S. But that doesn't mean that I shouldn't try. On the other hand, they were quite pleased when I stopped seeing you-know-who. They never liked him. They never liked anyone I ever dated. How about you? How was your summer break—eventful?" I asked Dong Yi.

"Well, you could say that. First, there was the news about Liu Gang. Do you remember Liu Gang?"

"Of course, we went to his birthday party. He graduated last year, didn't he?"

"Yes, he did, but now he is unemployed and has come back to Beijing. He is going to stay with me for a while."

"I am sorry. How's he doing?" I was surprised by the news.

"Many people in the department, including professor Li Shuxian and her husband, professor Fang Lizhi, are helping him," said Dong Yi. Professor Fang Lizhi was a physics professor who had been China's leading opposition figure for many years. In 1987, he was expelled from the Communist Party for supporting the 1986 student demonstrations. His writings on human rights and democracy had brought him international recognition and plenty of trouble with the government. His wife, professor Li Shuxian, was Dong Yi's professor and also a prominent figure in China's Democracy Movement.

Dong Yi continued, "By the way, if anyone asks you about Liu Gang, don't say anything. We believe that the secret police have been to the campus looking for him."

"The secret police? Why?"

"He caught the attention of the secret police when he was the editor of the magazine *Free Talk*. Since returning to Beijing, he's become even more vocal about political reform. He has been giving speeches at public rallies on campus."

I interrupted Dong Yi as I suddenly realized that he might be in danger as well. "If the secret police are watching Liu Gang, then you are not safe either."

"Don't worry about me. I am OK. Honestly, I am fine." He smiled.

"What else? You said this was the first news," I asked excitedly, partly to change the topic, and partly to satisfy my curiosity. I wanted to find out everything about him as quickly as possible so that I could start to tell him about my plans for the future.

"I got married." This time his voice was calm, as if he were telling me that he had just bought a new shirt, or changed the calendar on his wall.

"What?" I was stunned, had no idea what to think. I felt as if the life had been drained out of me. "Have you been planning this for some time? Why didn't you tell me?"

"No. I did not plan it. I did not even know that it was going to happen. When I was at home, everyone in both our families wanted us to get married. At first I thought it was just another round of the show they put on every time I am at home. But this time it was different. Do you remember that evening last year when I'd just come back from Taiyuan? I came to see you. I wanted to tell you that I was thinking of leaving Lan. I had thought so much over the summer about you and about what I wanted from life."

I was shocked to hear these words, and my surprise numbed my tongue. Even though I had often tried to guess what he'd wanted to tell me that evening, it had never occurred to me that his leaving Lan was a possibility.

"I thought about what you said about *Anna Karenina*—the doomed love story." Dong Yi carried on, "And it would not be fair for Lan either, I thought, to marry her if I did not love her. I came to tell you all of this. But you were back with your diplomat. What's his name?"

"Yang Tao," I said.

"I could not compete with Yang Tao. I could not buy you jewelry or afford expensive restaurants. You seemed happy. You seemed to have patched up your differences."

Was I that shallow? Yes, I was. But if only he'd known the reality of my relationship with Yang Tao. If only he'd known the loneliness I felt without him.

"Why didn't you at least tell me?" I asked.

Why didn't he come and rescue me? Didn't he know that I would have let everything dear to me go, if he had called me to go to the edge of the sky with him?

"It does not matter anymore. The truth is that as every year went by, it became harder and harder to end the relationship. Everyone said that if we didn't get married, Lan's reputation would be ruined. She would never be able to find someone good to marry."

"What do you mean?"

"Because, well, how can I put it, Lan was no longer a virgin."

I was surprised to hear this, knowing the harsh morality of inland China. Perhaps Lan was more progressive than I gave her credit for; perhaps they loved each other enough to brave the hostility of society. Perhaps . . . then I stopped my train of thought abruptly. I felt sad, jealous and angry—this is more than I care to know, I said to myself.

Dong Yi continued, "When I told Lan about you, I hurt her badly. I couldn't bear to see her unhappy. We have loved each other for so long. I needed to make it up to Lan and to do my part to bring happiness back to our lives."

"But we never even kissed," I stammered.

"It did not matter to her. It was the feeling I had for you that she resented. In many ways she was right—a purely physical thing would have hurt less. She also resented that we stayed close friends. She asked me why. I could not say. She believed that, like the Party, I 'prefer the new to the old.' She said that since I had come to Beijing

University, I looked down on her and I was ungrateful for all the things she had done for me—caring for my parents, cooking, cleaning and so on. Everyone around her said the same thing."

Dong Yi lowered his voice to a whisper. "Lan told my parents and her family about you. They all took her side. Wei, you know how complicated life can be, don't you?"

He paused. Did he expect understanding or sympathy from me? My love, what do you expect me to say? I wanted to lose myself in his eyes, for they were so gentle. But I was devastated. And so I said nothing. I could not help him, not at that moment.

"So we did the easiest thing and got married. It was time to end all the suffering."

"Yours or mine?"

"Don't be cruel, Wei. I wish I could be more like you. In fact I have never known anyone like you. At the drop of a hat, you can start your life all over again. On the contrary, I am a coward. But I think this is the best for everyone. I am everything Lan has, but you have the whole world at your feet."

"Don't be too hard on yourself," I said. Suddenly I was aware again of where we were, of the shouting of freshmen and the smell of cooking fat and spicy sauce in the student canteen. "You are not a coward. You are just nicer than I am."

At that moment, drowning in the sound of the busy world around me, it came home to me that, sitting opposite, was the man who embodied everything I had ever wanted, and everything that I had lost. Dong Yi had entrusted himself, and his future happiness, to another.

Five

Gold Rush

There will come a time, when wind breaks the waves.
Then we shall raise our sail, and go to the sea.

—Li Bai, eighth century

I met Eimin in the spring of 1988, three months before my graduation, at a party hosted by the Psychology Department. He had just returned from Scotland with a PhD and been appointed an associate professor. The department chair respectfully asked him to speak to the students about his experiences in the UK; this was a real honor as the department chair was older than him. Eimin surprised us; instead of a lecture, as we were used to in China, he had a different style—the Western style. He answered questions and engaged the audience. He had a natural ability to make you believe that you were there with him, walking, seeing, exploring and evaluating, everything from psychology, and Western decadence, to the Loch Ness monster. Sitting at the back of the room, I heard something in his voice that seemed to come from a faraway place.

Eimin was twelve years older than me, and had spent his youth on a remote People's Collective Commune in the Cultural Revolution. When Deng Xiaoping reopened the universities in 1977, Eimin borrowed books from fellow send-down youths and read them under oil lamps through the night. His father was a college professor who had questioned Mao's role in the Cultural Revolution to a close friend, in confidence. The friend turned him in. He was tortured and sent to do forced labor, his family thrown out of their home, his children transported to separate People's Collectives around the country. Eimin was fifteen when he went to shovel cow manure in the Great North of China. He spent the next eight years there, and was not allowed to visit his father.

What Eimin had experienced was so different from my own life. He had lived through, and survived, the Cultural Revolution. He had been in the West for five years, and he had seen more than just what went on inside classrooms. To me, he was mature, enigmatic, successful and intelligent, all the things I found attractive in men. He also suited my mood at the time: my desire to break free from my past.

The fact that Eimin was my professor added more charisma to his allure. In Western culture, a student is asked to respect her teacher and, sometimes, to see her teacher as a friend. In Chinese culture, a student is asked to devote herself to her teacher and to see him as an inspiration. Romance between a professor and his student is deemed inappropriate in the West, but in China romance occurs frequently between teachers and students. Such romance is the common theme of Chinese martial arts novels.

Eimin and I had been friends for some time when, one night in November, he invited me to a dance on campus. I had by then left Beijing University and moved back to live with my parents. My days were filled with English lessons, in preparation for studying in America, and my evenings with homework. I missed the campus life and so I happily accepted Eimin's invitation.

But Eimin was a lousy dancer. I wondered why he had invited me there. But I did not care; I had a wonderful time dancing through the whole evening. For his part, Eimin sat out most of the dances, watching me from the sidelines and smiling.

We were among the last to leave the dance hall. It was past midnight and Eimin said I should not attempt to cycle back to my parents" apartment so late, and in the cold. He offered to let me sleep over on his sofa. Eimin had been given a small room on the first floor of the Young Faculty Building when he returned from Scotland. There was a telephone in his building, which I used to call my parents. I told them I was staying with a girlfriend in her dormitory. It is fair to say that we both knew what was going to happen that night, and that it was something we both wanted. When he came to me in the dark, I opened my arms and kissed him back.

Soon I was in love with Eimin and by February 1989 I began to spend a lot of my free time with him in his small but private room. I had just completed, in January, the GRE and TOFFLE exams that were required for my applications to universities in America. I had applied for a place in their next academic year, beginning in September. Unfortunately Eimin was somewhat of an ambitious workaholic, who spent much of his time teaching and conducting experiments. One evening, I had expected to see him but he was carrying out a survey somewhere on campus. So I went to visit Chen Li, who I knew would liven up my evening.

The campus was quiet after a day of excitement. The evening was balmy and pleasant, and the yellow sand that had blown in from the Mongolian Desert and been floating in the air all day had settled.

We met at the Spoon Garden Bar. We went through a small door and down a narrow stairway leading to the basement. The bar was simply a large room, undecorated and with only basic tables and chairs. But it was the hippest place to go on campus. Spoon Garden was a residence complex of three buildings that housed foreign students and visitors to Beijing University. Chinese students were not allowed inside the buildings unless invited by a resident. The Spoon Garden Bar was opened two years earlier, and it was the only place in the complex that Chinese students could enter freely. Foreign students spent most of their free evenings here, sharing their stories about China or about home. Chinese students came here, despite the high prices, to gain a taste of foreign lands and to feel just a bit exotic.

We took off our heavy winter parkas and sat down at a table near the entrance and ordered coffee. The air in the bar reeked of the scent of sweet tobacco. Poor lighting became romantic in the smoke. Speakers blared out a mixture of some of the most popular English songs then current in China: the Carpenters, Lionel Richie and Wham!

I looked around and saw fashionably dressed Chinese girls scattered around various tables. Their long jet-black hair shone like satin, their lips were red and moist. Dating a foreigner was risky, but many tried. Marrying a Westerner was the dream of many Chinese girls, for then they could leave China forever. Some foreign students seemed to enjoy their popularity, like kings enjoying the worship of their subjects. They came to the bar to be surrounded by Chinese girls, to get drunk and to be seduced by the sights and scents of Oriental femininity.

Chen Li was in a happy mood that evening. He had just found out that he stood a good chance of being assigned to Shenzhen after graduation. For a long time, he had wanted to go to Shenzhen, a city across from Hong Kong and the first special economic zone in China. Shenzhen was not only the first, but also the most successful of the special economic zones initiated by Deng Xiaoping.

"Do you know that the average income in Shenzhen is already ten times that in Beijing? Free market economics have worked miracles there. Imagine what China would look like if Shenzhen spread to the entire country!"

"Don't you want to stay in Beijing? After all this is the capital and where the policies are made," I asked.

"Many of my classmates want to stay in Beijing, in fact some are desperate, doing whatever they can, going through back doors or trying bribes. Not me. I am not interested in policy. Well, that's not fair. What I mean is that I want more to do with the real economy itself. You have always told me that I looked more like an engineer than an economist. I am more of a field economist—similar to engineers, I like to get my hands dirty."

The image of Chen Li working in a field seemed to suit him. The only son of factory workers, Chen Li was always more interested in real problems and solutions. I liked Chen Li for many of his qualities, among which was his naïve enthusiasm. He genuinely believed that there existed black and white, good and evil, right and wrong, and behaved accordingly. His confidence in such a simple vision of the world was particularly refreshing after having spent most of my time with someone who was twelve years older, in whose view everything was complicated, gray and uncertain.

I sipped my coffee slowly and listened to Chen Li's plans. It is so good to be excited about one's future, I thought. I wished that I were as positive about mine. At that moment, Hanna came in.

Hanna was the daughter of a family friend and my mother's ex-student. A year before she had dropped out of university to go to America. Her distant aunt, a well known Chinese actress in Hollywood, had agreed to sponsor her. I understood that it was in the bag, and was therefore shocked to see that she was still in China, and in the Spoon Garden Bar of all places.

"Hanna, what are you doing here?"

"Oh, I tutor Chinese to *Lau Wai* [foreigners]. By the way, this is Jerry, my student." She looked around and said, "Do you mind if we join you? It looks full tonight."

"Sure," I said and introduced Chen Li.

Hanna looked happy and more radiant than ever. A great natural beauty, Hanna, at five foot nine, with tanned skin and a curvaceous body, recognized her assets and was not afraid of flaunting them. When she laughed, her entire body waved with her hair. Every man in that room was looking at her, and once they did, they could not take their eyes off her.

"Jerry is a professor at the University of Kansas."

"What do you teach?" Chen Li asked in English.

"Asian History," Jerry replied, in near perfect Chinese.

Hanna put a cigarette to her lips and Jerry lit it for her. "Jerry is very good with languages. His Chinese was already quite good when he answered my ad, now four months later, it is almost perfect. Jerry also speaks fluent Japanese."

Though in his early fifties, Jerry was still a handsome man. He was tall, muscular, with distinguished silver hair and an air of superiority.

"Hanna is the best tutor one can have. I am very fortunate to have come across her." He looked at her with adoration, while she reciprocated with a beautiful smile.

"How come you are still in Beijing?" I asked.

"I can't get a student visa, can you believe it? You'd think that my aunt's backing would be enough. She's very rich. But this silly man at the American Embassy still wants to see a college acceptance. My aunt is working on that. In the meantime, I needed some money so I came to Spoon Garden and put my card up in the lobby."

At this point, Jerry joined in and started to explain how difficult it was for foreign students to get into American colleges. "It's not just about money. You'd need sufficient exam scores, such as SATs [Standard Assessment Tests]."

"But it is too late to take the exams for this year." Hanna puffed away. "God forbid that I have to stay in China one more year. I will go to America one way or the other. I have to. I can't get the kind of job

I would like in China. Do you know how much they pay for freelancing if you don't have a college diploma? Close to nothing. That's why I came to teach Chinese at Spoon Garden. It's good money. But this isn't a long-term solution. After all, I studied English and journalism. What am I doing teaching Chinese?"

"China is wonderful. I really like the country," said Jerry. "But I think young people should go abroad to see how other people live. For example, the other day," he gestured at Hanna and then continued, "I was just telling Hanna that I had never seen such a panic among people as I saw when I was getting on a bus in Beijing. Every bus seemed to be the last bus. People trying to get off pushed those who wanted to get on, and vice versa. As a result you end up with a bus that is not moving at all because everyone is stuck where they don't want to be." He mimed shoving and pushing and squashing actions as he said this.

We all laughed. Jerry was delighted with our reactions and went on, "I love Chinese women, beautiful, gentle, caring, sensual and feminine. But when I watch them pushing and shouting, trying to get on buses, I just want to run away."

I started to feel slightly ashamed of my gender and of my country. When someone points out ugliness that's inherent in your own country, you feel somehow partly responsible, even though you may hate it as much as anyone.

Chen Li told Jerry and Hanna about his plans for after graduation. Jerry became very interested and started to ask a lot of questions about Shenzhen and the special economic zone. Soon, Hanna seemed bored. She wanted to go to the counter for some snacks. I went with her. As we stood up and walked toward the glass display cases, many eyes followed our steps. Hanna tossed her thick, long black hair to one side so that her beautiful face was fully in view for her many admirers.

"How do you like Jerry?" she asked me.

"He seems very nice, and funny."

"He is so much more mature than these adolescent boys." She tipped her head toward the wandering eyes all along the bar. "He is divorced and has a teenage son who lives with his mother in Philadelphia. They are great friends. They go horse riding together; they do sports together. Imagine that in China, father and son good friends! You'd never see it." In China, the relationship between a son and his father is characterized by obedience and respect for the older man, not friendship.

"Do you know that he is an Asia expert?" Hanna continued. "He can teach me about Chinese and Japanese history! He has traveled around the world giving lectures. You have to let him tell you about the places he has been to, beautiful tales he tells." She took a small plate of salted peanuts and went on, "I want to see those places, which means I need to leave China for a country with an open border, where people are allowed to have passports and travel as they wish."

"Is that why you want to go to America, to travel around the world?" I asked.

"Partly. What's your reason? I heard that you are trying to go to America too."

"I want to make changes in my life." Then I thought about it and said, "And I suppose, just like you, I would also like to see the world."

Presently, a young American whom I vaguely knew walked up to us and said hello. "Who is this beautiful lady, Wei?" His breath was soaked in alcohol and his eyes bloodshot.

"Tony, this is my friend Hanna."

"Are you a student at Beijing U?" Tony lifted his glass. "How come I have never seen you around? I must be blind."

"You are not blind, but drunk," Hanna said in perfect English. Then she turned around and took my hand. "Let's go back to our table."

I said good-bye to Tony. We left him standing at the bar uncomprehendingly—perhaps he did not expect so brutal a rejection from a Chinese girl.

"Little boys. I have no patience for them. They are so immature and self-absorbed," Hanna said.

We sat down and passed around the roasted peanuts and hot chocolate. Chen Li and Jerry were now discussing history.

"How can you be so sure about it after what happened in your history?" Jerry fixed his eyes on Chen Li. "After all the Cultural Revolution only ended ten years ago."

"I don't know much about the Cultural Revolution. I was eleven when it was over. But I think if there was anything positive about that period of Chinese history it would be that the Cultural Revolution educated people about what it meant to be poor and isolated. People like my parents are in fact very pro-reform, not because they understand economics. My parents never finished high school. What they know is that they don't want to go back to the time of Cultural Revolution. Deng Xiaoping once said famously 'let some people get rich first.' Now others have seen how good life can be and want to follow suit."

"You are a student of political economics: do you think that economic prosperity could continue without pluralism and democracy? Some people, such as professor Fang Lizhi, believe that corruption is the direct result of the lack of democracy in the political system, which would inevitably clash with economic policies. Do you hold the same view?"

This was also Dong Yi's view, I thought to myself. I wondered if he read Professor Fang's work.

Chen Li answered, "I can't say that I know Professor Fang's full views. Much of his writing is banned in China. But I do think that, at some point, China will have to deal with political reform as well, which surely will be more painful than economic reform. But for now, lack of democracy does not seem to have stopped economic growth in, for example, the special economic zones."

"But what about freedom of speech—don't you want it? I mean . . . liberty and freedom are, after all, God-given rights."

I envied Americans their easy assumption that they could say anything they wanted without worrying about the secret police or prosecution. The world was open to Jerry, but not yet to Chen Li and me.

"What about the negative aspects of freedom of speech? Won't too much of it lead to disorder and chaos?" I said to Jerry. Though I agreed with Jerry that freedom of speech is a basic human right, his air of superiority, the fact that he had such freedom and we did not, made me want to argue.

"I don't believe there are negative aspects to such freedom. On the contrary, when there isn't freedom of speech, injustice will happen. Injustice is what leads to disorder and chaos," responded Jerry.

"Politics again?" Hanna put a stop to the conversation. "Jerry, tell Wei about what happened to you in West Berlin. I told her that you had traveled around the world, and Wei would like to hear some of your stories."

Jerry was happy to oblige. His stories took hold of our imaginations, and, sitting in the Spoon Garden Bar, we dreamed of exotic places.

As the evening went on, the bar got more crowded and the crowd got rowdier. A group of Japanese students was now singing and shouting. At the next table, a Chinese girl was reading the palm of a blond American boy, while her girlfriends giggled loudly. Chinese spoken in English, Japanese or German accents mingled with English spoken in Chinese accents. George Michael was singing "Careless Whisper." We talked more about China, America and the world, and drank more coffee (Chen Li and me), beer (Jerry) and champagne (Hanna).

The gold rush was in high gear that spring, to America or to the special economic zones. The new prosperity, and the freedom it promised, seemed within our grasp.

Six

Funeral

We cannot keep the spring, no matter how birds cry,
littered on the ground are shattered red and
dirtied glory.

—*Wang Ann Gou, ninth century*

The spring of 1989 changed everything in China. The death of one of the highest-ranking Communist Party leaders triggered a movement that would become the largest mass demonstration of the century, and bring China to the world's attention.

But as the snow started to melt away in March, no one was aware of such things. Beijing was, as usual, full of anticipation. Decorations for the Chinese New Year celebrations had been stored away, red lanterns taken down from the doors and paper cuttings of *Shuang Xi*—Double Luck—peeled off the windows. A warning sign stood next to the abandoned ice rink. The first south wind replaced the north wind.

I had been waiting anxiously throughout the winter for news from the American universities I had applied to. To take my mind from the agony of waiting, my parents found me some freelance work at the holiday tour company owned by my father's office.

This was the beginning of China's journey toward prosperity, and everyone wanted to board the bus. State-run enterprises, such as the one where my father worked, had spun off all sorts of moneymaking subsidiaries. Tourism seemed to be the perfect choice for my father's office, as their responsibilities included all the parks of Beijing. Bureaucrats became tour operators; new logos were painted on buses belonging to the department; tours were advertised overseas.

I was grateful for this opportunity. The year before, after I had dropped out of graduate school, I went back to my old department and requested a job. (For a country where only one percent of the population makes it to college, I knew I was qualified, even without being the first in my class at Beijing University.) But I was told that the job allocation had been completed a few months before. In the centrally controlled Chinese system, every bolt has its fixed place; I was the one who left my given position, and as a consequence I became unwanted. Professor Bai, my sympathetic Department Chair, told me that they could send my *Hukou*, or residence permit, back to my parents. I could at least be listed as a dependant there.

"But what about your file?" queried Professor Bai.

Where would I put my file? I asked myself.

In China, everyone had a file; no one knew exactly what was in her own file. But we did know roughly what might be there—things we had said about the Party, self-reflections, self-criticisms we had to write over the years, evaluations of us by Party members, secret reports others had made on us . . . Only Party leaders had access to the files. A person's file forms a secret profile, and wherever one went, the file would follow. It was always being added to. In China, this is called *Gua Dang*, which means, literally, hanging a file. Everyone needed a place where she could hang her file and thus have an official existence.

Now that I had fallen out of the system, where would my file go? Without my file, I did not exist as a person in China and thus would not be given a passport.

So I went home with my *Hukou* and my father managed to let me "hang my file" in his office. But I did not draw a salary and was in effect unemployed. Instead of finally paying my own way with a graduate school scholarship, I came to depend on my parents again for everything. I was only too happy to take tourists on trips, so that I could ease, slightly, the burden on my parents.

Unfortunately, it was not a job I enjoyed. I was always caught in the middle, for the Chinese had their schemes and the tourists had their complaints. Most of the tourists I encountered were aging overseas Chinese coming back to seek their roots and, probably, see the country for the last time. Many of them were from Taiwan, and had traveled a long way, via Hong Kong, to the mainland. Typically, the night before the end of the tour, the Chinese guides and drivers would threaten not to take the tourists to the airport if certain amounts of off-book tips were not paid. Their argument was that the tourists were rich and thus could afford such tips. They argued that they wanted tips equivalent to the amounts that a tour guide or a driver could make in the West. They completely ignored the fact that the standard of living in China was much lower. "Why should we be paid less just because we are Chinese?" they'd say. The tips they demanded were more than a year's salary for an ordinary Chinese. They were also cheerfully complacent about the fact that they were not providing the same level of service as is standard in the West.

The tourists always paid up in the end. Being a freelancer, I was not included in the schemes. But I still felt terrible because I knew what had happened, which made it difficult when I had to say goodbye to those grandpas and grandmas at the airport. I felt sad for them. They had returned to China to trace their roots and to see a homeland that they might never see again. But what memories were they taking back? I felt ashamed of those I had to work with, ashamed of their heartless greed and the fact that I was somehow party to it. Every time, I just took my weekly wage of sixty yuan and walked away as fast as I could. (Sixty yuan, then, was about $10. Twenty yuan would buy you dinner. Several years later it buys you one ice cream.) I told my father about the demands for off-book tips, but he wasn't able to do anything; corruption was everywhere.

Meanwhile, I was still waiting for the call, or the thick envelope, from America and, one sunny spring morning, a large and heavily stuffed envelope did indeed come for me. I had been told that thin letters meant rejection while thick ones meant good news. My parents, watching nervously, had to wait for me to tear the envelope open to tell them: I had been accepted by the University of Texas at Austin and they had given me a full scholarship. A day later I had a call from the other university I'd applied to, the College of William and Mary in Virginia. They too offered me a full scholarship. I threw my arms around my mother and screamed with joy. Spring arrived in Beijing, fulfilling its promises.

I waited for Dong Yi under the big oak tree outside the English Hall. A few months before, we had taken English lessons together, and the GRE exam. Campus was quiet, most students had gone to read, or lie down for an afternoon nap. Sunshine came through the leafless branches and landed on my face with tender warmth. In the distance, color had just begun to return to the hills. Purple lilies budded in patches along the south slope of the lake.

Dong Yi emerged, a lone figure on a bike, the sun behind him, like a prince arriving in shining armor. I have always thought that the best kind of love is the one where, when you look into a pair of eyes, you see home. That afternoon, I still saw home in Dong Yi's eyes when he sat down next to me. How I envied Lan. I sighed. The thought of the woman who possessed the love I could not have depressed me. But I didn't say so. Instead, I told Dong Yi about the scholarships.

"Two scholarships! How wonderful! Which schools? When do they want you to start?"

I told him about my offers in detail.

"Congratulations! It looks as if you're set to go." Dong Yi seemed sad. But soon his smile returned.

"But this is not all that I have asked you here for," I said. "There is something I would like your advice about. Please tell me as honestly as you can because your advice is the most important to me."

"Of course," replied Dong Yi.

"You know that Eimin already has his PhD and so he cannot go to the U.S. as a student." I looked at Dong Yi, who nodded, little suspecting what I was going to say, and went on, "He said that finding a job in the U.S. is close to impossible and may take years. If I want him to come to the U.S., the best way is for us to get married."

Dong Yi fixed his eyes on me, without moving at all, for a long time, and the smile drained from his face. He did not say a word. I waited, biting my lips. Then he spoke in a voice that I had never heard before, "Have you lost your mind, Wei?"

I looked at Dong Yi's stern face and started to cry. Only a few minutes before, we were laughing cheerfully. Now I was in tears. "I want to be happy, Dong Yi—you know that better than anyone else. It has always been happiness that I am looking for. What if Eimin is my happiness? My going will leave me without it."

"Eimin is not your happiness."

"How can you be so sure?"

"Because you are not sure. Wei, please listen to me. How long have we known each other? Three years now. I think I could say with confidence that I know you well. You are passionate, trusting and full of life. Eimin doesn't seem to trust anyone. He is different—and I don't mean that he is older. You deserve someone who loves you and whom you truly love."

"Well, you got married," I said sharply. There was a brief silence.

"I am sorry. I did not mean to be nasty." I knew what I had said was uncalled for and I regretted it immediately. "But I don't want to be alone, particularly in America—I am scared."

On the outside, my life could not have been better, or my future brighter; but deep down I was desperate. I had lost happiness once, and looking at Dong Yi only reminded me of the pain of that loss. I could not afford to do it again, even if it meant marrying someone less than perfect for me. Being loved was better than being alone.

Dong Yi took out his handkerchief and gently wiped away my tears, which only made me sadder. He let me lean on his shoulder and then put my hand in his and held it tightly.

"Please don't marry Eimin, Wei, I beg of you. Focus on going to America. You have a lot of paperwork to do. Don't give up. Happiness comes to people who wait."

He spoke as if he were making me a promise.

On 14 April, Eimin and I walked to Spoon Garden under a clear sky filled with stars. It was deep into the evening in Beijing, and about ten o'clock in the morning in Virginia. On our way, we passed the brightly lit library full of hardworking students with their heads buried in books. Outside the library, some people were walking in pairs, apparently on a break from studying. Girls held hands like sisters; lovers whispered to each other.

Spoon Garden was the only place on campus where one could make international calls, for a month's wage a minute. I had decided to go to the College of William and Mary because there I would be doing a Master's degree as opposed to a PhD at the University of Texas. I felt I did not know enough about America or my own interests to go straight into a PhD program. When the voice of the Psychology Department Secretary at the College of William and Mary came on the line, I was surprised by how clear she sounded, as if she were only in the next room. She said that they were expecting to hear from me and asked me whether I had any questions about the offer. I said no.

"Then do you wish to accept it?"

"Yes," I said firmly. My future had, at last, started to take shape.

We heard about Hu Yaobang's death on the evening news the next day. The former Party General Secretary, the number one man in the Chinese Communist Party and the Chinese Central Government, had died of complications from a heart attack. Like the rest of the country, I was shocked and saddened by the news. Hu Yaobang was a reformer and an open-minded leader who sympathized with student protests, and so was viewed by Chinese intellectuals and students as a friend. Many believed that his sympathy toward students and intellectuals had led to his fall from power in 1987. The death of Hu Yaobang was all anyone could talk about that evening on campus.

Overnight, wall posters—tributes, articles and poems—appeared in the Triangle, a location normally used by the university to post announcements or awards. Most of the articles remembered the integrity of Hu Yaobang and his contribution to reform. Many questioned his unfair dismissal and, by implication, the judgment of the leaders of the Communist Party. Some called him the "Soul of China." As more and more wall posters began going up during the day, on 16 April, calls for democracy and freedom also appeared.

By the afternoon, the Triangle was filled with articles, poems and open letters. A large crowd had gathered here, mostly to read and reflect. I walked along the walls covered with wall posters, finding so much to read.

"Comrade Hu Yaobang used to say 'work until you die and when you die it is over.' Now he is dead, our beloved friend . . . Hu Yaobang never abused his power or sought favors. He was always concerned about the people. He will live in our hearts forever."

"Hu Yaobang was a friend of the students and an advocate of education ... But today our government spends much foreign exchange on luxury cars from Japan and West Germany, and little on education ... This is a critical moment for reform. Reform needs to continue."

I carried on along the wall and read, "Seventy years have passed since the May Fourth Movement. Still we have not got democracy and freedom. Comrade Hu Yaobang had to resign because he departed from the party line and supported the students . . . China needs democracy."

The May Fourth Movement of 1919 was a university-student-led movement that laid the foundation of modern Chinese culture. Students took to the streets calling for "Mr. Democracy" and "Mr. Freedom" for China. Today, my contemporaries naturally recalled the spirit of May Fourth and saw Hu's death as a threat to reform and a loss for the process of modernization.

How extraordinary, I thought, that people were mourning, but at the same time looking forward to the future. China—the sleeping giant—had finally woken up. The people were taking back control. Standing in the middle of the crowd, I too felt powerful.

Gradually, students in their hundreds filled the area and, as the crowd grew, some started shouting slogans. As if waiting for such a signal, the crowd became charged with excitement and strong emotion. Some students called for the mourning to be moved to Tiananmen Square.

"Let's make a wreath."

"Write some banners too."

More students came. The crowd started gathering materials for making wreaths. Some students passed around black armbands. I took one and put it around my left arm.

Tiananmen Square was not only the heart of modern China, it was also the place to which people gravitated whenever there was a public mood to demonstrate. Zhou Enlai, Mao's right-hand man for fifty years, and the Premier of China, had died at the beginning of 1976. He was also someone who showed compassion during the Cultural Revolution, rescuing many intellectuals and old revolutionaries from the Red Guard. For many ordinary Chinese, Zhou Enlai was a wise leader and a symbol of humanity. When the traditional 5 April *Qingming* festival, or Festival of the Dead, approached, mere months after his death, hundreds of thousands of Beijing citizens defied a ban by the government to gather at Tiananmen Square and mourn the passing of Zhou.

For the first time in the history of Communist China, the people had become defiant of the larger-than-life "heroes," those who had helped to found and run the Republic. People brought paper posters, white paper flowers, eulogies and poems to Tiananmen Square. Workers, teachers, schoolchildren, intellectuals, soldiers and the elderly laid wreaths in layers up the Monument, burying its base and reaching about sixty feet high. Many more people took off the white paper flowers they were wearing on their jackets and pinned them to the pine trees and bushes around the Square. These white paper flowers eventually covered the evergreens as if snow had just fallen on the Square.

I was ten, and I remember watching my mother and her colleagues making a wreath in our living room. Everyone in the room wore a black mourning armband—my mother had made an especially small one for me to wear as well. Few words were spoken. The only sounds were those of scissors snipping and paper folding. Steam from hot teacups lingered around, bringing warmth to the room. When the wreath was finished, my mother knelt down and said, "Wei, you've helped a lot tonight. Now it is late. You should go to bed. Mama needs to take the wreath to Tiananmen Square."

That night, security troops moved into the Square, and cleared away all the wreaths. When thousands of people came the next morning, they saw only the broken pieces left behind. Anger spread in Beijing. More wreaths were brought in, despite the blockades set up at the entrances to the Square. A police van urging people to leave was overturned. The gray three-story building used as the United Command Center, as well as a number of vehicles, were set on fire.

As we later learned, at around 9:00 P.M., the First Party Secretary of Beijing, Wu De, spoke through the loudspeakers and urged people to leave the Square. Many did, but about a thousand people refused to go. Three hours later, the floodlights went on and 10,000 army reserves as well as 3,000 police rushed into Tiananmen Square, surrounding those who remained, waving batons and huge sticks. Countless people were beaten and thirty-eight were arrested.

———

Thirteen years later, like my mother before me, I came to stand below the Monument to the People's Heroes. I had cycled for over two hours with Chen Li and a few of his classmates to Tiananmen Square. We wanted to see for ourselves the public mourning of Hu Yaobang, as well as to read the wall posters that were blossoming in their thousands. Over 100,000 students and citizens had gathered in Tiananmen Square on that day, 19 April, to mourn Hu. Wreaths and bouquets covered the entire base of the Monument, together with essays and poems mourning Hu and extolling democracy and freedom. At the very center of the Monument was a gigantic portrait of Hu Yaobang and a banner crying out: "Where have you gone? The soul comes back!"

As endless streams of people poured into the Square, new wreaths had to be passed over people's heads to be placed at the base of the Monument. Some people read poems out loud; some wept openly. More and more stood up to speak publicly—mourning Hu Yaobang, condemning corruption and calling for democracy. The audience applauded and cheered at every speech. Chen Li was very excited and applauded as hard as he could. His enthusiasm infected me too, and I began to cheer loudly as well.

After about half an hour of listening to the speeches, Chen Li and I walked around the Square reading the wall posters. A few articles exposing the web of "prince gangs" attracted my attention. Prince gangs were made up of the offspring of important officials and Party leaders, who used their connections to secure good jobs, money and power for themselves.

"No wonder there is so much anger around, look how they have profited from their parents' powers," Chen Li said after reading one of the posters. At the time, living expenses had skyrocketed for ordinary Chinese, inflation was rampant and the gulf between rural and city, poor and rich had widened dramatically.

"In comparison, Hu Yaobang lived a simple life and was devoted to the people. But now he is dead!" I read out loud, feeling a deep sorrow not just for the death of Hu but also for what he had represented—selflessness, honesty and love for his country. The death of Hu Yaobang gave the people of China an opportunity to voice their sorrow and anger, and their demand for change, a voice that was lost when the government had tightened its control of the press after the 1986 student demonstrations.

That evening I went to the Triangle to read the new wall posters. While there, I heard that the police had dispersed a crowd of 10,000 student demonstrators and spectators outside Xinhuamen, one of the entrances to the elite Zhongnanhai compound, which houses Party leaders. When the last few hundred students refused to leave, the police surrounded them, three or four to each student. They beat the students and then dragged them into buses parked nearby.

Near midnight, I was just about to leave the Triangle when several students began to pass around leaflets about the "truth of the tragedy of 20 April." A student holding a megaphone relayed the story of "the student beating" again and again to the crowd. The sober mood in the Triangle turned to anger. Although I was as furious as anyone there that night, I had become too tired to stay up. I had spent the day in Tiananmen Square, and the evening in the Triangle, and I was worn out. I took the leaflet and left the enraged crowd. The next morning, announcements of a boycott appeared all around campus. Students stood outside lecture halls and classrooms to persuade others to stay away. STRIKE TODAY was written across blackboards all over campus and, within days, students at thirty universities and institutions of higher education in Beijing had gone on strike.

The funeral of Hu Yaobang was to be held in the Great Hall of the People on the west side of Tiananmen Square at 10:00 a.m. on 22 April. Only Communist Party leaders and government officials were to attend. However, the hundreds of thousands of students who had been mourning Hu's death wanted to pay their respects. They wanted to see their friend for one last time.

I met Dong Yi for dinner on the evening of 21 April, the day he returned from Taiyuan. Afterward, we stopped by the Triangle to read the latest wall posters. The campus had begun to settle down for the night when, suddenly, sounds of shouting and singing came from the east gate. People in the Triangle started to run. Some jumped on their bicycles and flew towards the sound. "Forget about the bicycles, let's run. We'll get there quicker," shouted Dong Yi.

As we ran to see what the noise was, which was becoming louder and louder, more students sped by on their bicycles. People who were standing along the road began to run as well.

"What's going on?'one student called out.

We had reached the east lawn outside the library when I saw a large crowd marching toward us. At the front of the column, a large banner read: "Qinghua University."

"Qinghua lead the way!" they shouted. "Where are our fellow students from Beijing University?"

"Democracy for China! Freedom of speech!"

"How dare they!" shouted someone in the crowd that was now growing outside the library. "Beijing University is always the leader!"

Since the May Fourth Movement, in 1919, Beijing University has always been proud of its reputation as the cradle of democracy and freedom for China.

The news that Qinghua University students were marching onto campus to call on the students of Beijing University to participate in the Democracy Movement quickly spread to every corner of the campus. Thousands of Beijing University students carrying departmental flags and banners rushed to meet the marching columns from Qinghua University.

"Let's show them who is the leader of the Student Movement!" some shouted as they passed us. Thousands upon thousands soon congregated along the main path leading to the south gate, flags flying and banners raised high. With one voice, we sang the Chinese national anthem, "The Chinese people have reached the most critical moment . . ." and we sang "The Internationale." Our singing echoed across buildings into the evening sky.

Later, students from other nearby universities, such as the People's University, also joined in. When the road leading to the south gate became packed solid with people, tens of thousands of students marched out of Beijing University toward Tiananmen Square. Dong Yi and I waved and cheered our fellow students who marched past us. One banner read, "Long live democracy! Long live freedom!" Another read, "Grieving for the soul of China." And another, "Punish the bureaucratic profiteers." I read aloud, looked at Dong Yi and smiled. He smiled back. I felt my heart beating faster and faster, the blood rushing up to my face; such was the pride I felt that evening.

Along the streets outside, ordinary citizens cheered as the students marched by. They shouted, "Long live the students."

Though I did not want to leave the excitement of Beijing University, I went back to my parents" apartment that night as I had promised them I would. When I got up the following morning, I turned on the TV to watch the coverage of Hu's funeral, showing on all three channels.

"You must come and see this," I said to my mother.

There must have been 100,000 students sitting on the cold stones in front of the Great Hall of the People on the west side of Tiananmen Square. Three rows of armed police sat face-to-face with the student demonstrators. Sunshine reflected off the Monument to the People's Heroes and shone on the four huge characters, each four meters high and three meters wide, that spelled Sorrow.

From one corner of the Square came the national anthem: "Build a new Great Wall with our flesh and blood! China has reached a critical moment! Rise up! Rise Up!" The next wave of students then stood up and continued the national anthem. After the national anthem, came "The Internationale": "Rise up the cold and poor slaves of the world! Rise up the suffering people!" A national flag was lifted high and then lowered to half mast to pay tribute to Hu Yaobang.

Shortly before 10:00 A.M., the loudspeakers in the Square began a live broadcast of the memorial service inside, while all the TV stations broadcast the official service. Deng Xiaoping arrived at the Great Hall and was greeted by Party General Secretary Zhao Ziyang, Premier Li Peng, the adopted son of the late Zhou Enlai, and other Party elders. Zhao Ziyang delivered the memorial address that fell short of labeling Hu Yaobang a "great Marxist" and thus a national hero, as suggested by his family and leading intellectuals.

Half an hour later, the funeral came to an end. Luxury cars carrying senior Party leaders drove off behind the walls of police. Cameras were again turned to the Square. The crowd mourning there moved forward. They shouted, "We want dialogue! We want dialogue!"

A few student representatives started to approach the Great Hall to present a petition. As the student representatives talked to the staff at the Great Hall, the sea of mourners in the Square shouted rhythmically, "Li Peng come out! Li Peng come out!"

How ironic history can be, I thought, looking at my mother who had participated in the public mourning of Li Peng's father, Premier Zhou Enlai, in the same square thirteen years before.

At that moment the image that brought tears to the eyes of everyone in the Square, and to the countless millions sitting at home in front of the TV set, appeared. On the steps below the imposing columns of the Great Hall, three young men knelt down holding a petition over their heads. The Square fell into a sudden silence, then loud sobbing, like waves in a stormy ocean, broke through the crowd.

With tears rolling down their faces, young men and women in the Square cried and shouted to the three tiny figures on the steps of the Great Hall, "Get up! Get up! Get up!"

"Children!" my mother shouted at the TV set. I stared at the screen and my mind went numb. Words suddenly became inadequate.

The three young men did not move. A scene that had been repeated for 2,000 years in China was, once more, being played out at the end of the twentieth century. Kneeling before the Emperor was the method by which ordinary citizens begged their rulers to receive their complaints. Such an action had often brought death to the petitioner because it upset the Emperor. Throughout Chinese history, many brave souls who had dared to perform such an act had lost their lives. Many wondered, that day, whether this generation of Chinese youth were telling the world, by going up the steps of the Great Hall, that they were prepared to make a similar sacrifice.

The three young men knelt on the hard steps of the Great Hall of the People for forty minutes. Their petition contained three demands: (1) that the coffin be driven once around the Square so that the students could pay their respects one last time; (2) that Li Peng hold a dialogue with the students; and (3) that the news of the day's student activities be published in the newspapers.

But no one came out to receive it.

Seven

Divorce

I lived at the head of the Yangtze river, you at the tail . . .
When would this water stop?
When would this anguish end?

—*Li Zhi Yi, ninth century*

The day I met Dong Yi for dinner, 21 April, he had just come back from Taiyuan, where he'd seen Lan.

I waited for him outside the Little Peking Duck House. I was worried. Almost all his friends were involved in the Democracy Movement, and we already suspected that Liu Gang was under surveillance by the police. I was afraid that Dong Yi might be followed. But luckily my fears were, then, unfounded. This fear was new to me and I found it hard to adjust, but as the days went by it became familiar to me.

The original Peking Duck House was the most famous restaurant in Beijing; fabulously expensive, and booked up way in advance. Therefore a trip to the Duck House was only reserved for special occasions, such as my acceptance by Beijing University. Located near Tiananmen Square, in the center of the city, a trip there would take my family over two hours. Once we had picked the duck from the window, it went into the roasting oven (ducks used for this restaurant are specially bred at a farm outside Beijing). It took twenty minutes for the duck to be baked just right, its skin crispy and red. Thinly sliced duck was brought to the table, together with sweet wheat sauce, long slivers of spring onions and thin, warm pancakes. The bones were taken away to make duck soup. We used our fingers to roll up slices of duck, onion and sauce in the pancake, before greedily devouring them all. With every bite, red sauce dripped down our fingers. The taste was heavenly.

The Little Peking Duck House was the first offshoot of the original Duck House. It was opened in 1988 in Haidian village across the road from the campus. Since opening, the restaurant had become the favorite place for executives from nearby technology enterprises, as well as for students from Beijing University. Despite the prices, the restaurant was always full. Those who had money or something special to celebrate flocked there. Business was brisk.

But that night, what Dong Yi had to tell me was more a cause for pain than celebration. He had gone back to Taiyuan with the intention of asking Lan for a divorce.

Divorce was then very rare in China, marriage being viewed more as a family duty than anything else. Until Western ideas of love and marriage were introduced into China at the beginning of the twentieth century, the only escape from an unhappy marriage was death. But change happens slowly in China and, in the People's Republic, the law only allowed consensual divorce. If there were special circumstances, such as mental illness or counterrevolutionary activities, then nonconsensual divorce was permitted.

Some years before, when I was about seven years old, a famous painter had fallen in love with his student and asked for a divorce from his wife. The wife not only refused to grant his request for fifteen years, but also managed to rally the entire country to her support. Finally the reputation and career of the painter was destroyed and the student left him. This case even inspired a Women's Association which helped other women take revenge on their "flower hearted" husbands. And their refusals to grant their husbands the divorces they wished for proved powerful. Unlike their counterparts in the West, an unmarried couple in China could hardly have a life together; and it was worse, inevitably, when a woman wanted a divorce. She would have no sympathy from either men or women. In most cases, the woman would be branded a tramp or a "broken shoe"—a very graphic insult for a woman. Traditional Chinese values weighed much more heavily on a woman. She must be obedient and submit to her fate as a wife, no matter what. When daughters were growing up, they were told that once they married they would have to "follow the rooster if she married one, or the dog if she married one." At best, a divorced woman was branded with a black mark for the rest of her life. Few men would want to marry her again. Many were cast out of society. One female writer was scorned by society the first time she divorced. When she divorced for the third time, she was forced to leave the country and seek political asylum in Germany, on the grounds of being three-times divorced.

Divorce was therefore not for the fainthearted, and I had never personally known anyone who was divorced. I never thought Dong Yi would contemplate such a drastic act; he was too kind and too loving ever to think about hurting Lan. Initially, he told me, he had planned to leave China because he hoped it would be easier to divorce once he was in a faraway land. He told me that he had applied for places at American universities.

But now he wanted to risk everything. He did not want to wait any longer. Dong Yi was not the type who promised much in words. Yet I saw the promise in his eyes, the promise of love and happiness that I had been waiting for.

A marriage banquet was taking place in the Little Peking Duck House. The party occupied four large round tables, and commanded the attention of many waitresses. When Dong Yi and I came in, the party was just starting. The groom's father, who traditionally paid for the feast, had just picked the ducks. Beer and rice wine had been brought to the tables, the bride and groom were making their rounds, toasting the guests.

Dong Yi had abandoned his Beijing University T-shirt in favour of a smart white shirt, and the light reflecting off the shirt onto his face made his features appear serene. While we waited for our duck, Dong Yi asked me about developments in Beijing since he had left. The death of Hu Yaobang and the swift protests that followed had caught everyone in China by surprise. Dong Yi wanted to know every detail of what had happened on campus.

I was happy to talk about the Student Movement and to discuss with Dong Yi how things might develop. Talking about it allowed me not to ask about his trip home. Not to know whether Lan had agreed to a divorce. I was terribly nervous. I desperately wanted to know and yet was so afraid of finding out.

However, eventually, there was only one subject left to discuss: Dong Yi's trip back to Taiyuan, and Lan.

Dong Yi's parents lived in Taiyuan, the capital of Shanxi, a northern province in the Yellow River region. Shanxi was a stronghold for the Communist Party. The People's Liberation Army liberated Taiyuan in 1948, a year before the founding of the People's Republic. My grandfather was one of those who marched into the city on that day; he stayed on to form, and then run, the provincial government. His stay lasted for the rest of his life. My mother and her siblings grew up in the provincial government compound in Taiyuan.

By the end of the 1980s, however, Taiyuan was still a poor and backward inland city; the new era for China had been a long time coming and had not yet reached Taiyuan. Dong Yi's father wanted to go back to his hometown, Guangdong, where economic reform had brought people prosperity, but his request had been lost somewhere among stacks of paperwork. Time moves slowly in Taiyuan, and Dong Yi's parents were still waiting for their request to move to Guangdong to be granted.

Dong Yi was the apple of their eye. He was the kind and honest son they had taught him to be, as well as the best student at his high school and university. As expected of an eldest son, he had brought them honor and respect among friends, colleagues and acquaintances. Dong Yi's admission into the graduate school at Beijing University gave them pride and joy beyond anything they had ever imagined.

But, when Lan came to them in tears and told them that Dong Yi had fallen for someone in Beijing, they were shocked. They sat down and talked to their son about honor and respect.

"You told her that you loved her since you were both nineteen, how could you change your mind now? You gave your word to that girl and for goodness' sake you ought to keep it," said his father. "You cannot go about ruining other people's lives because you want someone else, or another kind of life. A man without honor is a man without friends and respect."

When Dong Yi got married, they gave them a grand banquet and their life's savings. They wanted Lan to have the best they could afford. They wanted Lan to know that she had their support and love. Dong Yi understood this. All his life, he had tried to live up to his father's example. Every time he thought about the years that his father had spent sweeping streets during the Cultural Revolution, he asked himself whether he would have been as brave, whether he would give up so much for his honor. He respected his father all the more—honor was something one should not take lightly. And promises were made to be kept.

But Dong Yi had not been happy. He spent more time in Beijing and occupied his free time in political debates with people like Liu Gang. Slowly Dong Yi and Lan felt their sympathy, caring and tenderness chipped away. The cracks between them had widened.

So it was not surprising that, when he arrived home in Taiyuan, he had found it difficult to address the subject of divorce with Lan. But he had determined to do so when he left Beijing, he told me, on his train journey home. He watched the dawn from his window; "The sun was just coming up from the yellow hills of the Great North, golden light seemed to rise up from the fields to touch the sky above." Dong Yi anticipated a new beginning in his life as the day dawned. He saw the start of his new life as beautiful and as glorious as the morning outside his train. He wanted to shout to the fields and hills of his childhood. He felt the force of rebirth pushing him forward to embrace life.

But then the train arrived in Taiyuan, and the city closed in on him. As the bus took him closer and closer to home, his stomach started to twist and hurt. Someone seemed to be punching him in the abdomen again and again. He felt sick and started to lose, bit by bit, the strength that had carried him all the way there from Beijing.

When Lan returned from work and found him waiting, she was so excited and happy that she jumped into his arms.

"Why didn't you tell me that you were coming home? How long are you going to stay?"

Then she noticed his face, white as paper. Immediately she made his favorite sliced noodle soup and urged him to finish up everything in the bowl. When they lay in bed that night, she held his hands, kissed his chest and lips; she was so tender and sensual that night, as if there had never been any distance between them. She made love to her husband for the first time for many months. Afterward Dong Yi lay motionless in the dark. He tasted his tears. He had lost all the courage he had brought with him from Beijing.

Lying in bed next to his wife, Dong Yi remembered the last time that he'd wanted to leave Lan. She went to see his parents, her parents, her friends and everyone he knew. He told me how he had seen this fragile and gentle woman desperately fighting to save their relationship. He thought that he might just as well give up now, for Lan would never give him a divorce.

"The next day, when Lan was out working, I looked through our photo albums," said Dong Yi. There was their wedding photo, taken in the studio at a downtown photo shop. Lan looked beautiful in the picture; but he looked sullen and unhappy. He remembered that they spent hours in the studio, Lan doing her makeup and deciding on poses. In the end they had a big fight. He was so frustrated that he just wanted to leave.

Dong Yi wondered how he had come so far with Lan. He wished that he had never gone further than the summer of two years before. That was the first time that he had realized just how far apart they were, with his growing interest in politics and the outside world, and her focus on domestic routine. He looked across the table at me. "Wei," he said, "I realized that I had made a huge mistake. But by the time I came back to Beijing, it was too late." He hated himself for having waited so long. He retreated to his old world, marrying Lan just as she and, it seemed to him, everyone else wanted.

For the past two years, he endured the false life he had made for himself. He said, "But the walls were closing in on me, and I wanted to leave my wife's world, to get as far away as I could."

As the days went by, in Taiyuan, Dong Yi gradually regained his strength. The inevitable decision came slowly but clearly; he must tell Lan of his true intentions. Lan would be better off if she knew the truth, he told himself. It was only fair to divorce if love no longer existed in their marriage.

"It was Sunday. Lan had planned for us to go shopping. I asked her to stay and I told her about my decision. She was shocked; she'd never realized that I was so unhappy. She cried. I felt her pain. I wanted to stop her tears. Then Hu Yaobang died suddenly. I read avidly about the student demonstrations, and watched everything on TV. I thought of you, Liu Gang, Professor Li Shuxian and the others. I had no doubt that China was coming to a crossroads. I said to myself, something wonderful and exciting is happening there and I want to be part of it. And so I thought," he said sincerely, "that this was not the time to indulge our personal lives, particularly not in a time-consuming divorce."

"My adviser had already asked me to do a PhD with him," continued Dong Yi. "So I won't be going to America this year. Nor will I go back to Taiyuan either. Maybe I will go to America, maybe next year." He held my hands.

"Don't worry. Eat your duck soup. It is getting cold." I could see clearly that his heart was torn between the two women in his life. I wondered whether the death of Hu Yaobang had simply given him an excuse to avoid a difficulty he was not really prepared to face. Then I stopped myself thinking such things. I needed to trust him—without trust where would love be?

I also thought of Eimin. We are both in a jam, I thought. What am I going to do?

There were no more classes: classrooms empty, chalk untended on desks, chairs collecting dust. Beijing University students had gone on strike.

Since 15 April, Eimin had been dutifully going to his lectures, office and laboratory. Although he also spent evenings at the Triangle reading wall posters and listening to the public speeches of student activists, he was not caught up in the storm, as all the other students were.

"I have had enough involvement in political movements in my time, now I just want to do my research, teach my classes and live my life in peace."

I could not say that I understood his motives, but I certainly understood his background. At the beginning of the Cultural Revolution, he was as active as any other fourteen-year-old in China. He went with his friends and Red Guards to "seize power" from the old establishment. But, one day, a group of Red Guards came to his home and took his father. They tied his hands behind him, put a tall hat on him and hung a big sign saying "black gang member" around his neck. He was then dragged out of his home, paraded through the streets of Nanjing and taken to a people-beating meeting in the central square. The beating lasted the whole night. When Eimin and his mother finally managed to carry the professor back home the next morning, he was covered with blood and could hardly walk. His clothes were torn to pieces, his face was painted with black ink and half his hair had been shaved off. Many of the Red Guards who beat him that night were his former students.

Overnight, Eimin fell from grace. He became a "black gang bastard." After his father was sent to labor camp, his family was separated, and Eimin was sent to a People's Collective Commune in northern China. Even there he had no peace. The Red Guards who ran the camp told him to "eat manure," and gave him the worst tasks. There was little to eat, except corn buns and diluted rice soup. It wasn't until a year after he arrived at the camp that Eimin made a friend, a retired army soldier in the village. His friend taught him Kung Fu. Every night, after a day's work in the fields and everyone else had gone to bed, Eimin would practice his Kung Fu movements outside. In the moonlight, surrounded by nothing but silence and deep snow, he found peace and strength. He shut his heart to the rest of the world and vowed not to be part of any movement ever again.

It was these stories of Eimin's past that kept me from telling him about Dong Yi. Eimin was wary of people. I was the only person, other than his father, who he trusted completely. I could not bring myself to betray him and destroy that. In many ways, I loved him, particularly his strength and his will to overcome and triumph over the adversity of his youth.

But now there seemed to be a slim chance that Dong Yi and I could be together, something I had wanted for a long time. Something in which I had lost hope so many times that I did not want to lose it again. But the choice before me was cruel and, for the first time in my life, I had a real dilemma on my hands. I began to understand Dong Yi and how difficult his choices were.

I decided to tell Dong Yi that I would like to see him less, rather than more, as he wanted, and that I needed time to decide what to do. I was learning that we did not live in a vacuum isolated from others, and that our actions affect people all around us. I needed the right time and right words to make the right decision.

I did not want to spend much time with Eimin either, so I went back to my parents. I spent most of my days preparing to go to America, which meant making my passport application. In the evenings I read wall posters posted by the students of the university where my mother taught. The escalating conflict between students and the government conveniently provided me with a diversion and a breathing space away from my own problems.

Two days after Hu Yaobang's funeral, on 22 April, over 50,000 students boycotted classes in thirty-nine universities in Beijing. At the same time, students at Beijing University set up a student radio station in the number twenty-eight building, next to the Triangle. Some of my friends were emerging as organizers of the Movement. My friend Li, who was two years ahead of me in psychology, and was then in her second year at graduate school, became actively involved in the radio station, broadcasting announcements, news, recorded speeches from student activists and messages of support from parents, citizens of Beijing and friends living overseas.

While the students organized themselves in Beijing, some students traveled to other provinces to drum up support. Red Guards in the Cultural Revolution first used this method of networking—*Chuanlian,* or linking up—to spread revolution. Back then they traveled on trains to every corner of the country, into factories, offices, schools and People's Collective Communes. Now Beijing students used the same method to inform others of what was happening in Beijing. This was the way that information—other than that allowed by state-controlled media—was transmitted in China. Two students from Beijing visited my sister, Xiao Jie's, university in Shandong province. Students at her university soon began to boycott classes as well.

Back on the campus at Beijing University, more wall posters were going up every day. Professors such as Professor Li Shuxian at the Physics Department had come out in clear support of the students, while others offered advice on how to further the Movement. Foreign journalists were now flocking to the campus, interviewing students, and photographing and videotaping their activities.

On the evening of 25 April, the main text of an editorial that was going to appear in the *People's Daily* the next day was broadcast by national radio and TV programs. The editorial, which many believed was the view of Deng Xiaoping, was entitled "The necessity for a clear stand against anarchy." It read:

> This move is a well planned conspiracy. It is intended to confuse people and throw the country into anarchy. Its real aim is

to reject the leadership of the Chinese Communist Party and the socialist system. This is the most serious political struggle that concerns the whole Party and nation.

I had come to see Eimin early that afternoon. Sitting in front of the TV in his room, I could not believe my ears. This was the first time that I had come close to a political struggle, and I was shocked. Having experienced firsthand the cruelty and evil of the Cultural Revolution, Eimin had no doubt that this was the prelude to severe retribution.

"I am afraid this is it. The editorial has labeled the Movement as anarchy. This is the Party's official evaluation. The Party will never reverse this assessment. The students need to retreat if they are to avoid a disastrous end."

Eimin became genuinely worried. I believe it was from that moment on that he became involved, however unwillingly. He knew what punishment could mean in China and he did not want that to happen to his innocent and naïve students.

We went downstairs to the Triangle, where people had already started to gather. Different views were floated; some called for retreat, others for caution. Some students wanted the newly formed Autonomous Student Association to come up with a resolution for a response. As the evening wore on, more and more people came to the Triangle. Presently a wooden cart arrived. A young man was standing on it, urging people not to retreat, and to carry on until democracy triumphed in China. He told the crowd that, yesterday, the Autonomous Student Association had been formed to represent all the universities in Beijing. He finished with the now familiar rallying cry, "The Movement is not 'anarchy'!"

It was Feng Congde, one of the student leaders. He had apparently been rallying students around the campus to attend an emergency meeting at the Triangle that evening. The student radio station began to rebroadcast the *People's Daily* editorial. Roars of protest erupted from the thousands now gathered at the Triangle. I went over to say hello to Feng Congde. He was married to my old roommate, Chai Ling, and I had not seen her for a long time. I wanted to know how she was doing.

"How is your wife?" I asked.

"She is doing well. In fact she is coming to the meeting later."

———

It was almost an accident that Chai Ling became my roommate. She had transferred to the class ahead of me from geology. It was the first time that such transfers were allowed in Beijing University. Many people had reservations about the new system and thought the transfer allowed people who did not score highly enough in college entrance exams to move to more desirable departments.

Psychology had, at that time, one of the highest entrance score requirements in Beijing University; the feeling in the department was thus particularly hostile toward the transferees. No one wanted to room with them.

I had been the odd one out since I entered university. There were nine girls in my class, one more than a room could accommodate, and thus one person always had to room with the girls from another year. Having been on my own since I was twelve, at boarding school, I did not mind being the one chosen. As a result, I had spent my first year rooming with the final-year students, and then the next year with the first years. The girls from my class lived a few doors down the hall, but I rarely saw them outside classes.

Naturally when the transferees came in, I was asked to room with them. The department felt that since I had so far not had a stable group to room with, it wasn't likely that I would mind being moved again, this time with the transferring students. I didn't mind a bit: I was used to being an outsider.

The transferees knew that they were unwanted and not welcome, so they trod carefully in their new home. They were extra kind and sweet, and watched warily for others" reactions before speaking. It was as if we were all in some extension of our psychology classes, the new students scared of putting a foot wrong. Well, almost all of them.

Chai Ling was small, with a round face and thin but kind eyes. She always kept her hair short, just brushing her cheeks. She was free spirited, rebellious and, at times, disagreeable. She never seemed to be afraid of speaking her mind, and did so in a curiously soft, high-pitched voice.

Because Chai Ling had much to catch up with in her new degree, she took classes with us as well as with her own class. Sometimes we would spend most of our days together, exchanging notes and helping each other with our homework. Despite her late start in psychology, Chai Ling progressed rapidly, and, a year later, scored well enough in the graduate school exam to be given a place.

Unfortunately, the professors were not pleased with her, probably because of her rebellious personality. Many in the department regarded her as too difficult to work with and thus did not want to accept her. In the end, after persistent pleading from Chai Ling, the department agreed to let the professor with whom she wanted to study decide.

By this time, Chai Ling had moved to a small corner room down the hall, and I was finally with my own classmates, following yet another room reshuffle. One day she came to see me.

"Wei, you are the best student in your class, all the professors love you. Could you please talk to Professor Wang for me? I really would love to study human emotions with her."

I went to see Professor Wang and pleaded for Chai Ling, but she was adamant; she wouldn't work with Chai Ling. I felt terrible when I told Chai Ling about the result of my conversation with Professor Wang. So it was inevitable that when the department eventually agreed to admit Chai Ling into the graduate program, under the supervision of another professor, Chai Ling rejected the offer, and said she'd rather study elsewhere than with a professor of someone else's choice.

A few months later, she enrolled in the graduate school at Beijing Normal University.

Many people in the department—including me—were surprised by her decision, believing that she was being obstinate and inflexible, and as a result suffered unnecessarily.

A few months after Chai Ling graduated, she came to my dorm room. I had run into her a few times on campus when she came to visit her boyfriend, Feng Congde.

I was happy to see Chai Ling. We talked about her new life as a graduate student and how she liked Beijing Normal University. Then she dropped her bombshell: she and Feng Congde had married. At that time in China, young people had to wait until after university and their twenty-third birthday to marry. Chai Ling had then just turned twenty-three. "I had no idea that you two were married." I apologized for having just called Feng her boyfriend, and hurriedly congratulated her.

"We have rented a place outside campus," she said. "You must come and visit us."

It was uncommon back then for ordinary people to rent rooms from private citizens. No one owned property, and renting properties owned by the state was illegal. I had heard of people doing so, but they risked imprisonment. The majority of these people were farmers coming to the city for work, who had no other choice and were too desperate to care about such punishment. But Chai Ling did not belong to such a desperate group. Married graduate students lived in their separate dormitories, which was considered generous, as most people had to wait, sometimes for years, for their work units to allocate housing to them. Many young people had to continue living with their parents and grandparents.

I was therefore shocked by Chai Ling's unconventional behavior, while at the same time intrigued; this was a new way of living that I had not come across before, so I readily agreed to visit her.

Chai Ling's rented room was part of a traditional courtyard house, located inside the village of Haidian, across the street from the campus at Beijing University. Chai Ling led me through the narrow courtyards and deep alleyways. Here families were crammed into small courtyard houses that I never knew existed, surrounded by a maze of walls. It was approaching dinnertime and smoke billowed everywhere, as many families were cooking on coal-burning stoves in the courtyards. Above our heads, the sky was dark and filled with heavy clouds. Autumn winds had begun to bring a chill to the evenings.

This was a world different from that at Beijing University, with generations of one family living together, children running noisily in the courtyard, laundry hanging on clotheslines and dirty water pouring onto the streets. As we walked along, I wondered how Chai Ling and Feng Congde had found this place. And why did they prefer to live here, instead of living on a beautiful campus, where every aspect of life was neatly organized by the university?

After about ten minutes, I was completely lost. We walked on for another ten minutes, finally arriving at the house. An elderly lady squatted at the low entrance, cooking. Either the clouds above had thickened or the courtyard house was naturally dark, but I could hardly see more than two meters in front of me. I slowed down, fearing I'd trip. Chai Ling introduced me to her landlady, who smiled generously, showing a few missing teeth. They chatted happily about the day. I was surprised to see Chai Ling so at ease with the old lady; I felt terribly out of place, not knowing what to say. Ever since I was twelve years old, I had lived within the walls of elite boarding schools and universities. I knew little about life beyond those walls.

We went into Chai Ling's room, so dark that she had to switch on the light, a bare lightbulb hanging down from the ceiling. A double bed, two trunks, a desk and two chairs were the only furniture. A few minutes later, once we'd gathered up the things to cook with, we went out to the courtyard again, where Chai Ling began to light her small cooking stove. When the fire caught, she bent down to blow on the coal inside. Smoke rose up, making it even harder to see.

I asked her how she found the place, and she told me it was through some friends. Their landlady had recently lost her husband, and needed money.

"Aren't you worried about being caught?"

"No," she said, and went on to explain to me that more and more people had to do this now. The government couldn't catch everyone. "But of course I'd appreciate it if you don't tell anybody about it."

I asked her what she liked about living here. She said that life was more real outside than inside the ivory tower. She felt comfortable being with people like her landlady, and humbled by real life and real problems.

Chai Ling cooked a couple of simple dishes and some rice. Feng Congde could not join us because he had a class that evening. We chatted about old times and the future. At ten o'clock I had to go back because the door to my dormitory would soon close, so I thanked her for inviting me over and for the dinner, and then I hurried back.

I was wide awake for hours after the lights were turned off in our dormitory. My roommates had long gone to sleep, and Wei Hua was, as usual, talking in her sleep. But my visit to Chai Ling kept coming back, filling my mind with images, conversations and my own thoughts. Chai Ling had not changed since I met her more than a year before. In fact she had become more determined not to let anyone tell her how she should live her life.

Perhaps it was this determination and yearning for freedom that was eventually to give her the courage to rise up and fight for the students' cause.

———

I didn't see Chai Ling till the following day. To my surprise, my old roommate looked younger and more radiant, her eyes alive with excitement. She was burning with a determination to fight for democracy in China.

The biggest battle between the people and the Communist Party was quickly taking shape.

Eight

Marching

With enough will, we can move mountains
with our hands.

—Folk story, AD 200

The 26 April *People's Daily* editorial marked a turning point for the students, the word "anarchy" igniting strong emotions on campuses across Beijing. Overnight the flame of anger was set burning among hundreds of thousands of students and faculty. Naturally, this sentiment was strongest at Beijing University.

I was woken in the early morning of 26 April by shouting and loud noise. I looked at Eimin, who was still sleeping, got out of bed, dressed and hurried over to the window that opened onto the Triangle. I saw a large crowd already gathered there. Blue sky had broken through the thin clouds, promising a bright and warm day ahead.

Suddenly there was rapid knocking on the door and the voice of Li yelling "Eimin! Eimin!"

Eimin quickly opened the door. Li had come to take him to an emergency meeting at the Psychology Department.

"The Autonomous Student Association decided, last night, to organize a mass protest in response to the editorial," said Li, trying to catch her breath. "The president of the university has asked all departments to discuss the situation and come up with an official stance from the faculty and the university."

Eimin hurried away with Li. After they left, I locked the door and went downstairs to the Triangle.

The Triangle was in chaos, and I'd never seen such a mess. Fresh wall posters had, overnight, covered the entire length of the wall and more were being put up even as I watched. Along the wall, a crowd—four layers deep in places—read and discussed the posters. Standing at the back of the crowd, I could see only those wall posters posted high up on the wall. From time to time, I had to stand on my tiptoes to continue reading the passages at the bottom of those wall posters. Once or twice, I lurched forward after standing on tiptoe for too long. People in front turned around, clearly irritated, so I apologized and moved away.

After drifting around the Triangle for a while, I became frustrated with not being able to read the majority of the wall posters. More people came; some pushed their way through the crowd. The crowd was also getting noisier, with people calling out to friends, talking about the events and arguing about the the pros and cons of the wall posters.

"This is ridiculous!" I said to myself. I felt cut adrift from the views of my fellow students. "I've got to get in there." I began to push my way further toward the wall, braving a few angry looks.

Presently more people brought in new wall posters and discovered that the wall had run out of space. "Over here!" shouted a young man, carrying a bucket of wheat paste—the traditional homemade glue for wall posters. The students who were holding up the corners of the wall poster began to run. Quickly the crowd followed. The young man ahead brushed the paste generously on the side of the faculty building, and the wall poster went up.

This time I was in a rather good viewing position.

"What have we done wrong?" I read. "We spoke the truth on behalf of the people. We want to root out corruption and privilege. We want the rule of law not the rule of man. We want democracy not dictatorship. We demonstrate peacefully. What have we done wrong? Parents, we are not wrong."

"Wei." I heard a voice calling softly and was startled by it. I turned around and saw Chen Li standing right behind me.

"Hello." I was so pleased to see him. "How long have you been standing there?"

"Since you came to stand here," said Chen Li, smiling. "But I thought I'd let you finish reading it."

Seeing Chen Li there, amid thousands of strangers in such a tense political atmosphere, seemed to me to be like meeting an old friend in a foreign land. That morning, his gentle smile seemed even more heartwarming. I had not seen him since our trip to Tiananmen Square almost ten days before. I wanted to tell him about my scholarship to America, but decided that it was not the right time, nor the right place.

"Have you been taking part in the demonstrations?"

"Yes I have. In fact I was in Tiananmen Square for Hu Yaobang's funeral," said Chen Li, as we moved away from the crowd at the wall.

"You were!" Immediately I envied his having been so personally involved with the demonstrations. The images I'd seen on TV a few days earlier were still vivid in my mind. "Tell me about it please," I asked impatiently, wanting to know right away all the details of that day in Tiananmen Square. Through Chen Li, I felt that I too was personally connected to the three brave but anonymous young men kneeling on the steps of the Great Hall of the People.

Embarrassingly, my stomach decided at that moment to remind me that I had not yet had breakfast. Chen Li laughed and accompanied me to the university store to buy something to eat. Then he told me about that day, how he had entered the Square after hours of marching through the city, how the citizens of Beijing brought food and donations to the students, and how angry they felt when the government refused to receive the petition they had brought. He told me that when the three young men went down on their knees on the steps of the Great Hall of the People, many of the students around him cried.

"I'll never forget that," said Chen Li. "I realized right there—at that moment—that our government had betrayed the trust of the young people of China. I felt that not only we the students—those who were in the Square that day and those elsewhere on campuses around Beijing—but also our country had been insulted. I felt ashamed because I am a member of the Party."

I looked at Chen Li. His eyes shone with emotion. His voice began to break up.

"Chen Li, don't blame yourself for something that is not your doing. You joined the Party because you believed it was the party of the people. I still think it is." I thought of my parents who had maintained their faith in the Party despite having suffered in the Cultural Revolution. "Not everyone in the Party is bad, most Party members, like my grandfather and my parents, are wonderful people who want to do their best for the country."

When we came out of the shop, the temperature had risen. The crowd at the Triangle had thinned out, as more and more people went to lunch. Directly in front of the number three canteen, a camera had been set up; a foreign news crew was preparing to interview students. Two young men from Beijing University were piling up copies of the *People's Daily* in front of the camera. Further down the long wall, another cameraman was taping scenes of people reading the wall posters.

> The Autonomous Student Association last night voted overwhelmingly for a mass demonstration tomorrow. We protest [against] the charges that have been levelled against us. We do not wish to overthrow our government or bring chaos to our country. On the contrary, we want prosperity and freedom for the people of China . . . the Student Movement is not anarchy. Our peaceful demonstration is protected by the Constitution!

I guessed that the interviewee was either a spokesman for the Autonomous Student Association or one of its representatives.

After the student answered a few questions on camera, the cameraman turned his lens to the pile of the *People's Daily* newspapers. A few students set the papers on fire. One young man picked up a burning sheet from the pile and waved it in front of the camera, shouting into the microphone held up to him, "These are lies!"

"Burn lies! Burn lies!" other students shouted.

Presently more copies of the *People's Daily* were brought over and thrown onto the burning pile. The flames of the fire grew bigger and sparks flew up. I could feel the heat radiating toward me.

Then came a formal announcement from the Autonomous Student Association: "Tomorrow, there will be a major demonstration of students from all the institutions of higher education in Beijing. The demonstration will begin at 8:00 A.M. We hope all our fellow students are fully prepared."

"We should join the march tomorrow," I said, feeling the heat of the fire mirroring that of my excitement. I felt a sudden urge to be a part of what was going on and guilt for not having been with my fellow students on previous marches. Chen Li and I decided to meet outside his dormitory at 7:30 A.M. and then go to the south gate together.

In the evening, when Eimin came back, he told me about the discussions the faculty had had. Most professors were worried about the rapid escalation of the conflict. They feared that the demonstration tomorrow could further worsen the already fragile situation and bring grave danger to the students.

"So the faculty does not support the demonstration?" I asked.

He said that the university thought a better response would be for the faculty, and some leading intellectuals, to write an open letter to Deng Xiaoping, asking that the wording of the editorial in the *People's Daily*, and the word "anarchy," be changed. "I also attended a meeting, on behalf of the Psychology Department, at the university. That's why I have come back so late," Eimin explained. The university had asked the students to remain calm and exercise caution and restraint, viewing the demonstration the next day as too confrontational.

I told him that I had agreed to go on the march with Chen Li. Eimin was at first surprised and then worried. "Obviously if you want to go, I can't stop you. But I want you to think about it very carefully." He went on to say that he admired the courage of the students, but believed theirs was a lost battle. He couldn't see that a few thousand students could go against the might of the Chinese government and the army without it becoming very dangerous. "The army and the police will be well prepared and waiting for you. If you go tomorrow, you will be working directly against the Party leadership. Think about America. You could easily be stopped from leaving the country." We carried on arguing about this for a while, until, an hour later, on the evening news, as if someone wanted to confirm Eimin's fears, the Central Broadcasting Corporation of China and Beijing Television rebroadcast the Beijing Municipality's "Ten Regulations for Demonstrations." They warned those who planned to participate in the demonstration the next day of grave consequences.

These broadcasts cast a dark shadow over the campus at Beijing University. For the first time in this Movement, students were faced with the real possibility of danger or even death. But the students were determined. That night, many of them wrote their wills. Some of those wills were posted at the Triangle on 27 April, as the march was leaving the campus.

"Remember me, Beijing University."

"Please forgive me, Mama. I have to go. Your daughter loves you, but she loves her country too."

The day of the march, 27 April, began like any true spring day, bright, cheery, birds singing happily in the morning sunshine. The trees arching over the road leading up to the south gate were just beginning to bud, with tiny tender green leaves, and the air was fresh. Chen Li wore a pair of jeans and a stone-colored light jacket. I wore a thick red sweater over a white shirt.

We were among thousands of students marching out of Beijing University. More students stood on either side of the road, watching and cheering. Some had climbed up to the trees to gain a better view.

Chen Li and I were walking at the front of the march. As we passed the south gate, I turned around and saw row upon row of demonstrators, walking close to each other, blurring the divisions between the rows. Red departmental and university flags stood out against the background of blue sky. I could not see where the flags and banners ended. And beneath them was a mass of people.

Over our heads, on top of the walls of the south gate, sat about a hundred students, squeezed closely next to each other. Across the road, hundreds, if not thousands, of ordinary citizens stood and watched solemnly. As we turned on to Haidian Road, we waved victory signs to the spectators.

Organizers of the demonstration ran up and down the ranks, sometimes telling us to move faster, while other times to slow down. Chen Li and I were close to the front of the march, where a red banner and the flag of Beijing University flapped in the fresh spring wind.

"Peaceful student demonstration is not anarchy!" I chanted in unison with Chen Li and my fellow demonstrators. Thousands of Beijing citizens lined the streets, while more watched the marching columns from the windows of their apartments. The warmth of the spring sunshine and the excitement of marching in unity with my fellow students made me feel alive, in a way that I had never felt before.

Spring, what a wonderful season! I thought.

Out of death and poverty comes life.

I looked at the budding aspen trees.

I exchanged smiles with Chen Li, as we followed our section leader, who was walking backward with his megaphone and chanting, "Not afraid to shed our blood and give our lives!"

I was excited to be part of life and renewal. I looked ahead and saw students marching in step, flags flying high above their heads. I looked behind and saw tens of thousands doing the same. The enthusiasm of my generation shot excitement into my veins. "There will be a new world!" I thought.

Two groups of students came running hand in hand, on both flanks of our column. We were told that these students were there to prevent outsiders from entering the ranks of the Beijing University march—there was always the possibility that the secret police would use the march to discredit the students.

Among these students, I saw a familiar face, that of Cao Gu Ran, a former classmate of mine, who was now a graduate student in psychology. I had not seen him since our graduation day almost a year before. I waved and moved to the side with Chen Li.

Cao Gu Ran wore his favorite uniform—a navy blue tracksuit and running shoes. His face was dark and rough. He was not tall, about five feet five, but muscular. Throughout his university days, he religiously kept his body fit by running many miles a day. Once I asked him whether he was doing too much, but he said that exercise was nothing compared to the fieldwork he used to do back home. Cao Gu Ran came from a poor peasant village in Hunan province, where schooling was scarce and most children only received primary education. I never knew what he had had to do to score one of the highest college entrance exams in his province. His parents never came to visit him in Beijing because they could not afford it, but I knew that Cao Gu Ran lived his life at Beijing University as if they were there with him every day. He wanted to make them proud, which he had done by graduating with top grades and becoming a graduate student at the best university in China.

"I can't believe it's you," said Cao Gu Ran, panting as he ran. "What are you doing here?"

"The same as you," I replied cheerfully. "Nice to see an old friend, especially today."

I introduced Cao Gu Ran to Chen Li. "Petition for the people!" we all shouted, as we marched on.

It turned out that Cao Gu Ran had also been actively involved in the strike and the demonstrations from the outset. He was, like Chen Li, in Tiananmen Square on the day of Hu Yaobang's funeral. He too was moved to greater involvement with the Movement by the actions of the three brave young men on the steps of the Great Hall of the People.

"But things are different today," said Cao Gu Ran. "The *People's Daily* editorial has raised the stakes. We can't afford spontaneous acts anymore. We have to be more organized."

"How can you organize tens of thousands of people?" asked Chen Li.

"Or hundreds of thousands of people. The number of students in all the higher education institutions is huge," Cao Gu Ran replied. "It is going to be difficult. So far a lot of organization has been at the departmental level. Over at psychology, we have our demonstration representatives, security people and home-support organizers."

"What do you think will happen today?" I asked, recalling my argument with Eimin the night before.

My old classmate warned me that he was sure there would be a show of force by the government, after all the students had come out in defiance of the editorial and the warnings. He saw major confrontations ahead. "No matter what happens, I am here now and will be till the end. If anything should happen to me personally, I only hope that my parents will understand. I have written a letter to them explaining why I am doing this, and my roommate will mail it for me if I don't get back."

I was touched by his words, knowing how much he meant to his parents and they to him. I began to feel the enormity of what we were attempting almost as a physical weight upon me.

"I also think something big is going to happen today, somewhere along our marching route," said Chen Li. "This is why there are more reasons today than ever to keep our demonstration peaceful. We mustn't let the blood go to our heads. We cannot give the government any excuse to use force."

Suddenly we halted. We had just passed the People's University, and the intersection at the Friendship Store, a shop designated for foreign shoppers, could already be seen. A huge crowd of spectators in their thousands had gathered here. Some of them shouted, "Don't beat the students!" About twenty yards away, we could see two police cars and six police vans, and five rows of the People's Armed Police, in their deep green uniforms, blocking the road. The front of the march had stopped face-to-face with the police. The chanting stopped, and a strange silence fell, suddenly, among the ranks of students.

This was it, the moment we'd been expecting. It was close to midday, and the sun was shining so brilliantly that it was becoming blinding. My vision blurred, the color of the blue sky and the budding trees melded together; the people standing on the side of the street became colorless. Yet staring straight ahead, my heartbeat racing at one hundred miles an hour, I saw clearly the faces of the policemen. They had faces just like the young men next to me—but I couldn't guess their thoughts or feelings. Their faces were expressionless, and so they seemed to me like aliens from another planet.

We stood there in silence for perhaps five minutes, but it felt like an eternity. I recalled the story my mother had told me about how police and army reserves had beaten up demonstrators at Tiananmen Square thirteen years before, when they had gathered to mourn Zhou Enlai. I wondered whether the policemen in front of me also carried iron bars? Would they be as brutal, in broad daylight, as their predecessors had been thirteen years before, in the middle of a dark night? I thought about my parents, who did not know that I had come out here. Their faces refused to leave my mind, no matter how I tried not to think of them. I suddenly wondered if I would see them again.

"Police, make way! Police, make way!" the citizens on the side of the road shouted. A large group of them began to rush over. At the same time, our column moved forward. The students in front of us locked their arms together. The police line was pushed back, but did not break. Cao Gu Ran and his comrades tried desperately to keep the citizens who were rushing toward the police from breaking into the march. The police pushed back. People were shouting, but I could not hear anymore. All I heard was the beating of my heart and the sound of our steps on the asphalt beneath us. Chen Li locked his right arm with my left.

Another wave of students came up from behind. I felt the pressure and I could taste the acid coming up from my stomach. But my feet walked on. My body threw itself forward. Arm in arm, we charged at the police again. I came so close to the police lines that I was able to stare straight into the eyes of one of the men. We stared at each other, shoving this way and that, as he pushed me back.

To the surprise as well as good fortune of everyone there on that day, the police were not carrying weapons. In the end, they could not withstand the sheer number of people charging at them, the police blockade was breached and we got through.

Cheers rang out from the thousands of spectators. "Long live the students!" they shouted. People came out onto their balconies and tossed down food, money, colored paper and strips of cloth to show their support. The entire front including Chen Li and I jumped up and down with joy. Soon the policemen withdrew to their vans. As they retreated, some of them smiled at each other and gestured that there was nothing they could do. The seemingly endless marching column of students flew through.

When we began moving again, our arms locked in each other's, we sang "The Internationale" loudly. Two people from the medical team came running with a first-aid kit. The red crosses on their white head-bands burned brightly under the spring sunshine. One guy, three rows ahead of Chen Li and me, was taken to the roadside for treatment. Thousands more students from other universities joined us at the next street crossing. Flags and banners converged. The sound of chanting and singing echoed across the buildings and streets of Beijing.

"There will be a new tomorrow!" we chanted.

Nine

Hunger Strike

May the pledge that we write with our lives clear the
skies in our Republic.

—*Declaration of a hunger striker, 13 May 1989*

As it turned out, over 100,000 students had marched on 27 April, while a further one million citizens watched along the marching route, or joined in the demonstration. Chen Li and I finally returned to Beijing University with our column in the early hours of 28 April, after marching more than thirty miles on the second beltway around the inner city. When we approached the south gate, we were greeted by gray-haired professors and university administrators, lined up to welcome back their students. They were so happy that we had returned safely. The air was filled with the sound of drums and gongs, while firecrackers exploded into the night sky.

I spent most of the next few days at home with my parents, preparing my passport application. A division had surfaced at home, with my mother supporting the students and my own involvement, and my father believing confrontation was not the means to a resolution but the prelude to disaster. We argued over dinner. But regardless of our views, we watched the TV news reports as a family (later on, the government censored such reports). The impact of the 27 April demonstration in Beijing soon reached other parts of the country. My sister

wrote home to say that she had taken part in similar student demonstrations in Qing Tao, where she was going to university, and that
the students at her university were all encouraged by the prospect of a
public student—government dialogue.

In early May, the government, represented by the State Council
spokesman and the vice minister of the State Education Commission, held several meetings with student representatives. However,
the government only agreed to talk with the official student body, the
Student Association of Beijing, whose members were not elected but
appointed by the Youth League and the Party Committee at each university. I thought of Yang Tao, and how he had told me that this body
had spied on the unofficial student groups, and knew with a sinking
heart that this was less likely to mean that we'd make some kind of
progress but really that it was window dressing—these people's interests didn't lie with the Student Movement but more with their own
political ambitions. Most of the meetings were televised. Every day,
the students at my mother's university packed into the two TV rooms
on campus: they were so crowded that some students even came to our
home to watch the meetings. We were all frustrated by what we saw—
rather than engaging in a discussion about the students' demands, the
officials instead used the talks to deliver lectures and even warnings to
the students.

Yet many student leaders believed that victory had been won and
declared the end of the strike on 5 May 1989. Students returned to
their classrooms. Small-scale protests still continued, but were now
confined within the campus. From time to time, I still went to Beijing
University to read the wall posters. The students at Beijing University
had voted against the recommendation of the Autonomous Student
Association and continued their strike, though even there the mood
had changed and become quieter. The excitement of the past few days,
when tens of thousands of us had marched out of the campus, seemed
to have fizzled out.

On one of those days, I also went to see Dong Yi. He was unshaven
and looked tired. I wondered what he had been busy doing; after all
there was still a strike at Beijing University. I told him about the march
on 27 April and how Eimin and I had had an argument the night
before. But our conversation was cut short.

"There is a meeting at the Writers' Association downtown. I need to leave for it right away. When will you be on campus again? Let's meet then."

Together, we walked downstairs. "You can't imagine how many times I wanted to find you and talk to you; so much has happened," said Dong Yi, his tired eyes shining with excitement. "But you wanted some time to yourself, so I thought I should wait for you to come to me."

Outside the dormitory, he unlocked his bicycle. "Now you are here, but I have to go. I am sorry, Wei. I will tell you everything when we meet again. Let me call you at your parents'."

"When?" I asked as he mounted his bicycle.

"Soon," he assured me.

But he did not call.

On 11 May I went to Beijing University again. The campus was once more buzzing with excitement, but with an air of something altogether more serious than before. One lone wall poster, written by a group of graduate students, had appeared at the Triangle, proposing a hunger strike at Tiananmen Square. The poster had set off an intense debate among the students. I ran into Li's boyfriend, Xiao Zhang, who was taking food to Li and the others who were working at the radio station. He told me that the radio station had been inundated with articles and requests for airtime by students and that Li, being one of the key organizers, had not been able to rest or eat.

"Is this what we want to do? Is this furthering our cause?" Many students asked such questions, and argued about the merits of taking such drastic action. Some speeches pointed out the scheduled visit by Mikhail Gorbachev on 15 May.

"Let's greet Mr. Gorbachev with our hunger strike at Tiananmen Square!"

"Mr. Gorbachev has pushed through much tougher political reforms in the Soviet Union. Let him come and speak to the students!"

Among the many who debated the Movement's next steps, as well as how to use Gorbachev's visit to advance the student cause, was Chai Ling, who, speaking from the radio station, argued furiously for an immediate hunger strike. The next day, the Autonomous Student Association put up sheets for volunteers for the hunger strike to sign.

It was set to begin at noon on 13 May. At the same time, the students delivered a petition to the Party Central Committee demanding that Party and government leaders talk with representatives from the elected Autonomous Student Association. The officials were told that the students would begin their hunger strike if such demands were not met.

By the morning of 13 May, the Government was still refusing to yield to the students' demands. So the moment had come for the hunger strikers to depart.

"In this bright, sunny month of May, we have begun a hunger strike," read the declaration of the hunger strike, posted at the Triangle.

> In the glorious days of our youth, we have no choice but to abandon the beauty of life. Yet how reluctant and unwilling we are! . . . We do not want to die. We want to live, and live fully, because we are in the prime of our lives. We do not want to die; we want to learn all we can . . . what are we to do?
>
> Democracy is the noblest human aspiration; freedom is a sacred human right, granted at birth. Today both must be bought with our lives . . . Farewell, friends, take care. Loyalty binds the living to the dead. Farewell, loved ones, take care. We don't want to leave you, but we must. Farewell, mothers and fathers, please forgive us. Your children cannot be loyal citizens and worthy children at the same time. Farewell, countrymen, let us repay our country in the only way left to us.

Thousands of people had come to read the declaration and to see the hunger strikers off. Around 10:30 A.M., in front of the number twenty-nine building, below the loudspeakers from the student radio station, 150 determined young men and women gathered to pledge themselves to the Beijing University Hunger Strike Group.

All the hunger strikers wore white headbands. Young as they were, they seemed strangely mature. In contrast to the high emotion on the faces of the people surrounding them, they looked calm. Once again I saw Cao Gu Ran, in his favorite blue tracksuit. He wore a white sash on which he'd written the words, taken from the American revolutionary hero Patrick Henry, "Give me liberty or give me death." Looking straight at the student who led the oath, with his right fist raised up, he repeated solemnly with the other hunger strikers:

> I solemnly swear that, in order to promote democracy in the motherland and to bring prosperity to the country, I will go on a hunger strike. I resolve to obey the rules of the hunger strike group and will not break my fast until we have achieved our goals.

Silence reigned among the packed crowd of spectators. I watched in disbelief, wondering how we had come so far so quickly. Most of the hunger strikers, particularly the women, were small and thin. It seemed as if a mere gust of wind would carry them away. How would they survive the next few days, denying themselves food?

"Take a good look at them now, breathing and alive," I told myself. I tried to burn their faces into my memory, searching each one in turn, while a dark question kept invading my mind, bringing tears to my eyes. Which of these faces might I not see again?

Then they began to move. Loud applause broke the silence.

"Dialogue now, no more delay!" the crowd chanted. "Down with corruption! Down with dictatorship!"

We followed the hunger strikers to Yanchun Garden Restaurant where the young faculty of Beijing University hosted a departure banquet for them. The young lecturers, Eimin included, had donated their salaries to give their students a decent send-off. The crowd waited patiently outside.

After their last lunch, the hunger strikers marched to the south gate, followed by their classmates, friends and thousands of fellow students. Three hundred or so supporters, including monitors, first-aid staff, propaganda workers and others who would help organize and protect the hunger strikers were already waiting at the south gate. The two groups converged. Basking under the glorious May sunshine, they marched out of Beijing University, carrying with them the university flag and a large banner with the words "The Beijing University Hunger Strike Group."

We shouted, "Farewell our heroes! We will be here to wait for your return!"

The hunger strikers marched into the Square prepared to die. The nation was shocked and, at the same time, touched by their bravery. The campus radio station broadcast news from Tiananmen Square. "Over 1,000 students are now taking part in the hunger strike that began at 5:40 P.M. yesterday," said the announcer, the excitement in her voice mixed with concern, "and the number is growing as we speak."

But I felt an overwhelming sense of grief. I was terribly sad.

The campus was alive with activity; many people were going to Tiananmen Square to support the hunger strikers. A plea for emergency donations had been posted at the bulletin board at the south gate. Money was needed to buy water, blankets and medicine for the hunger strikers, and to rent trucks so that support personnel could be transported in and out of the Square. Two female students were collecting the money at the south gate. Another group, at the next table, was asking people to sign a petition demanding a meeting with Gorbachev. I gave the girls my week's allowance, five yuan, and signed my name to the petition.

I felt sad for them, for myself, and all the good people of China. For such a simple request—to be able to speak freely and to live free of fear—the young had to put their lives on the line. But why did their choice have to be death, today in the twentieth century? My beautiful but long-suffering motherland, why is it so hard for you to gain anything: independence, respect, prosperity? Must every step of your journey be tainted with blood?

I felt isolated, sad and depressed. I needed Dong Yi. I needed him to listen to my thoughts and share my burdens. I needed to hear his voice, reassuring me. I went to see him.

Dong Yi was not in his room, so his roommate let me in. He was a first-year graduate student whom I did not know well. We chatted a little bit about the weather and my going to America, and then he left. I sat on Dong Yi's bed, flipped through that day's *Beijing Youth Daily*, the official newspaper of the Communist Party Youth League, which at the time was sympathetic toward the students. But Dong Yi still did not return. I paced around in the room, glancing out of the window at the few runners on the racetrack, and then sat down again, picking up Dong Yi's copy of *War and Peace*.

Three hours later, Dong Yi came back. He was surprised and yet very pleased to see me there. "Have you been waiting long?" But before

I could answer, he took out his washing bowl and said, "Give me five minutes to clean up, then I will be right back."

When he returned, he had shaved and washed. He told me that he had just cycled back from the eastern part of the city, where he had been meeting with several writers and intellectuals. "Let's go to Weiming Lake. We have not been there for so long." Dong Yi was clearly in high spirits.

So we cycled to Weiming Lake, with me sitting on the back of his bike. When we got to the top of the hill, Dong Yi let the bicycle coast down. Immediately we picked up so much speed that I had to grab hold of his waist, my hair and purple dress lifting in the breeze.

On the banks of Weiming Lake, life was in full bloom. All along the path, bushes of spring ivy blossomed with what looked like large balls of fire. Dong Yi parked the bike at the sports hall on the east bank, and we walked down to the water.

Dong Yi told me that in the past couple of weeks, he had been talking to intellectuals around Beijing to gain support for the students. "If you look back at the history of China, student movements alone have never mounted any real threat to the government. The Party understands this," explained Dong Yi. "This is why we believe that unless we have broad support from the people, whatever we gain from the demonstrations will be lost."

I had no doubt that the "we" he was talking about referred to people such as professor Fang Lizhi, professor Li Shuxian and Liu Gang.

Then he told me about the May Sixteenth Statement, which had been signed by around thirty prominent authors, artists and scholars. The statement strongly criticized the government's handling of the crisis and called on the intellectuals of China to participate in the Movement. "The intellectuals of China are speaking out as a unified force for the first time in our history," Dong Yi said eagerly. "A march of 30,000 intellectuals is being organized and will take place tomorrow at Tiananmen Square. Wei, the hunger strike is uniting the country."

Dong Yi sat down on a large rock on the lake bank and said, thoughtfully, "Now my task is done, it's time to go and see the hunger strikers. They are the real heroes."

"Take me along with you!" I said. Through Dong Yi my determination that one day we should have freedom was rekindled. Through his eyes I was reminded of tens of thousands of courageous people. I wanted to join him, to be part of a grand march; even if it led to death, I did not care. I would go with him, to the march, for China.

"Give me liberty or give me death."

On 15 May, Mikhail Gorbachev became the first Soviet leader to visit China in thirty years. With his visit came the world's reporters and TV cameras, which by midday, had converged on Tiananmen Square to cover the student protests.

When Dong Yi and I arrived at Tiananmen Square on our bicycles, we saw tens of thousands of people marching around it, waving banners of support for the students. Among them, we saw columns of workers waving their union cards, staff from the government ministries and ordinary Beijing citizens. The white banners of the Bank of China were particularly eye-catching. Eventually 100,000 people came to Tiananmen to support the students. Among these 100,000 were 30,000 intellectuals.

Dong Yi and I brought water and soda for the hunger strikers. Student monitors had circled off the hunger-strike area so that outsiders would not be able to enter and cause problems; everyone going in was checked. Dong Yi showed his student ID card to one of the guards and told him that we had come to see the hunger strikers from Beijing University. We were then shown the way into the hunger-strike area. There must have been tens of thousands more students in and around that area. Among them, we saw banners and flags from about thirty universities. Some of the banners read: "Freedom of the press!" Others: "Hunger strike—demand dialogue!" And yet others: "The country will have no peace as long as dictatorship lives"; "Corruption is the cause of anarchy" and "Hunger is bearable, lack of democracy is not." I couldn't help smiling when I saw one large banner written in English, which said: "Welcome, Mr Gorbachev!"

In front of the Monument to the People's Heroes I saw the large banner with the simple message: "Hunger Strike." The Hunger Strike Command Center had been set up there, with Chai Ling elected as the commander in chief. As the hunger strike entered its third day, the number of hunger strikers had grown to almost 3,000. The students were now demanding dialogue as well as to be recognized as patriotic and democratic.

Surrounding the hunger strikers were thousands of students who had come to show their support. They gave speeches and sang patriotic songs like "The Internationale," the national anthem and "September Eighteenth." (On 18 September 1931, Japan occupied the three northern provinces of China, forcing millions of Chinese to flee their homes.)

When can we go back to our beautiful homeland?
When can we see our fathers and mothers?
Fathers and Mothers,
When can we reunite?

The temperature in the Square had risen to well above 25°C, but it felt even hotter under the bright sunshine. The students who had recently joined the hunger strike sat in small groups on the flagstones in the Square, wearing white headbands that read, "I swear to live or die with democracy," or "Fast until victory." Those students who had been fasting for three days were lying down, some on bedrolls, some resting their heads on rolled-up blankets and padded coats. Though the days were warm, the nights were still cold.

The Beijing University Hunger Strike Group, having grown to almost 500 people, was by far the largest. Dong Yi found the group of students from his department. I helped him pass around the drinks, and watched as Dong Yi spoke softly to the hunger strikers he knew, asking them how they were holding up and what they needed, such as more blankets for the night. Up until then, no one had thought that the hunger strike would have to go on for much longer. Instead, there was a sense of confidence among the students that the government would soon give in.

After we finished passing around the drinks, Dong Yi stayed with the students from the Physics Department. I went to look for Cao Gu Ran. Some yards away, I found the cluster of nine hunger strikers from the Psychology Department. Most of them were first- and second-year students whom I only knew by sight. But I did not find Cao Gu Ran there or anywhere else.

"Have you seen Cao Gu Ran?" I asked.

"He fainted and was rushed to the emergency center," answered one of the young men from the Psychology Department.

Immediately I was worried. Horrifying thoughts flew through my mind.

Suddenly I heard Dong Yi's voice. "Someone has fainted over here!" As I looked up, two first-aid staff in white coats ran past. Soon sirens wailed beneath the blue sky and the young man was rushed to an ambulance. The Red Cross and the Beijing government had organized ambulances to transport hunger strikers to emergency centers near the Square. A few minutes later, the ambulance sped away from the Square.

Half an hour later, sirens went off again, another fainting hunger striker was taken away. While more hunger strikers fell, others including Cao Gu Ran came back. Cao Gu Ran had changed. His face was white. He walked slowly, at times unsteadily, and had to be supported by two first-aid staff. His headband was now twisted and half folded, showing only the words "liberty" and "death." He was pleased to see me. He sat down on a sheet spread out on the ground and told me about what had happened. He had fainted in the morning, and was given a saline drip at the emergency center, and then allowed to recover for four hours. "I feel fine now," he said, but his voice was not strong.

"Be careful—what you are doing is dangerous. You could seriously damage your health," I said to him.

"My health will be fine. Remember, I am fit," replied Cao Gu Ran, trying to be cheerful.

Presently, two professors from the Psychology Department came to the hunger-strike area. The department chairman, Professor Bei, and Professor Wang, both in their early sixties, had cycled all the way to the Square to beg their students to think about their health and return to their campuses.

"Look at them," Professor Wang, who became very emotional, said to me. "They are too young for this and certainly too young to die. What can I say to change their minds? I am desperate. They are only children."

"I am sure that they appreciate your worries," I replied. "But I don't think you will be able to convince any of them to stop fasting."

When Dong Yi and I finally returned to campus, it was shortly before dinner. Both of us were exhausted, physically and psychologically. The pale faces of the hunger strikers weighed heavily on our minds and consciences. We walked slowly to the Triangle, side by side in comfortable silence, the silence of mutual understanding and contentment.

Once we arrived at the Triangle, Dong Yi went to the number three canteen to buy some food so that we could eat outside while listening to the broadcast from the student radio station.

I waited for Dong Yi and my dinner, leaning against the long wall. The student radio station announced, "Today, Gorbachev came to visit China. But his welcome had to be held at the airport and not at Tiananmen Square as is traditional." The crowd in their hundreds cheered and applauded loudly. "We have once again shown the Government that the students are a force to be reckoned with!"

Then the announcer read letters of support from parents and students in universities across China, and gave news of donations from overseas. "Chinese students studying in California have donated $8,000 for us!" I looked over to the number three canteen, hoping to see Dong Yi coming out with our dinner. I was hungry, and the sweet scent of lilacs in the evening air only made me hungrier. Then I saw, emerging from the crowd, an extremely beautiful young woman, who seemed to be looking for someone. She had a perfectly balanced face, large brown eyes, full lips and creamy white skin. Her nose was high and straight. She looked youthful but at the same time mature. She was not only pretty but also sexy, which was rather rare at that time in China.

Then to my surprise, I saw her talking to Dong Yi's roommate. Before I could make any sense of it, Dong Yi came out of the canteen with our food. Just as I was about to wave to him, I saw the young woman rushing toward him. When I looked at his face, I realized immediately who she was. That was how I saw Lan, for the first and last time.

She was not what I had imagined her to be. Though she may have been physically vulnerable, she had a hidden strength. I watched them walking away, smiling, talking, as husband and wife should. Dong Yi's roommate came to tell me that something urgent had come up and Dong Yi had to leave. I pretended I hadn't seen anything and walked as calmly as I could to the canteen to get myself dinner.

Even today, as I think back to those years in Beijing, it was that moment, more than any other, that I can recall with undiminished accuracy. The way their eyes met, and Lan's face lit up. The way they rushed toward each other and then clung to each other as they walked away. My heart stopped, I couldn't breathe, I felt as if I was no longer alive.

I knew I could not compete with her. She was beautiful and sexy; any man would want to be with her. What on earth made me think that I could take Dong Yi away from her? No wonder Dong Yi couldn't bring himself to go through with the divorce.

My dream was shattered, my future bleak. I saw this as clearly as I saw the fire hidden behind those gorgeous wide brown eyes. Had Dong Yi's roommate said anything to her? Did he tell her who I was? Were those glances and that fire directed at me?

Inside the canteen, I moved through the lines and bought something to eat, I had no idea what, and sat down at one of the long tables. Dong Yi and Lan had long gone, but I still saw her, her glowing face and those sensuous lips, tilted slightly at the sight of Dong Yi. Those images replayed in my mind, over and over again, like a movie, some segments in slow motion, depending on how my panic, sadness or anger informed them. I am sure the canteen was noisy that evening, just like any other dinnertime, but I heard nothing other than my own thoughts.

I did not eat anything, I no longer felt hungry, happy or hopeful. I went back outside, but nothing seemed to have changed the way I'd changed. The evening air still smelled of lilacs, while twenty yards away, the student radio station continued to broadcast news from Tiananmen Square. I stood in the crowd, hearing the voice of the female news announcer drifting faintly in the air around me, like smoke, here one moment and gone the next.

What should I do now? I moved on, trying to shake off the images that haunted me. I wanted to be alone. I did not want to go home because going back to my parents" apartment would inevitably mean talking about my day, about Tiananmen Square or the hunger strikers, and Dong Yi. Nor could I sit in my room without thinking of my future without him. And I couldn't go back to Dong Yi's dorm building, where I had left my bicycle.

I felt so lonely surrounded by the crowd, and at the same time guilty that my mind was preoccupied with my own unhappiness while a much more serious crisis was taking place in Tiananmen Square. I could not help but think about Dong Yi and Lan, wondering why she had come to Beijing. Had something happened to Dong Yi's parents or his sister? Perhaps Lan had come to be part of Dong Yi's life, particularly in this dire moment, to show him that she shared his thoughts and beliefs? Had Lan come to fight for her husband?

Seeing Lan in person, the opposite of everything I'd imagined her to be, prompted more questions than I could handle. I wanted to know who she really was, what she thought and felt. I had cared little about Lan in the past. She was shapeless, hollow, colorless, invisible and faceless. She was a ghost. Now she appeared, alive, colorful, breathing and smiling. I wanted to know everything about her, to speak to her and to hear her speak. I wanted to find out the truth about her, not just what Dong Yi had told me. I wanted to know the real meaning of their relationship.

As these confused thoughts filled my mind, my legs took me slowly away from the crowd and the tensions at the Triangle, toward Weiming Lake. In front of the library, small groups of students sat scattered, talking softly or reading, while one couple seemed to be having an argument.

On the winding path behind the butterfly-roofed biology building, I was joined by others, mostly couples. Less than half a mile away from the Triangle, Weiming Lake was another world, peaceful and gentle. The great events of recent days seemed to have bypassed the lake, leaving it unaffected, a refuge for lovers and friends. I walked through the red stone gate to the rocky bank. Here an empty bench under a weeping willow overlooked the tranquil blue waters. Soft colored twilight cast long shadows on the lake.

I wondered what Dong Yi and Lan were doing. Were they having dinner at Yanchun Garden, the campus restaurant not far from Dong Yi's dorm building, where the two of us used to go? Or were they at one of those small family restaurants that lined the busy Haidian Road just outside the south gate? What were they talking about? After dinner, would they go and listen to the broadcast from the student radio station, as Dong Yi and I had planned to do? Slowly my anger grew, not toward Dong Yi or Lan, but toward myself. I realized just how ordinary I was. For what I thought were the special things I shared with Dong Yi, the buzz of city life, our love of words, the so-called intellectual conversations, our thoughts about the future, the Student Movement . . . suddenly I saw them for what they were: the currency of any relationship. There was nothing special here—Lan could easily fit in. And sitting next to her must be such an ego-boost for Dong Yi; she was simply the most sensual woman I had ever seen. What would happen in the days to come? When would I see Dong Yi again? What news would he bring when we next met?

As my mind turned to the distant days ahead, the day itself came to an end. Streetlamps shone around the lake, while the gentle evening wind now turned stronger and chillier. I could no longer see the strangers who had also come to the lake. Perhaps they had left long ago, or disappeared into the woods up the hill behind me. Suddenly I was struck by the thought that Dong Yi and Lan might come to the lake. I jumped up, looked around, alarmed, and started to move away. I did not want to see them together again, not so soon, and definitely not here. But as I walked quickly along the path, I could not get certain images out of my mind. I kept imagining them together, in an intimate way, in a way that Dong Yi and I had never been together. Eventually I managed to shake myself free of those images.

But I could not get the image of Lan's wide brown eyes, sparkling with desire, out of my mind. She stared straight at me. The wind rose from behind the trees to my right, chilling my bones. I turned around swiftly: the road sweeping down to the lake bank was empty. I turned back, the road ahead that turned at the biology building was also empty.

I almost ran down the hill. As I was about to emerge onto the brightly lit square in front of the library, I stopped and looked back at the road behind me, now in dark shadow. There I saw Lan again, smiling a victorious smile.

"You are right, I can't win," I said to her and then I ran into the light, noise and reality, without looking back again.

The Triangle was still full of people, some listening intently to the debate on the radio station, some arguing. Compared with a few days before, there were more middle-aged men and women standing shoulder to shoulder with the young. Some of them were professors and administrators at the university, while many others were locals, citizens who had more recently joined the crowd at the Triangle for news they could trust from the life-and-death battle in Tiananmen Square.

I cut through the crowd, passing between the rows of wall posters. As I turned the corner, I looked up. The corner window on the first floor of the Young Faculty Building was lit. On such a night, that softly illuminated window was like a lighthouse in a storm.

"Look who is here!" Eimin opened the door. Judging from his voice, I knew that my coming was a pleasant surprise.

I smiled and stepped inside his tiny world. Books and papers littered his desk. How can he still write his book while the world is being turned upside down under his window? I wondered. But I decided not to ask, for I was too distracted. Who am I to judge? I thought again, my mind going back to Lan and Dong Yi.

I stepped toward the desk, leaving Eimin standing behind me, smiling. I leaned forward to look out of the window at the silhouette of the large aspen tree against the dark, clear sky. I thought he must be wondering why I had suddenly come to see him at this time of night, but I didn't say anything. At that moment, I didn't particularly care what he thought.

Eimin's right hand came to rest on my shoulder. I did not move, but stayed staring out of the window. He came closer and put his left hand on my waist. His right hand moved under my hair and began slowly to stroke my neck. His left hand was now circling my stomach, rotating and circling, stirring my senses. Then he pulled me into him and began to kiss my neck and the tiny but sensitive spot behind my ear.

I still did not move. I closed my eyes and let his hands and lips work on me. Then my breath became as heavy as his and I turned around and began to kiss him back. Eimin turned off the light and guided me down onto his bed.

Lan's wide brown eyes had gone.

I saw nothing but darkness.

Ten

Heavenly Peace

Flowers falling in water, spring is disappearing,
spirits rising to heaven.

—*Li Yi, ninth century*

I spent the next day drifting between a determination to forget all about Dong Yi, and a burning urge to see him and to know what was going on between him and Lan. Meanwhile, life was passing me by out in the Triangle and Tiananmen Square. Great things were happening in China. Students were standing together as never before, to make a difference and to change the course of history. Why was I still living in the past, waiting passively for someone to tell me how my life might turn out?

"Do something! Make your own life, Wei," I said to myself.

These thoughts lifted my spirits and I became genuinely happy for a while. But soon my strength drained away again, and, by lunchtime, my desire to see Dong Yi had reached an overwhelming level. Eimin and I usually had lunch at the number three canteen around the corner. The canteen had recently become extremely popular with the students because of its proximity to the Triangle. As a consequence, the lines inside were enormous, almost all the time. Yet, we'd still go, for you could be sure you'd see your friends and so discuss the current events with them.

Dong Yi had only been to number three canteen occasionally,

and mostly with me. I thought that my chance of bumping into him would be greater in another canteen closer to his dormitory. So I persuaded Eimin to go there, and we went as soon as it opened for lunch. Knowing that they would take some time, I asked Eimin to get me two dishes from the small wok—where they served freshly made stir-fries. I kept my eyes on the door for the one-and-a-half hours we were there, hoping that Dong Yi and Lan would show up. But they did not. Though I would not have known how to react if I'd actually seen them together, I wanted so much to see Dong Yi.

Since the moment I saw Lan, I had asked myself a hundred questions without knowing any of the answers. Yet, among all the speculation, suspicion, love and hateful feelings, there remained one mystery—the purpose of Lan's visit. Why had she come at this particular time? Was she bringing news that might change everything?

Dong Yi was not at the Triangle that evening either. I walked around and through the crowds over and over again and saw neither him, Lan nor his roommate. He seemed to have suddenly disappeared into his other life. Our paths no longer crossed.

I resented Dong Yi deeply; not because he was now with Lan—after all, she *was* his wife. It was because he had left me with a cursory "something has come up," passed on by his roommate. I wished that he had felt he could let me know what had really happened. Didn't I deserve at least that?

I looked at Eimin, who had been reading the wall posters with great concentration. Suddenly I wished that Dong Yi had never mentioned divorce. My life would have been so much less complicated, and perhaps happier.

I went back to my parents' apartment, determined to get on with my life. I was by then spending half my time with Eimin and the other half with my parents. That evening, before going to bed, I laid out on the desk all the required paperwork for the passport application and then put it neatly into a large brown envelope.

Lying in bed at the apartment where I had spent my teens and young adult life, I imagined I saw the porcelain bodies of Dong Yi and Lan folded into each other like a pair of hands. Then I told myself that I had gone crazy, imagining and thinking of another woman's body, especially someone I had only seen from a distance.

But I couldn't help wondering whether Dong Yi loved her. He had told me he did, and it seemed obvious—from the moment his eyes met hers with joy and affection. That gaze had pierced my heart with unbearable pain. But how much did he love her? Did he love me more? And would he ever walk away from her? Then I remembered the fire behind those wide, sensual brown eyes. Lan would never let him go. My heart sank deeper and deeper into endless darkness. Love without hope is the most miserable kind of love.

Eimin was the one who loved only me and no one else, I told myself. He was the one who was there for me when I needed someone, as he had always been. He hadn't questioned me when I turned up out of the blue. He didn't ask where I had been or why I had come, but simply accepted me, was simply there for me. Why shouldn't I marry him? We could go to America and start a new life, where there'd be no more pain and waiting in vain. With such thoughts, a strange sense of peace slowly came over me, and I went to sleep, knowing that in a few hours a new day would dawn.

When I was fourteen years old, I thought the easiest job in the world was to be a weather forecaster in Beijing. All you needed to do, it seemed, was to predict that it would be sunny, and you'd be right at least nine times out of ten.

The dawn came, and the day was inevitably sunny again, boringly bright and warm. At Yellow Village, the large chestnut trees that lined the road were covered with deep green leaves that cast lace-patterned shadows beneath them. I was riding on my bicycle up to the gate of the People's University where, three weeks before, I had come face to face with the police during the first march, when suddenly I heard familiar voices calling out my name.

I turned around and saw Hanna and Jerry pedaling up from behind.

"Where are you going in such a hurry?" Hanna asked loudly, catching her breath. "We've been calling to you to stop for the past twenty minutes, but you were too far ahead to hear us!"

"To the city center," I replied, nodding to Jerry with a smile.

"So are we," said Hanna. "Why don't we go together?"

The three of us rode on in a row, with Hanna in the middle, passing little traffic except the trucks loaded with flag-waving students.

Hanna was wearing a red T-shirt and a pair of shorts, showing her perfectly toned long legs. Jerry, with his white short-sleeved shirt and long trousers, appeared pale beside her radiant tan.

"Are you going to Tiananmen Square?" Hanna asked, and we slowed down so that we could all talk. "Jerry and I have been there almost every day. Such an exciting event, especially for an Asian historian like Jerry." Then she leaned toward me and said rather proudly, "Jerry is thinking of writing a book about it."

I told her I was going to the passport office to put in my application. I was a little embarrassed, so I added, "but the passport office is not far from the Square. I will stop by to show my support afterward."

Hanna was surprised I hadn't applied already. "I thought that you'd received your scholarship some time ago, why have you waited so long to apply for your passport? Having a passport could be very useful, particularly now." She lowered her body as well as her voice so that the other two-dozen people riding around us couldn't hear. "It's all going well at the moment. But you never know what might happen next, the army could take over the city and the borders could close. I have my passport with me at all times just in case." At this moment she sat up straight on her bicycle and laughed, "My problem is that I don't have a visa to go anywhere."

"But that could change very quickly if there was a political crisis here," said Jerry. Because he was riding on the other side of Hanna, he had to raise his voice so that I could hear him. He tried to reassure us that foreign countries, including his own, would help the students.

"Do you actually think something like what Hanna said will happen?" I asked.

"Of course not," said Jerry. "We're just speaking hypothetically, aren't we?"

"Not me," retorted Hanna. "Anything is possible in China."

Presently we stopped at a traffic light. Jerry tipped his bicycle slightly, shifted his weight, and stood tall over his bicycle like a movie star. Some fifteen other cyclists also stopped at the light. All of them, men and women, turned to look at us—the two Chinese girls and the tall foreigner.

An open truck full of students pulled up at the crossing. A large red flag, "Beijing Institute of Steel and Iron," slowly fluttered as the truck came to stop. Together with twenty or so other cyclists waiting at the light, we waved and shouted our support.

"Thank you for your backing! Fasting until victory!" The students in the truck cheered back.

I noticed that some of them were wearing red crosses on their arms. They must be the medical support team for the hunger strikers, I thought, knowing that every day thousands of student volunteers were working in shifts to look after the hunger strikers in Tiananmen Square. The news from the Square had been worrying; more and more hunger strikers had to be treated for dehydration, although no casualties had yet been reported.

Presently a half-full bus pulled up behind the truck. Some passengers leaned out, perhaps noticing that we were also students, waved to us and called out, "Long live the students! Have a good day!"

Hanna, Jerry and I looked at each other and laughed out loud. "Good day to you too!"

The lights turned green. We waved the students on as their truck pulled ahead loudly, thick smoke gushing from the exhaust pipe. Bicycle bells rang out around us, sending the truck on its way.

Old chestnut trees soon gave way to young willows and vulnerable new aspen trees. The road widened after the crossing at Beijing Zoo. New matchbox residential buildings lined the street, laundry tangled over balconies like flags on an ocean liner. The sunlight became blinding, bouncing off the gray walls of the buildings.

We stopped at a small *Lengyin Dian*—a cold drinks shop. The shop was full of local workers, residents and the traveling public, but few stayed. People poured in and then rushed out with their purchases. Aside from the three of us, there was only one other customer, a pimply faced boy of about fifteen. He was having a glass of red bean ice— sweet red bean soup poured over compressed ice. While we ate our ice creams, our neighbor slurped and loudly crushed the ice between his teeth.

Infected with the happy mood surrounding us, I said excitedly, "At this moment I don't want to live anywhere but Beijing. You'd think this was the friendliest place in the world. I feel that I am connected with everyone, no matter who they are, old men carrying their bird cages, middle-aged mothers with shopping baskets, even children."

"Even I feel at home here, which is pretty extraordinary for a foreigner, if you ask me." Jerry was quick to echo my sentiment. "It almost feels as if I've been suddenly allowed inside a forbidden temple, to see China as it really is."

"I hope he is not scaring you—these days all he can talk about is this 'real China' stuff—how it is and how it should be," said Hanna, her lightheartedness mixed with concern. "I don't understand why he should suddenly feel so *personal* about China."

As she effortlessly dropped an emphasis on the word "personal," Hanna did her trademark sexy move—tossing her hair aside while glancing over to look at Jerry, her youthful body flipping upward like a dolphin, as if pulled up by her long locks. Hanna's sexuality was so different from Lan's, so much more overt. Hanna was voluptuous, and like a volcano filled with red-hot lava, unstoppable, inflaming everything in her path. What was it that Dong Yi saw in Lan? Did she, too, provoke a burning desire in him?

"So what is the real China that you have been allowed to see?" I asked Jerry.

"To begin with, I think China is much more similar to the West than people are led to believe," he replied.

"Isn't it just so typical? Foreigners think that they have understood China after being here for a measly six months," Hanna interrupted. "Talking about the real China—what nonsense! No one knows about the real China! I have lived here all my life, but if someone asks me about what China is really like, I would have no clue."

"But sometimes people from the outside offer great insights because, well, exactly because they have not lived here all their lives," I said. "They may be able to see things that we don't, or don't want to, see. As the poet Li Bai said, 'being inside the mountain makes you not able to see it.'"

"Remember the last time we met, when we talked about parallelism of politics and economics?" Perhaps Jerry had been encouraged by my comments, or maybe he intended to state his views about China despite Hanna's protest. "What was the name of your friend, Wei?"

"Chen Li."

"Right. Well, he did not believe that China needed political reform. I told him that China's economic reform would stall if political liberation was not forthcoming. I told him that freedom of speech was a basic human right that one cannot live without, and that democracy is the only future for any country. Look at the tens of thousands of people in Tiananmen Square—they understand and agree with me."

Without waiting for me to respond, Jerry continued his speech to his newfound audience. "The perception that the Chinese live contentedly under tight controls by their government and never complain is absolutely untrue. I say to my friends, 'Look at those students, they are willing to give their lives for freedom and liberty. Where else can you find this?' I tell my friends that the Chinese are the most courageous people. The Chinese students have given hope to the rest of the world."

"But do you think the students will win in the end?" I asked.

"I would say yes, because you are on the right side of history. Democracy will prevail." Jerry was becoming very excited. His voice became even louder, which made me nervous. "The students are doing the right thing, keeping up the pressure. This is a great opportunity for China as well as for the world. Imagine what an effect such changes in the world's most populated country would have on the rest of us."

In those days, optimism was everywhere, among the students and their supporters—which meant just about every ordinary citizen in Beijing. Many local citizens, workers and civil servants were initially suspicious about the Student Movement. Though many hundreds of thousands of people watched and cheered the first student demonstration on 27 April, most of them did not join in the march. Most student movements in Chinese history have been ill-organized, wracked by friction among different groups and so, ultimately, they have failed. When the students started the hunger strike on 13 May, they did not only show the people of China their determination and bravery, but also their ability to organize themselves under a united front—the Autonomous Student Association. Support for the students grew rapidly across the city. Soon many factory workers, small business owners, government employees and intellectuals took to the streets too.

By 17 May, the support for the hunger strikers had reached a new level, as over a million people, including students, intellectuals, shopkeepers and workers marched to Tiananmen in a show of unity. I had a glimpse of it when I passed the Square on my way to the passport office.

When Hanna, Jerry and I came to within half a mile of the Square, all traffic had virtually stopped. Groups of people walking around with flags and banners, people pushing bicycles, trucks carrying student monitors and supply vehicles transporting blankets were all tangled together in the crush. At first, truck drivers honked their horns trying to push forward, student leaders shouted from the top for people to give way. But the groups marching in formation did not move to let them pass. They clearly had the right of way and moved on as they wished, shouting loudly themselves. Cyclists rang their bells, and then got down and walked instead. Everywhere there were walls of people. By the time we came to the southwest corner of the Square, those walls were ten people deep.

"My goodness, how many people are here today?" Jerry exclaimed, standing two heads above everyone else, looking into the Square.

"More than yesterday?" asked Hanna.

"Definitely. The beltway and the Square are solid. I'd say at least double the number that were here yesterday."

The newspapers estimated that there were 50,000 people in the Square the day before.

Instead of being pushed by the slow flow of traffic on the beltway, Hanna and Jerry decided to try going toward the Great Hall of the People. Jerry wanted to climb up the steel fence surrounding the Hall to take photos for his future book. I said good-bye to them, watching them trying desperately to cut across the marching columns and through the walls of spectators, and then I began my slow journey to the east and so to the passport office. A few minutes later, when I turned around to look for them, they had already been swallowed by the crowd: they had disappeared without a trace.

From inside the slow-moving walls of spectators I could see that people from all walks of life had come out to support the students. A column of grade school students marched by, led by their teachers. The red scarves around their necks were especially eye-catching. But my attention was drawn to a large sign among a group of union-card-waving workers, saying "Deng Xiaoping resign!" I understood that it was a response to a televised meeting between the Party Secretary General Zhao Ziyang and President Gorbachev the previous day. At the meeting Zhao told Gorbachev that although Deng Xiaoping had officially retired, he was still the man who made all the important decisions. Every Chinese person who watched that broadcast understood that Zhao was in fact using the opportunity to tell the nation the truth about Deng. It was no surprise that much of the anger was now directed at Deng Xiaoping, the ultimate decision maker in China. But the sign calling directly for Deng's resignation startled me. I remember clearly that it was at that moment that I felt a terrible fear that all this would end badly. The battle had become personal, for both sides.

At the passport office, the atmosphere of promise, of hope, seemed to have gone into overdrive. There was a cheerful buzz about the place, despite the long lines and confusion as to where one should go for a form, or to get an answer to a question, or simply to hand in a completed application. The noise level inside was further aggravated by the fact that everyone was offering often not useful, and sometimes simply wrong, advice to everyone else.

"Do you know whether these photos are OK for a passport?" someone behind asked me.

I turned around, gasped in surprise, and exclaimed, "Minnie Mouse!"

"Wei!" my old roommate from boarding school screamed back at me. Min Fangfang—Minnie Mouse—had indeed transformed herself into a womanly, fashionable lady, just as Qing had told me. She had ditched her thick, black-framed glasses for contacts, and her straight hair was permed into soft and large curls. Her eyes were skilfully painted and her lips cherry red.

"How come you are here in Beijing? I thought you were at graduate school in Shanghai," I said to my friend.

"I was. But now there are no more classes. Many of my classmates have come to Beijing to take part in the hunger strike, those who stayed on campus are demonstrating in Shanghai," Min Fangfang replied. "It was great. I took the train back from Shanghai for free. Not only did they let us on without a ticket, the staff as well as passengers cheered us on all the way to Beijing. They said, 'You youngsters are so brave. Go on, we support you.' Some of them thanked us because they said that we were doing it for them."

My friend looked at me with a wide smile, "What a surprise! Where are you going, America?"

"Yes, to Virginia, a small college called William and Mary. And you?"

"Boston. University of Boston."

Then we talked about what had happened to our old classmates. I was surprised to find out that a number of them had already gone to America to continue their education. After about two hours, we both handed in our applications and finished our long conversation about those we knew. We said good-bye to each other outside.

"When do you plan to leave?" Minnie Mouse asked, already on her bike.

"September."

"Same here. Bye and good luck." Then she waved and sped off.

When I returned to Beijing University to see Eimin, I was still in high spirits, lifted by my unexpected reunion with my old roommate. Eimin was happy that I had finally handed in my passport application, although his congratulations came with asides such as "My little bird will leave me and fly away," which made me feel bad.

These comments about my going to America had become a real sticking point in our relationship. I did not like the way Eimin seemed to insinuate that I cared little about him or our relationship and that I was heartlessly and deliberately destroying what we had by leaving China. He also managed to drive the point home with his consistent declaration of devotion that usually followed these remarks: "But I still love you despite what you are doing," or "Let's make the best of the little time we have left." These words made me feel that I had to defend my honor by restating my love and appreciation for him. The more I did it, the more uncomfortable I felt because as Eimin liked to point out, "If you love me as you say you do, you know exactly how we can be together in America."

I knew what he meant. I asked myself the same question too. If I loved him, as I said I did, why didn't I marry him? If we didn't get married, it was clear that Eimin would not want to continue the relationship after I left. Thus, in this subtle, or as I later realized, rather explicit way, he was giving me an ultimatum.

That evening he took me to the Yanchun Garden restaurant to celebrate another milestone in my going to America. Yanchun Garden was the campus restaurant in a high-roofed dining hall near the track field, frequented by students with a bit of extra cash, or those who had friends and family visiting. This was the place where the hunger strikers had had their last meal, a banquet organized by faculty members like Eimin.

Presently our conversation was interrupted. "They just called our number. Wait here, I will get the wonton soups." Eimin got up and walked to the counter.

I looked around and saw only strange faces. I had hoped that I would have heard from Dong Yi by now, but I had not seen him for three days. I could only assume that Lan was still here. What had they been doing for these three days? What had they been talking about? Was I ever part of their conversation? How would it end?

"Here we are." Eimin showed up with two large bowls of wonton soup, steaming hot. He handed one to me, the porcelain spoon stuck inside. "This is yours. I have put lots of chilli sauce in mine."

Eimin loved chilli sauce, which he added to everything he ate.

"You need not be scared." He picked up from where we had left our last conversation, while stirring the soup in a circular motion to cool it down. "There will be a lot of men who would love to help you. Don't be offended. I am just saying it as it is, because I have seen it happen so many times when I was in Scotland. There were very few women overseas, mostly wives, and way too many men."

I knew that he was talking about the community of overseas Chinese students, to which he belonged for five years.

"You will be very popular, young, pretty, unattached, all on your own. But be careful. They will take advantage of you," Eimin went on, now trying to cool down a hot wonton in his mouth. "I am not trying to scare you. I am simply telling you what to expect when you go to America, especially in America, where there is a lot of crime. It will not be easy for a young girl like you."

I ate my wonton soup quietly. Had I been ten or even five years older, and known more about the world outside China, I might have questioned what Eimin said. But at the time, he believed that he painted a realistic picture of my life in the faraway and unknown land to which I was going. And I believed that he did so because he loved me and was concerned about my well-being. It was tough love from my lover, a man of experience and, in my eyes, a man of the world.

To my own annoyance I had recently grown more and more scared about going to America. Perhaps I was increasingly afraid of the fact that I was about to leave behind everything I had ever known. Perhaps the hopeless situation with Dong Yi had drained my strength. I thought about my parents too. When I left, I would leave them too, perhaps for a very long time. Who would care about me and help me when I needed a helping hand?

I wanted so much to see Dong Yi, if only for just a few seconds, from a distance, even if we did not speak. I thought that just the sight of him might bring peace to me. But I could find no peace that evening. On our walk back, I looked out for Dong Yi but could not see him at the Triangle. Perhaps he and Lan had been and gone, I thought; perhaps they did not come that day. Eimin ran into a colleague of his, and they chatted. I walked around to read the new wall posters, at the same time hoping to see Dong Yi.

But soon night fell, and there was no sign of Dong Yi.

As Eimin and I walked back to his room, we passed a table on which lay a petition urging the Communist Party leaders to start a dialogue with the students.

"Have you signed the petition yet?" asked one of the young girls at the table.

"Yes I have," I said.

"How many signatures have you got?" Eimin asked, looking through the long paper roll.

"Six thousand! Many prominent intellectuals including famous professors have signed," the girl answered excitedly. She then rolled the paper up to the last page so that Eimin could add his name.

After we got to Eimin's room, I asked him why he'd signed the petition. He had always been cautious about these things, especially petitions. He had told me, on more than one occasion, that one should never sign such things because it could become the evidence by which one would later be destroyed. "You can demonstrate, and as long as there is no hard evidence, such as photos, against you, you can always deny it. But you cannot deny your signature," he had always said.

I thought he was clever. I knew that he was experienced in such things because of what he had to go through in the Cultural Revolution. If he were to be caught doing what he did tonight during the Cultural Revolution, he would surely have ruined his career, his life, been imprisoned or forced to work until he died in a hard labor camp.

"Well, there are over six thousand names on the petition, what would the government do to me?" he said. "Besides there are much bigger fish to fry if they want to." Eimin drew the curtain. "Anyway," he said, "I did not sign my name, but printed it. So if anyone asks, I can still deny it and say that someone else put my name down." He turned around and smiled. "I am smart."

I could not deny that. If there was anything I was certain of, it was that Eimin was an intelligent man.

The next day, 18 May 1989, I wore a large straw hat and a white linen dress. An early morning rainstorm had cleaned the streets of dirt and litter, which were now piled up along the sides. The temperature had cooled; I could feel the caress of crisp, fresh air on my face and my body as I rode my bicycle. I felt silly with my hat, but Eimin had insisted on my wearing it, because it would cover up my face. "Believe me, the secret police will be taking photos," he said. "You don't want to be caught on film and jeopardize your chance of going to America."

Eimin and I were on our way to the bus depot, at the beginning of the Western Boulevard of Eternal Peace, to take part in the second march of one million people to Tiananmen Square.

In the Square, the hunger strike was going into its fifth day. Over 700 hunger strikers had already collapsed and the number was going up fast. But the government continued to refuse to talk to the students about their demands. To millions of ordinary Chinese citizens this was shocking, shameful and anguishing. It seemed clear to everyone but the leaders of China that if dialogue did not take place soon, someone would die in Tiananmen Square and that would be a great tragedy for China. Perhaps the government understood the situation clearly and simply chose to ignore the hunger strikers. To entertain such a possibility was to make the situation much worse. It meant accepting that the government could be coldhearted, arrogant and have little concern for life. This inflamed outrage and disgust among the people.

When Eimin and I found the flag of the Psychology Department within the mile-long column of Beijing University students, my old classmates, who were by now graduate students, were very happy to see me and welcomed me back to their ranks with the greatest enthusiasm. Li was, as usual, busy organizing the columns. Lu Bin, the tallest and strongest senior, was to carry the departmental flag. Li exchanged a few words with the other organizers about whether the march should be done by cohort.

"This way we can make sure that there are no infiltrations," urged one of them, a young man whom I did not know. He must have been a first-year undergraduate.

"Too difficult to maintain. We would be better off if we let everyone walk wherever they want. I would be happy to walk around to make sure there are no strange faces," said Su, a graduate student.

"I agree with her. Let's all be vigilant—why don't you do the security with Su," said Li, turning to the young first year.

Presently an old fragile man with a walking stick appeared at the edge of the crowd. He stood impatiently waiting for the march to begin. Li rushed over to greet him, and those who escorted the old man.

It was Professor Huang, who had retired five years before from the Department. I had met Professor Huang on a few occasions when he attended departmental functions, such as the ceremony in which the Nobel Laureate Herbert Simon was made an honorary professor of the department. Later on, when I was thinking about going to America, I called upon Professor Huang, who had a PhD from Stanford, for help. He was already in his eighties, not in good health and spent most of his time sitting on the sofa in his living room. But his mind was still active. We talked about the department, about my future plans and his experiences in America almost fifty years before. When I showed him my transcript and asked whether he would mind giving me a recommendation, he said, "These are the best grades I have seen. Of course I wouldn't mind."

"Thank you so much for coming, Professor Huang," said Li loudly, holding his hand. I could hear the gush of emotion in her voice.

"I am happy that you have invited me to come. I feel good today. Being with you young people makes me feel ten years younger," the professor replied with equal excitement in his voice.

"Professor Huang has come to march with us!" shouted Li to everyone in the Psychology camp. Her voice was immediately drowned by loud applause.

But it was not until almost two hours later that our section of the march was able to move forward. It turned out that the six-mile long Western Boulevard of Eternal Peace had been jammed with people, with more joining in from both the north and south. The sun was burning brightly when our column moved on, Lu Bin waving the red flag, sending it flaming up. I walked next to Professor Huang, trying to support him with my arm. But the elderly professor needed no help. He walked proudly in his washed off-gray Mao jacket, chin up and steps steady.

The journey to Tiananmen Square was a slow one as too many people and vehicles were trying to get to the Square. It was later reported that 18 May saw the biggest demonstration ever in Beijing, with the total number of people estimated at one and a half million. At a few junctions, we had to come to a complete stop before finally, after more than an hour, reaching the Square. Here more people, flags, banners, trucks and vans blocked the beltway. We stopped at the corner. The students from Fu Dan University in Shanghai marched by in formation. The staff at the *People's Daily* marched with a large banner saying, "We did not write the 26 April editorial!" attracting applause wherever they stopped.

Soon we turned right, marching south, passing the Great Hall of the People. Somewhere in the walls of spectators, I spotted Jerry's tall figure, snapping pictures, and then I saw Hanna next to him, glowing as usual. I waved at them, but neither saw me.

"It's Hanna and Jerry. Hanna was not joking—they are here every day!" I said to Eimin. I told Eimin that I would like to go over and say hello to them, but he warned me against that, saying that if I were to be photographed talking to a foreigner at the Square, I could easily be branded as "liaising with a foreign country," a serious crime.

Many spectators had cameras with them. Sometimes the demonstrators also took photos of themselves, of friends holding their hands up in the victory sign or banners that caught their eye. It seemed all innocent and harmless. But I took Eimin's advice and stayed put. I did not doubt what Eimin said: I believed that the secret police were there, in civilian clothes, recording as much as they could about the people and the events in the Square.

We moved on, marching alongside the staff of the Wangfujing Bookstore, the largest in China, and the workers from the Beijing Second Pharmaceutical Company in their white coats, as well as the thousands of fellow Beijing University students. Unlike the day before, I was no longer nervous about the banners demanding Deng Xiaoping's resignation, as they had become a common sight, like bamboo shoots springing out of the ground after the first spring rain.

That day, 18 May, was the best day I had ever experienced in all my years of living in China—it felt as if the people could finally say anything they wanted to say, openly, without fear of retribution. That day was the closest we ever got to real freedom of speech.

An hour later, we arrived at the southern tip of the Square. Not far from us, a truck was unloading people. Then a small blue bicycle was handed down. The sight of the bike immediately caught my attention, and, just as I was beginning to realize what it reminded me of, I saw my mother climbing down from the truck.

She was wearing the lily print shirt that she had made herself and a pair of black trousers which stopped just short of her ankles. My mother was then in her early fifties. But from the way she moved around busily and with great agility, you would never have guessed her age.

I left my column and ran over to see her. Two students had offered their hands to help her come down from the truck, which made her rather uncomfortable. My mother was not someone who admitted to her age easily. As she moved quickly to get down by herself, she slipped, and had to hold on to the proffered hands, which made her even more embarrassed.

When I came over, she was standing safely on the ground and was saying something to her students, smiling and waving her hands.

"Mama, what are you doing here?"

"Oh, my dear!" she cried out when she saw me. Instead of answering me, she turned to her students and said proudly, "This is my daughter."

They said hello and I nodded back.

"You go ahead," she told her students. "Don't worry about me. I can cycle back to the university later. No problem."

"Are you here to demonstrate, Mama?"

"Officially I am only here to watch. You know that we have been told not to encourage the students. But my students were happy when I told them that I was coming and they insisted that I should not bicycle but take their truck," she explained. "How did it go at the passport office?"

"Fine," I said. Presently I saw my column moving forward. "I'd better go now."

My mother looked at me with the tender love I had been accustomed to my whole life, and said, "Be careful."

"I will, Mama. You take care too." I waved good-bye and then ran to catch up with my friends. When I caught up with Eimin and the rest of my former department, I turned around to look for her. But she had disappeared, swallowed up in the sea of people.

The rainstorm came again in the afternoon, pouring down with more anger than in the morning, soaking everything under the sky. The day turned into night. We were already on our way back to the bus depot to retrieve our bicycles when the sky turned black. The entire column became disordered, running for shelter. White banners had been abandoned: they lay dirty on the street, the ink washed off.

Eimin and I could find no place to hide from the rain that was slashing down. The few places, like the guide's house outside the Military Museum, were crammed with people. Most of the trees on the boulevard were too young to give any protection, and anyway, with the rolling thunder and the cracks of bright lightning, we knew better than to shelter under trees in a storm.

Eimin and I decided to ride back in the rain, since we were already soaking wet. But a few hundred yards later we had to give up because the heavy rain completely blocked our vision.

Instead of stopping as abruptly as it started, like most summer storms, this one became a blanket of light rain, which looked as if it would continue for some time.

When we finally got back to Eimin's room, rid ourselves of our wet clothes, dried and drank hot boiled water, it was time for the seven o'clock evening news. As usual the first report came from the Square, together with the government urging the students to end the hunger strike.

"The hunger strikers have refused to take shelter from the rain. The conditions in the Square have worsened considerably."

A doctor was interviewed. "The hunger strikers are now very weak, with a diminished immune system. The number of people that have been at the Square, plus the rain, could trigger an outbreak of infection." The doctor then looked into the camera and said, "Dear students, for your own health, please end the hunger strike and leave Tiananmen Square."

Then the news program broadcast the meeting that took place during the day between President Li Peng and student representatives in the Great Hall of the People. Wang Dan, from Beijing University and Wuerkaixi, from Beijing Normal University, both prominent leaders of the Student Movement and both nineteen years old, were among the thirty student representatives.

Not long after the meeting began, the student representatives went into direct confrontation with Li Peng who warned the students not to stir up trouble in China. We knew immediately, without needing to hear it from the student radio station, that the meeting would be rejected by the students, who continued to demand the retraction of the *People's Daily* editorial which had labeled the Student Movement anarchic. The government had again refused to change their assessment. They also refused to acknowledge the meeting as a way of dialogue.

But for me, the news I had been waiting for did not come; there was nothing from Dong Yi. That night I was exhausted not only by the events of the day but also I was emotionally drained. I thought of Dong Yi, Lan, the students lying unprotected in the Square, Hanna and Jerry, Eimin . . . My heart was broken. It was time, like those who fasted in the Square, for me to take control of my life. Why wait for someone else to tell me how it might or might not turn out? I told myself, in my mother's voice, that I should stop chasing impossible dreams and be happy with what I had. Happiness was what I wanted and felt I deserved.

I turned off the light and went to bed. In the dark, I whispered to Eimin, "What do we need to do to get married?"

Eleven

Letter from America

For true friends, the edge of the sky is as
close as next door.

—*Wang Peng, eighth century*

Because of the rain, only a small number of people went to
Tiananmen Square on 19 May. More hunger strikers had
collapsed from a combination of lack of nutrition, wetness
and cold. To help the ill-equipped students cope with the sudden
change in the weather, the Beijing Red Cross delivered ninety buses
to house the weakest 1,000 of the 4,000 hunger strikers.

"Now we are broadcasting an important newsflash!" Beijing TV
station's regular news broadcast was interrupted. A caption appeared
on the TV screen, "Important News: Zhao Ziyang and Li Peng visit
the hunger strikers at Tiananmen Square."

"Come and see this!" I screamed at Eimin, who was working on
his book.

The picture showed a commotion on the edge of the Square. Then
a group of people in gray Mao suits appeared through the drizzle. The
camera moved swiftly toward them. Walking at the front of the group
was a man in his sixties, slightly taller than those around him. He wore
a pair of oversized square glasses and a light-colored sports jacket.
A young man sheltered him with an umbrella. The rest of the group
walked respectfully behind him.

"Zhao Ziyang, the General Secretary of the Communist Party Central Committee, and Li Peng, Premier of the State Council, went to Tiananmen Square at 4:45 A.M. this morning to see the students who are on a hunger strike."

I could hardly believe my eyes or my ears. The man who held the highest position in the land had come to Tiananmen Square! For weeks the government had refused to hold talks with the students. Only yesterday, Li Peng had again called the Student Movement "anarchic" when he met with student representatives. How extraordinary and strange that Zhao Ziyang should now come to the Square! Did this mean the government was considering shifting its position?

"What's going on? I thought the government wasn't talking to the students." Eimin had come to sit down on the sofa.

"Maybe this is it—they have given in," I said, although I suspected that was too good to be true. But I truly wished for such a miracle. I wanted to see a victory for the students.

In the Square, two student representatives dashed over to greet the General Secretary. Zhao shook their hands. A few minutes later, more student representatives appeared. Zhao Ziyang and Li Peng boarded a bus, shaking hands with fasting students. "Where do you go to school?" asked Zhao in a heavy Hunan accent, familiar to all Chinese thanks to his predecessor, Mao Zedong.

"Beijing Normal University," the student answered.

Our eyes were glued to the TV screen, disbelief mixed with wonder at this affectionate scene in Tiananmen Square. To most Chinese, the Party leaders were gray men who lived in their elite compound—Zhongnanhai—and traveled in dark-windowed luxury cars. They were not real. They were symbols of power. They gave speeches behind closed doors only to so-called People's Representatives. But today, the General Secretary of the Party had not only come to the Square, but he was walking with, and chatting with, the hunger strikers. He was showing concern for their well-being. At that moment, Zhao Ziyang became human and a friend to all the students.

A young man lying under a gray blanket tried to sit up. Zhao stopped him.

"We have come too late," he said, speaking into a small megaphone handed to him by a student, as he stepped out of the bus. Zhao Ziyang had tears in his eyes.

Tears came to my eyes. Tears came to the eyes of everyone who heard him.

"I am sorry, fellow students. No matter how you have criticized us, I think you have the right to do so. Please think of your health and leave the Square before it is too late," he begged the students. "It is not easy for the state and your parents to nurture you and send you to college. How can you, at the age of only eighteen or nineteen, or in your twenties, sacrifice your lives like this? We demonstrated and lay across railroad tracks when we were young too, taking no thought for the future. But today I ask you to think carefully about the future. Many issues will be resolved eventually. I beg you to end the hunger strike."

His speech was greeted with applause. Many hands stretched out from the bus windows toward him. As he passed by, more students came, handing over anything that they could find, a hat, a notebook, clothing, asking for his autograph.

But Zhao was right. It was too late for both sides, as we discovered later. Zhao Ziyang, the reformer, left the Square exhausted, already a broken man. Li Peng, a hardliner, now held sway in Zhao's place. The hunger strike continued.

The next day, I went with Eimin to see someone from the University Communist Party General Committee. We sat in a large classroom with dark desks and long benches. It had been raining nonstop for the previous two days. The air was now cool and damp inside the classroom. I waited for the meeting to start. There were three small windows on one side of the room, which let in just enough light on a normal sunny day, but were hopeless on a dark day like this. I did not understand why the meeting was taking place here, but then nothing was normal anymore. Sitting in this empty room, I had the eerie feeling that I was inside a tomb.

The middle-aged woman with short hair and a round face from the University Communist Party General Committee had a pair of small eyes, which seen from a distance, seemed almost invisible. She greeted Eimin warmly, reminding him of the last university meeting that they had both attended. I could tell, from her carefully chosen words, that she thought highly of Eimin's credentials.

The sound of paper shuffling between her fingers echoed in the room. When she lifted her eyes, she spoke only to Eimin. "I am afraid you can't get married, Dr. Xu. According to this application, comrade Little Liang is not yet of age."

"No. But she will turn twenty-three next month."

"Why not wait till then?" She glanced quickly at my face and then my stomach. Right away, I felt the sting of her suspicion.

"Wei is going to America soon. We don't have much time to establish the, er, 'husband and wife relationship.' Comrade Chang, as an important member of the Committee, you have seen much and know more than any of us. It may be some time before Wei and I can see each other again. That is why we are here today, to request special permission from the Party to get married."

The Party woman's eyelids twitched.

"I understand what you are saying." She nodded knowingly at Eimin, as if there was some kind of secret code that they shared.

"Personally I would do everything to help our returned-to-motherland PhDs," she continued, "but exceptions are difficult and not something I can decide here and now. I will have to talk to the other Committee members."

"Of course. We appreciate your sympathy and understanding," Eimin complimented her with a broad smile.

The Party woman was clearly glad to hear Eimin's praise. "Many people think that we Party officials are brain-dead, rule-obsessed bureaucrats. But you are highly educated. You know better."

We reached the door. Casually, the Party woman turned to Eimin and asked, "Have either of you been involved with the Student Movement?"

"No." Eimin spoke without the slightest change in his expression, holding the door open for her.

"I didn't think you would," she said, stepping outside. "But I had to ask, you understand?"

She looked at the sky. A few raindrops were coming down.

"I have always known that the demonstrations would end badly, I said so from the outset. Look what it has brought us."

"The students are too young to understand the consequences of their actions," agreed Eimin.

"'Students' wrongs, teachers' faults.' Many of our faculty have failed to do their duty," said the Party woman.

"Well, thank you again for seeing me at such short notice. I look forward to hearing your decision." Eimin shook hands with her.

"No problem. Anything for you, Dr. Xu. Besides, I don't have much to do these days. You know what I mean." She smiled again, as if secretly she and Eimin shared membership of a special club. "Goodbye. I hope I can get back to you very soon."

We parted. I felt a sense of relief. Finally the conversation, during which I was not asked to participate, was over.

That morning, martial law was declared in Beijing. I had to go home because I knew that my parents would be worried about me. The mood at the Triangle had sobered, compared with a couple of days before, and when I passed by to go home, I found many students reading the details of the martial law order that had been posted on the walls since the morning:

1. Beginning at 10 A.M. on 20 May 1989, the following districts will be under martial law: East City, West City, Chonwen, Xuanwu, Shijingshan, Haidian, Fengtai and Chaoyang.
2. Under martial law, demonstrations, student strikes, work stoppages and all other activities that hinder public order are banned.
3. People are forbidden from fabricating or spreading rumors, networking, making public speeches, distributing leaflets or inciting social anarchy.
4. Foreigners are forbidden from involvement in any Chinese citizen's activities.
5. Under martial law, security officers and PLA soldiers are authorized to use all necessary means, including force, to deal with prohibited activities.

I wondered exactly what these words meant. It was the first time that martial law had been imposed in China and, like most people, I had no idea how it worked or what might happen. One thing I knew for sure was that the army was going to take over the city. But how many soldiers would there be and what would their duties be? What did they mean by "all necessary means"? What kind of force? Images from the million-people march of two days before filled my mind. What would the government do if it happened again? It would not be possible to arrest ten thousand people, let alone a million.

I pondered these questions all the way home.

Little had changed on the streets to indicate that the city was now under martial law. There were no soldiers or army vehicles, which I had imagined swamping the city. Here and there, I overheard travelers cycling nearby speculating on some of the same questions. It seemed that people were scared, but few knew what might happen.

As soon as I opened the door at my parents', I knew that something was wrong. The normally quiet apartment echoed with loud voices; my parents were shouting. And why was my father at home in the middle of the day?

"You must talk to her. She is at Lao Chen's home waiting for us to call," said my mother urgently. "I told her that she must come home immediately. The sky is falling in!"

"What are we waiting for then? Let's go to the post office right away. She must come home. That's an order," asserted my father.

Back then all long-distance phone calls had to be made at the post office.

"What's happening?" I closed the door behind me. My parents were startled. They hadn't heard me come in.

"It's your sister. We heard from her yesterday, saying that she had been demonstrating in Qing Tao with her classmates, stopping supply trucks." My mother clutched her handbag tightly as if she were strangling it, her voice shaking. "Why is she doing something this dangerous? We sent her to college to learn, not to die!"

At the time my sister, Xiao Jie, was in her third year of college, studying oceanography at university in the picturesque coastal city of Qing Tao, an old German colony on the east coast of China. In addition for its famed brew—Qing Tao beer—the city was also home to a Chinese naval base.

"It is not that bad, Mama," I tried to calm her down.

"No? What she is doing is disrupting transportation and supplies, stopping factories' normal work. Haven't you heard? The army can shoot anyone carrying out such acts!"

"Your mother has asked your uncle Chen to fetch Xiao Jie from school," said Baba. "You are all fools. It's no longer a student demonstration, it's a matter of life and death!"

"What do I have to do with her not coming home?" I protested, but they ignored me.

"Let's go before the post office closes or the army shuts down the city." This time it was my mother wanting to leave. "She is coming back on the first train to Beijing! Whatever happens from here on, I want my children near me."

"OK, let's not cry again," said my father. "Thank heavens nothing has happened yet. I told all of you that it would end badly. The whole thing was just a foolish game. Now do you believe me?"

"Let's go. Let's go," my mother interrupted, one foot already out of the door.

After my parents left, I took out a bottle of Coca-Cola from the refrigerator and went to my room. On my desk lay a letter from America. Immediately I recognized Ning's handwriting.

I picked it up quickly, wondering why the stamp was Chinese. I opened the envelope. The letter was written on three pages of smooth white writing paper. In the middle of the carefully folded pages was a check for $1,000. "Dear Wei," I read, and I could almost hear Ning's gentle voice:

> I was overjoyed to hear about your scholarship to America. Congratulations! The happy thought of your coming must have done me a world of good, for my experiments are producing fantastic results! I know that the beginning—before receiving your first "paycheck"—will be the most difficult and thus enclose a check for $1,000. You can use it to buy your airline ticket or pay rent when you arrive at William and Mary—use it however you want. Please don't worry about paying me back. It comes from my savings and I don't need it.
>
> What about Dong Yi? He told me that he was also applying for graduate schools in America. Has he got in anywhere? I have not heard from him for a while. What is he up to? Has he gone back to Taiyuan?
>
> On second thoughts, I don't suppose Dong Yi would

stay in Taiyuan while there are fireworks in Beijing—how exciting it must be for you. I do envy the two of you. Not only do you have each other—great friends just around the corner, but you are also able to be part of such an extraordinary time in history. I wish I was there. I want to be there. I want to join you and our fellow students at Beijing University and fight for China's tomorrow.

But I cannot, not physically anyway. I have to be here to do my experiments. Some people from my university have gone back to Beijing to take part in the Movement. The rest of us, four hundred or so, are staying here and doing our best to drum up support financially as well as politically for our fellow students at home.

Yesterday we organized another fund-raising event at the student union. Female students made Chinese dumplings and spring rolls. Two students demonstrated Chinese brush painting. They were really good too. Many students donated ornaments and mementos they brought from China—arts and crafts from their region, family jade and silk. Over three thousand students attended the event. By the end of the evening, we'd sold everything and raised almost two thousand dollars!

Like every other Chinese student on campus, I have set up a donation basket at our lab. My fellow students and professors have been very generous with their donations. Before this I did not particularly socialize with the American or European students in my department. Now people come up to me every day to chat about what is happening in China and what they have seen on TV the night before. We get into long discussions about China, politics and democracy.

Have you taken part in the marches? Of course you have. How silly of me! Every night, after I get back from the lab, I switch from channel to channel to watch as much coverage of the Student Movement as possible, searching for familiar faces. So many times I've wanted to see you, but also feared to find you there. For as much as I support the students and the hunger strike, I hope that you are not one of the four thousand fasting in Tiananmen Square. As a friend and someone who cares very much about you, I hope that you are well and safe.

As I am writing to you, the sun is sinking into the red desert. I understand that Beijing is getting very hot too. Though I am here, sitting in the lab, having to wear a sweater because the air conditioning makes it quite cold inside, my thoughts have gone back to Beijing. What has happened in China today? Are my friends safe and well? Will tomorrow be the better day that we are waiting for?

You must come to visit me after you are settled in Virginia. We will go to the Grand Canyon. Believe me when I say that there is nothing more breathtaking.

Please take good care of yourself! Hope to see you very soon.

Forever Yours,
Ning

PS: A friend of mine is going back to Beijing tomorrow. He will bring this letter and mail it to you there.

Ning's letter made me think of happy days—white boats at the Purple Bamboo Garden, high school graduates singing together, the moon over Weiming Lake, hearts filled with hope . . . his letter opened the dam. Suddenly I felt an unbearable longing for love—the kind that would lift my spirits, fulfil my dreams and touch my soul. My thoughts flew to Dong Yi and I wondered where he was. Why he hadn't come to talk to me. I wanted to hear him say anything or nothing at all. I just wanted to hear his voice and be in his presence for a while. I missed him.

I put the check in the drawer and the letter back in its envelope. And I decided that not a second must be wasted. I must go to Dong Yi. I left a note on the dining-room table telling my parents that I had to go back to campus immediately.

"Please don't worry about me—I am only going to see Dong Yi, not to take part in anything. I am not going to Tiananmen Square."

———

First, I went to the Triangle to see whether Dong Yi was there. The Triangle was more crowded than it had been in the afternoon and there was a feeling of the night before battle. Some people were courageous, some fearful, everyone was involved. The student radio station was broadcasting live news and announcements.

"Zhao Ziyang is ousted. Li Peng is now in charge."

"The Beijing Autonomous Student Association has voted to end the hunger strike, which has achieved a great victory for the students."

As if there had been a sudden snowfall, the walls of the Triangle were covered with new wall posters. Some of the authors were extremely concerned, some proclaimed the coming of zero hour, some called for the government to withdraw the martial law troops and some, like the author of the wall poster in front of me, poured out their hearts to their motherland.

> I am hereby revoking my membership of the Chinese Communist Party. I am ashamed and outraged. The Party that bills itself as the servant of the people has just decided to send armed troops against the most innocent, vulnerable and patriotic people of all—the young students. A party that loved the people would not do this. A party that cared for the wellbeing of our motherland would not do this. Anyone who has any decency and humanity would not do this. The Party leaders are tyrants. From now on, I do not want to have anything to do with such a party.
>
> I call on my colleagues and fellow students who are CCP members to follow suit. Please join me to reject the Party that ordered force on its own people!

It was signed: Chen Li, Masters Degree Candidate, the Department of Economics.

I almost screamed. Only two weeks before, I had been talking to Jerry and Hanna about Chen Li, and reminding them of our discussions at the Spoon Garden Bar. But had he gone mad? Did he know what he was giving up? The job he had always wanted in Shenzhen, a promising career in a country where politics and the Party was everything?

He had not only written a fiery wall poster, but had also gone against the norm for the authors of wall posters, and signed his name and affiliation. He did not have to do that. Had he left it anonymous, like most of the others, no one would ever have doubted his courage and sincerity.

Then, in my mind's eye, I saw Chen Li's face, sincere and clear. He was looking at me with his honest eyes, which seemed to say, "I have never shunned responsibility for my words or my actions. I will not do so now."

I could not help but admire his courage. I understood that he was making a point too, to all the people of Beijing University, that the time had come for all of us to stand up and to be counted.

"Who is this Chen Li?" an undergraduate in front of me asked.

A huge crowd had gathered to read Chen Li's meter-high wall poster.

"I don't know. Never heard of him."

"Whoever he is, he is a gutsy guy! Look, he has signed his name, department, everything," said someone nearby.

The student radio station suddenly interrupted these observations.

"The Beijing Autonomous Student Association calls on every student who is currently on campus to go to Tiananmen Square. We cannot let our brave fellow students fall into the hands of the military!"

How times had changed since I last saw Chen Li, on 27 April, when we marched together. Since then our beloved city had seen hunger strikes, million-people demonstrations and now martial law.

"The Association also calls on everyone to block intersections against the army vehicles entering Beijing!"

"I must go and see Chen Li soon," I told myself. I missed my friend and our long and heated discussions about politics and the economy. I also must do my part at such a critical time and stand up and be counted. With martial law in force, the students in Tiananmen Square needed more support than ever.

But I was not going to do any of these things on that day. First, I needed to see Dong Yi.

I walked through the crowd, scanning them carefully, but I did not see him. I walked on, against the flow of people coming toward the Triangle, to Dong Yi's dorm building, clutching the letter from America in my hand.

The noise from the crowd at the Triangle gradually subsided. I had moved away from the battlefield. But the closer I got to the building, the angrier I became. The sense of peace that I had thought would come from going to see Dong Yi had not materialized. I began to ask myself questions. Why hadn't Dong Yi contacted me? Where had he disappeared to? Did he have any idea what I had done in his absence? Was he concerned at all? But, above all else, I was angry with myself for having waited so long to come, for being such a coward.

I made my way inside the building.

Three years before, it had been Ning who had led me to Dong Yi. Since then, I had walked along this hallway so many times, sometimes in love, sometimes with my heart breaking, and at different times full of optimism, shame or despair.

On that day I walked into the familiar building once more.

But had I come too late?

Twelve

Professor

Impossible to cut, but sorting out is even more difficult.

—Li Yi, ninth century

I was standing outside his door, in a red silk dress, not knowing what to do next. All along the hallway doors swung open, and young men in T-shirts poured out, flip-flops slapping on the floor, chopsticks knocking against aluminium bowls, as they chatted with each other. It was dinnertime and, as they passed me, I felt the curiosity in their glances.

My mind had gone blank. Half of me wanted to leave, to return to the peaceful equilibrium that I had finally achieved in the past few days. But the other half, alas my heart, wanted me to stay. I had left a note the day before for Dong Yi, and now I wished I hadn't. Now I wished that Dong Yi was not waiting for me inside. The courage that had exploded from my heart the day before, when I ran up the stairs, clutching Ning's letter, had now retreated to a secret garden where I could not find it.

Why had I come, to disturb his happy life and mine? The past was the past. Ning was in America. That morning, Eimin had told me that we had been granted special permission to marry. And Dong Yi must be happy with Lan, since he had not tried to contact me.

Then I told myself that I was being ridiculous and selfish. If I truly loved Dong Yi, I would want him to be happy, whatever the conse-

quence might be for me. And I knew that Dong Yi would feel and do
the same for me. We would always be the best of friends. We would
always have the past. With this thought in my mind, I knocked softly
on the door.

Dong Yi had been waiting for me, but alone. I quickly looked
around the room for signs of Lan, a suitcase, a silk scarf or a lipstick—
but found none. Perhaps she had left, I thought. When? And why
hadn't Dong Yi come to see me?

We stood in the middle of the room that had changed little since
the day I first saw it three years before.

"You look lovely today. Red always looks good on you." Dong Yi
spoke gently.

I could tell that he was happy to see me, but his tone of voice was
edgy.

"I wanted to see you earlier, because I have to go somewhere very
soon. But I did not want to go to Eimin's." Dong Yi sat down on his
roommate's bed. I understood that he had given me his bed, the clean
and neat one.

"How have you been? You just disappeared that day. What happened?" I pretended that I didn't know what he was talking about.

"Lan was here for a couple of days."

"Really? Everything all right in Taiyuan?"

"Yes."

The more reluctant Dong Yi was to speak, the more I wanted to
push him. I wanted to know what he was hiding from me. I wanted
the answer that I deserved and I wanted to make him feel the pain that
I had suffered.

"You could have told me. I would have liked to meet her."

"You would? Perhaps next time, when she is here for longer," he
said uncomfortably.

"Next time? For longer? Is that why you didn't even bother to
contact me for so many days? You have mapped out your future. How
lovely!"

"No. That's not the reason. I wanted to see you. But with everything happening so fast in and outside of Tiananmen Square, I didn't
have time. I am happy that you are here now."

But I knew that Dong Yi was lying, at least partially. I knew that
he would have been busy in his role as intermediary between the stu-

dents and the intellectuals, just as I knew that he was sincere when he said that he was happy to see me. But I knew Dong Yi too well—he was not telling me the truth, at least not the whole truth.

"Why did Lan come?" I stared right at him, knowing that he would not lie to me if I asked him a direct question.

"It's strange." He looked down at a ballpoint pen in his hands. "I've been thinking, for a few days now, about how to tell you. But I don't know. It's still taking time to sink in, for me. All I can say is that it feels strange, extraordinarily strange as a matter of fact." Then he looked up. When our eyes met, I felt as if my heart had stopped beating.

Slowly Dong Yi uttered the words, "I am going to be a father."

Fury melted. All my thoughts stopped, reasoning collapsed. This time it was my turn to be speechless. But then there was nothing more to say.

"You said in your note that you'd received a letter from Ning?" Dong Yi rescued me.

I searched in my bag, but could not find it. My mind was in turmoil, my eyes were looking, but not seeing, my hands were moving, but not knowing what they were seeking.

"Where could it be?" I started again, flipping furiously through my bag, sweating—finding a couple of lipsticks, a pen, two notebooks, a diary, my wallet, a pair of sunglasses . . .

"Not to worry. I won't have time to read it now anyway," said Dong Yi. "I need to go see professor Fang Lizhi." Professor Fang, the famous political dissident, was the most outspoken critic of the Chinese government.

I stopped my useless searching and looked up. I was met with a pair of eyes, full of kindness. Then I heard his equally gentle voice asking me, "Would you like to come along?"

Five minutes later, we were riding east on Haidian Road. It was a mild evening, perfumed with the sweet scent of white lilacs. People were out, taking their daily after-dinner walk with their families, clutching straw fans. Children played jumping jacks on the pavements.

But there were signs of abnormality. Before the Student Movement, this road would have been packed with stalls selling delicious snacks from across China—Tianjin pancakes, Mongolian roasted lamb, Shanghai wonton soup. But now all the stalls were closed down and piled up on the sidewalks. The intersection of Haidian Road and Zhongguancun Street that ran from north to south toward the city center had been blocked; a student checkpoint was in operation, inspecting passing vehicles. Such checkpoints had appeared around major university campuses in Beijing, aimed at stopping the troops from moving in.

The cool wind must have calmed me down. I congratulated Dong Yi on the news of Lan's pregnancy. It was clear to both of us that there was much that we needed to say to each other. But it was also clear that the timing wasn't right.

"I told professor Li Shuxian that I would be there at seven." Unlike most Chinese, Dong Yi was always conscientious about being on time. Professor Li was Dong Yi's supervisor and the wife of professor Fang Lizhi.

"Don't worry, we will be there on time." I pedaled furiously to keep up with him.

But we did arrive late. By the time we had parked our bicycles in front of the colorless matchbox building and run upstairs, we both had red faces and were sweating.

Professor Fang Lizhi himself opened the door. The professor wore a pair of thin-framed glasses on his round face, and he had a round body: not exactly how I had imagined "public enemy number one" would look. In a forceful and deep voice, so loud that there was an echo on the stairway, he greeted us.

"Sorry I am late." Dong Yi quickly shook hands with Professor Fang, and introduced me.

We followed him into the living room, which was airy and decorated in the same neutral style as the outside of the building. My eyes were drawn to the Chinese arts and ornaments scattered around the room, their rich colors contrasting strongly with the muted background.

Professor Fang led us to the window and pointed to the black car parked in the street below.

"It's the secret police," Dong Yi told me. The Professor had been under police surveillance since the American Embassy party incident. The Professor added that the police had become more blatant since martial law was declared, and that he had been told the day before that he'd better stay at home, and not talk to foreign journalists.

The American Embassy party incident happened in February,

1989, when the U.S. President, George Bush Sr., visited China. A barbecue party was held at the U.S. Embassy to welcome the president, and professor Fang was invited. The invitation infuriated the Chinese government, who prevented the professor from attending.

Professor Fang, who had been expelled from the Party in 1987 for supporting the students, sat down on a chair opposite us. He had been vice chancellor of the University of Science and Technology and so felt cut off from the live connection he'd had with students.

"How is the situation out there on the streets?" he asked us.

"Students and citizens of Beijing have come out in tens of thousands to protest against martial law," Dong Yi replied. "Earlier today I went to Tiananmen Square, where every intersection of the Boulevard of Eternal Peace was blocked."

"What kind of roadblocks?"

"Mostly empty buses, sometimes rickshaws or street stalls."

Professor Fang then asked us whether there was any news of troops coming in.

"Yes, but as far as I could gather, in small units only, and they have all been stopped by Beijing citizens and students." Dong Yi suddenly appeared better informed, to me, than all the other students on campus.

"Have you seen some of them?"

"As matter of fact, yes, just this afternoon. There was a platoon that entered the city center from the north gate. When we got there, they were already surrounded by a few hundred citizens. People were shouting at the soldiers not to use force on the students. One of them said, 'The students are doing it for our country and for you too!'"

"Were the soldiers armed?" Professor Fang was concerned.

"No."

"Then what happened?"

"For a while, the soldiers could not move forward, nor could they pull out. In the end, after the corporal promised that they wouldn't harm the students, the crowd let them withdraw."

Professor Fang leaned forward in his chair and asked Dong Yi how the intellectuals of Beijing had reacted to the news of martial law.

Dong Yi also leaned forward. It was clear from their conspiratorial pose that Dong Yi had some special knowledge about it, which Professor Fang had been waiting to hear.

"The leading intellectuals have called for the ending of martial law and the withdrawal of the troops. Similar sentiments have been voiced by intellectuals in the provinces and in Shanghai." Dong Yi spoke confidently. "The leaders of the Beijing intellectuals also voted to stand by the students to the end."

"What do you think the end will be?" Professor Fang stared intently at Dong Yi, and then glanced over to me.

My heart jolted.

Since martial law had been declared, Beijing had gone through a brief period of fear and panic. But that was quickly replaced by defiance and a sense of invulnerability. The more the students managed to stop martial law troops entering the city, the greater the spirit of the people. At times it seemed that the students would be able to take on the might of the Chinese army.

But the question of what would happen in the end always hung in the air. Only no one wanted—or dared—to ask it. I had pushed the thought of it out of my mind. The word "end" scared me; the possibility of a horrific end scared me even more.

I looked at Dong Yi, whose face showed no trace of fear. More than ever, I wanted to hear him speak, wishing that he would, as always, provide me with a refuge and say something that would allay my fears.

"This is exactly why I've come here today," said Dong Yi. So he had not been denying the thought of the end, like most of us, I thought.

"We wondered whether you could come and give the students your assessment of the current situation and what might happen in the days to come? I believe we need to start thinking about it and plan our strategies accordingly. We need to be brave, but also realistic." Dong Yi made his request calmly, but I guessed how important Professor Fang's answer was to him.

He did not say who the "we" in his group were, and Professor Fang seemed to need no such explanation. I never got a chance to ask Dong Yi about it. But knowing the type of activities he was involved with and the people he had been connected with, I suspected that it had to be people like Liu Gang.

Professor Fang declined the invitation, explaining that he was not concerned for his own safety, but for those who came into contact with him. He added that if he came with us, the government could easily say that the students at Beijing University were brewing an antigovernment and counterrevolutionary campaign with Fang Lizhi. He said contemptuously that he'd already been labeled the "black hand behind the Student Movement."

But Professor Fang did give us his analysis of the situation. Dong Yi wanted to note it down, but was told not to and that it was safer not to have anything written down.

An hour later, we said good-bye to the professors. When we were unlocking our bicycles from the rack, I glanced at the parked car. I wondered whether the secret police knew that we had visited professor Fang Lizhi? Would they stop and question us? Would we be arrested for breaking martial law?

The night had fallen on Beijing, and the pavements were now empty. The streetlights cast long shadows from our bicycles, as we rode down the narrow streets, the squeak of our pedals was the only noise. The closer we got to a streetlamp, the shorter our shadows. At the moment when we came directly under the light, they disappeared altogether. Immediately, another shadow started to stretch out, this time in front of us. Then we were in complete darkness. We rode speedily and did not speak to each other, looking back constantly to see whether we had been followed. My heart beat like a drum during the entire journey, fearful that we would be stopped before we reached the gate of our university. But we were not.

Dong Yi could not stay. He had to go and report back on his visit with Professor Fang. We said good-bye inside the south gate. The leafy path in front of us lay as straight as a knife cutting into the heart of the campus. I searched through my bag once again, and this time I found Ning's letter. I handed it to Dong Yi.

"I must go right away. People are waiting." Dong Yi got back onto his bike. "Has anything been happening in your life?"

"Nothing important," I lied.

He had to go. Tremendous events were happening around us. I had to wait; only I did not want to wait anymore. My heart could no longer withstand the suffering of waiting.

"Wei, we will talk soon." Dong Yi turned around and waved to me, and then he sped off.

As he disappeared into the blue evening, I wondered when "soon" might be, when I would see him again and we could speak about the future. But, if he couldn't bring himself to hurt Lan before, there was little chance that he would leave her now, or was there? The time had come for me to recognize that Dong Yi and I—us—was, by now, all but a dream.

In the distance, the twilight was approaching softly, like a lullaby at the end of a beautiful day. But everything that we had not said, now, had no time in which to be said. Hope was leaving me, and it felt as if this death of hope would be a long and slow death. It felt the way the silk strands look when they are being drawn from the soaked cocoons of silkworms.

Thirteen

Tanks at the Gate

A hundred battles, golden armor, yellow sand, shall not
return until I've taken the tower.

—Wang Shangling, eighth century

*I*t was a perfect day for a wedding. The sky over Tiananmen
Square was as clear as pale blue crystal, cool and flawless.
The sun had risen above the gray roofs of old Beijing
and was now shining without obstruction onto the magnificent
tower of Tiananmen—the Gate of Heavenly Peace. In front of it,
eight white stone bridges arched over the River of Golden Water
like a mother's arms stretching out to embrace her children in the
Square.

Martial law had been in effect in Beijing for a week. The thousands of hunger strikers had stopped fasting but still they refused to
leave Tiananmen Square. Every day, tens of thousands more came to
the Square, bringing food, water and blankets to their fellow students,
to show their support or to take the place of their friends who needed
rest. From a distance, Tiananmen Square looked like a wild garden,
with red flags and white banners.

The bride and groom were both graduate students. The bride, her
hair tied up in a bun, wore a red sleeveless *Qingpao*—the traditional
figure-hugging long Chinese dress, with a high collar and revealing
side slits. She stood shyly holding a small bouquet of red flowers, amid

hundreds of spectators and countless press cameras. Red is the color of luck and happiness in China. Her groom wore a slightly ill-fitting gray suit. Behind them, right in the middle above the central gate of Tiananmen, a dirty sheet was draped over the giant portrait of Mao Zedong. For the first time in the history of the People's Republic, someone had dared to throw ink onto the portrait of Mao.

The groom stepped forward, clearing his throat before speaking into the microphone. "Today we have come to Tiananmen Square to marry at a time when our motherland is going through the most critical struggle of a generation. We want to share our happiness with our fellow students in the Square, who have defied martial law to continue their protest. The hope of China is right here in front of us!"

The crowd responded with thunderous applause. Encouraged, the groom raised his voice and continued, "Today we declare our love and devotion to each other as well as to our motherland. Together we will fight for our country's tomorrow, together we shall see victory and a better China!"

Again the crowd applauded. Then Wuerkaixi, the dynamic and outspoken nineteen-year old student leader from Beijing Normal University, gave the congratulatory. The congratulatory is given at Chinese weddings by either a village elder or a special guest. Wuerkaixi had risen to national and international fame for rebuffing Li Peng during the televised dialogue meeting on 18 May.

He congratulated the couple and linked their happy marriage to the future of China. Their bravery, he declared, demonstrated to the government and the world that the students were not afraid.

By this time, the spirit of the crowd had reached sky-high proportions. People applauded every sentence from Wuerkaixi. Afterwards, a friend of the couple brought over a bottle of Wuliangye, the best Chinese rice wine, and filled up two shot cups. The newlyweds took the cups and drank. Behind them, two white doves were released into the air.

The crowd began to sing revolutionary songs, urging the couple to dance. I stood in the crowd, and I applauded and cheered. I thought of my own marriage to Eimin. Two days before, we had received the red book—our marriage certificate. That was all that marked our union. There was no wedding, no celebration and we told no one except our families about it—mine by phone and his by letter. My parents said nothing.

After I had last seen Dong Yi, on the evening of our visit to Professor Fang, I had thought hard about the sequence of events in my life over the past three years. The more I recalled the indecisiveness that had marked my relationship with Dong Yi, and the misgivings I had felt when I was with Yang Tao, the more I felt confident about my decision to marry Eimin. The lesson I drew from the missed opportunities and unrealized loves was that life went on; I could not mend what had happened in the past or change the choices I had made, but I could still make a new choice and hope the consequences would be better this time around. The couple in front of me would have to live with the choice they made today, just as the tens and thousands of students in the Square behind me would have to live with the consequences of their choices.

The only doubt that had lingered in my mind when I held the red book was that I wondered what Dong Yi's final decision might be, though I doubted that he would have chosen to leave Lan. Dong Yi was not someone who shunned his responsibilities, but I knew that if he had ever considered doing so, he would have come to see me to tell me about it. He might have been busy, as he said, with people to see and things to plan; but, still, I wished that we had had more time to talk. It would have made me feel better about what I had done, though I suspected that it would not have made any difference.

The wedding was the high point of the day, a much-needed lift for the mood in the Square. Since the ending of hunger strike, the Movement seemed to have lost much of its focus. It wasn't clear, now, what the Movement sought to achieve, through what means or to what end. Students from the provinces who felt that they had missed all the excitement of the hunger strike wanted to stay in the Square until the next meeting of the National People's Congress, scheduled for 22 June. Students from Beijing were tired, confused and disappointed, ready for an alternative course of action, wanting to leave the Square. We were told that the Autonomous Student Association had voted to withdraw. But, a few hours later, the decision was reversed. A couple of days later, a different vote emerged again.

Many within the Movement leadership, including prominent intellectuals, had called for an immediate withdrawal from the Square.

They believed that the students had made their point and nothing more would be achieved by continuing the confrontation. Instead they called on the students to return to their classrooms and then pursue the goals of the Movement, democracy and freedom, through peaceful and political means. But others, Chai Ling included, believed a withdrawal at this time, without their demands being met fully, would be political suicide. The concession that the students had won from the government—such as dialogue on improving education to be established at local government level—would be lost. If the students left Tiananmen Square voluntarily, it would also allow the government to declare victory, and then nothing would change in China.

That evening, in her small room on the same floor as Eimin's, Li listened with great interest to my description of the wedding. As I described the reactions of the crowd to her, I began to realize that the wedding had not only provided entertainment for everyone in the Square, it had also helped to remind us why we had come to Tiananmen Square in the first place, something which seemed to have been lost in our busy daily struggles.

"What a wonderful idea to get married in the Square!" sighed Li. "I wish I had been there to see it or I suppose, even better, that I could do the same."

"Are you thinking of getting married?"

"Not yet. But we have talked about it." She smiled, ducking her head down slightly. "I don't know whether it is just the time we are going through, everything is exciting and hopeful. But I just want to give, to make someone happy, to create a better tomorrow. Do you feel the same?"

"I don't know. Maybe not as much as you do, but I did get married." I thought that this was as good a time as any to tell Li.

"My goodness," she almost jumped out of her chair, "to Eimin? When did you do that?"

"A couple of days ago."

"Congratulations!" Li came over and gave me a hug. "How did you celebrate? A banquet?"

"No, we haven't done anything. Of course if we do so one day, you will definitely be invited. Maybe after all of this is over."

"How wonderful!" She sat back in her chair, avoiding the several piles of paper, newspapers and leaflets on the floor.

"I still can't believe what I am hearing. Congratulations, Wei. Marriage is such a big event in one's life. I am very happy for you. I am just surprised to hear about it, not that you two are not a suitable couple. I thought you liked someone in the Physics Department. But now it all makes sense, no wonder I've seen you here so often lately."

"It's over with the person in Physics," I told her.

I wanted to change the subject. Li's questioning was making me uncomfortable. Her casual remarks were feeding the doubts in my mind.

"What are these papers for?" I asked Li, pointing to the piles at her feet.

"Oh, they are for tomorrow. We are going to the western mountains. Over a hundred tanks arrived there yesterday, but they were stopped by students from Beijing Language University. Now those students need help." She passed me the newspaper on the top of a pile. It was a ten-day-old *Beijing Youth Daily,* the official newspaper of the Chinese Communist Party Youth League.

"Many of the soldiers have not been told the truth about the Student Movement. They had been ordered to come to Beijing to 'put down riots fanned by a small group of anarchists.' We managed to collect these newspapers. They were published before the government censored truthful coverage of the Movement. If they don't believe what we tell them, they must believe the official newspapers."

"Would you like some help with those?" I asked.

"Sure. I was going to tie them up in small bundles. I could use an extra pair of hands." Li handed me a bundle of string, of different widths and lengths. "But not those leaflets yet. Xiao Zhang will be bringing more from the printing room."

The next morning I set out with Li and twenty students from Beijing University to stop tanks from moving into Beijing. We carried small bundles of newspapers or leaflets on the back seats of our bicycles. We cycled west, passing the Summer Palace of the Emperors and along the winding alleyways of the last village on the east bank of Beijing Grand Canal. This canal is part of the Grand Canal that links the southern provinces of China with its northern capital, and it was built by the second emperor of the Qin Dynasty some 2,000 years ago, and then extended by other emperors throughout history. In the 1950s, a reservoir was built north of Beijing to serve as the main water supply to the city, and the canal became the natural waterway linking the reservoir and the eight million people living in Beijing.

As soon as we crossed the bridge, the narrow village main street turned into a straight, wide road, running along the west bank of the canal. Slender aspen trees with their white trunks lined the road. Except for groups of traveling students and citizens on bicycles, the road was free of traffic. The road ahead looked as if it were going all the way up into the sky.

After one-and-a-half hours of cycling, the western mountains came into view. These mountains have a special significance in modern Chinese history; in the years after the May Fourth Movement in 1919, many university students and activists took the mountain passages from here to the Yellow Highlands to join the Communist Party. Thus these mountains have always represented the awakening of university students, when they left behind their ivory towers and their comfortable lives to join in the real struggle of the people. In my youth, whenever I came into contact with these mountains, the images that appeared in my mind were always those of young men and women in their twenties, climbing the difficult terrain with each other's help. In that vision, they encourage each other, whenever they are tired or losing hope, and they tell each other that there is a brighter and better tomorrow on the other side—on the other side where the hope of China is. I had often wondered what it must have felt like to be one of those students, abandoning the past completely and starting life anew. How their hearts must have been stirred when they first saw the mountains. How exciting it must have been as they took their first leap into the future!

On that day the same thoughts appeared again in my mind and I felt that I was closer than ever to those students who had gone before me, who had also been on their way to build a better, brighter China.

Eventually we arrived at the foot of the mountain range. Miles and miles of corn and grain fields stretched away toward the foot of the first hill, where a village stood under the protection of the woods. A wide dirt path wound through the green-and-gold patchwork of fields. Lying along this path, like a great dead snake, was the long line of tanks.

In front of the snake's head stood the banner of Beijing Language University. Below the flag and in front of the tractor treads were twenty or so students. They were sitting or lying on old padded military coats. Li went to talk to the student leader from Beijing Language University, while the rest of us spread out, each taking a pile of printed materials.

Most of the tank crews were sitting on top of their tanks, bathing in the brilliant sunshine. They were no older than the students who surrounded them, though their faces were rougher. They seemed not to mind being stuck in the middle of nowhere, and they chatted happily among themselves. But it was impossible for them to ignore the voices of the newly arrived students, addressing them loudly from all sides.

"Why have you come?" one student asked. A soldier had taken off his hat and was now fanning himself with it. The student repeated his question. The soldier replied with a smile, "To protect the people."

"With tanks? The students in Tiananmen Square are unarmed!"

"We *are* the people and we ask you to turn back," another student bellowed.

"The student protest is not anarchic and it is not driven by a small group of counterrevolutionaries," I shouted as loud as I could so that the soldiers atop the tank could hear me. I stood on tiptoe, waving my newspaper. "If you don't believe me, read the *Beijing Youth Daily*."

But no one responded or took the paper.

"You have not been told the truth. The Student Movement is not antirevolutionary but patriotic." I waved the newspaper again, trying to make myself as tall as I could. But I was too short to reach the soldiers who sat idly on the top of the tank.

Placing the pile of papers on the caterpillar tread, I began to climb the tank. The burning sun had warmed the metal for hours, making it uncomfortably hot. Other students came to my aid while they cheered me on, pushing and lifting me up onto the giant machine.

There was actually very little space on the roof of the tank. Every time I took a step, I had to stop and rearrange my feet so that I could keep my balance. Four soldiers sat around the rim of the open roof, the top buttons of their uniform open. One soldier was fanning himself with his hat. It was much hotter on the roof of the tank where the sun burned down brutally and there was no shelter.

I stumbled toward them, trying to hold on to the newspapers and leaflets.

"Look, these are official Party newspapers." I shuffled the newspapers under their noses. "Let me read this one for you," I said, holding up a copy of the *Beijing Youth Daily*. "'Today, 18 May, a million people, including students from all the Beijing higher education institutions, factory workers, scientists, artists, store employees and ordinary citizens went to Tiananmen Square to support the hunger strikers and urge the government to start a dialogue with the students.' A million people! That is not a small group of people. And they are not trying to bring disorder to our country."

The soldiers did not take the newspapers, nor did they read the articles I had pointed out to them. But they had stopped chatting, and now looked uncomfortably away, into the cornfields.

"Here, this article says that the workers at the Beijing Gas and Electricity Company donated 10,000 yuan to support the students. Look, it says even the students at the Central Party School demonstrated."

The Central Party School was the place that trained and prepared outstanding Party members for important roles in government; its students were among the cream of the crop of the Chinese Communist Party.

I stuffed the newspapers into their hands and said, "Take them and read the articles, please. You will see that I am telling you the truth."

They seemed unsure how they should react to my persistent pleas that they read the articles. After a couple of minutes, the soldier who was trying to keep cool by fanning himself with his hat took the newspaper. The others copied him.

"Some cold water?" A local villager came by with two water buckets. He was about forty years old with hair like steel that refused to lie down. "Fresh out of the well." He filled a large wooden spoon with water and lifted it up. "Please drink. You mustn't get heatstroke."

The soldiers seemed more receptive to the offer of water than to my newspaper.

"We don't want you to go to the city and shoot the students. But we don't want to see you suffer either. We are all the little folks. We ought to look after each other. The big officials in Zhongnanhai won't care," said the villager earnestly.

Since the tanks had stopped here, local villagers as well as the students organized food and water deliveries to the soldiers. This made the interaction between the students and the soldiers friendly, despite occasional confrontations. The students had particularly emphasized that they had nothing against the soldiers personally; they said that the two groups shared the same patriotism. And so far, the relationship between the troops and the civilians had been relatively good.

But I wondered how long such a mood could last. Living conditions were deteriorating, particularly inside the tanks. The troops had been racing to get to Beijing for days. Now they were stopped in the middle of nowhere, miles from their destination and comfortable facilities. They could not get out of their tanks to shower or wash. There were no toilets except for the great outdoors. And, by the look of it, they might have to stay where they were for some time. Even for the most patient men, frustration must set in at some point.

What would happen then? Would they withdraw as the students demanded? Or would they force their way through?

Just as I was thinking about this, the tank leader emerged from the hole below, frustration written all over his face.

"Where's your order and discipline?" he said to the soldiers. "Look at you. Button up. And you, put your hat back on. You look as if you've already been defeated." He took away the newspapers from his crew, and was clearly angry that his soldiers had accepted them.

"Get down! Get down!" He leaned forward and waved his hand, gesturing at me to go. I was startled; I took a step back and lost my balance.

"Do not use force!" the crowd called out, thinking that he had pushed me.

The tank leader's face turned red and he fumed at his crew, "Go inside immediately."

After the soldiers had gone inside, perhaps for a dressing-down, followed by their leader, who closed the tank lid loudly behind him, I climbed down with the help of other students. The crowd applauded. I felt elated.

I looked around for Li and the rest of the group, but could not see them. More students and Beijing citizens had come to do their part, surrounding the tanks in large numbers. Many students had also climbed on top of the tanks, talking face-to-face with the soldiers.

"Here you are." Li suddenly appeared next to me. "All the material has been distributed. Everyone is waiting at the front."

We struggled through the crowd.

"The students from Beijing Language University have said that they need more help at night when the crowd leaves," Li told me. "Clearly, if the troops want to push through with force, it won't be during the day, in front of all these people, but at night."

"Don't they have enough people for the nights?" I asked.

"Apparently not. The university is not very big. Many of their students are in Tiananmen Square. Those who have been here since the first day are now tired. They think they can manage, but would appreciate some help from other universities."

"Can we help?"

"We are spread thin—not in actual numbers, after all there are twenty thousand of us at Beijing University. But the difficulty is in logistics and organization. That is why I want to get back as soon as possible. I need to find out whether we can organize some sort of reinforcements for them." Li was a natural-born organizer.

It would be two hours' hard cycling before we got back to the university. I thought about those young men and women lying in front of the tanks. The night would soon fall, and they would be alone against the might of the tanks and the army.

Fourteen

Tiananmen

You can hear the sound of weapons, of the army moving
in the middle of the night.

—*Bai Juyi, eighth century*

*M*y sister, Xiao Jie, came home as my parents had asked her to. I had not seen her since she left for school after the Chinese New Year in early February. On that day she was wearing a sleeveless pink cotton dress, and she looked tanned and healthy. Her long locks were now cut short to just below the shoulder.

"I was fine," she said. "Why did everyone think that I was in danger?" She became quickly irritated as soon as I asked about her days in Qing Tao. I suspected that my parents had already asked her the same questions, possibly more than once.

"Our parents just want you to be near in case things get worse. They were simply worried." I played the big sister.

"But why is Qing Tao more dangerous than Beijing? Which city is under martial law?"

"You know that it's not just where you are, but also what you do."

"Could you two go and buy some steamed buns for dinner, please?" Our mother had come in from the kitchen.

So we went out, on that warm summer evening, as we had done all our lives, to the university canteen to get steamed buns for dinner. "I don't think I did anything you didn't do, marching and demonstrating. I know that you've been to Tiananmen Square."

"Mama said that you had gone to stop military trucks. What was that about?"

"That was a few days after the hunger strike started. Some of the cadets from the Chinese Naval College who had marched with us said that there was talk of a military crackdown. So we went to stop trucks entering or leaving the naval base."

"How?"

"We stood arm in arm in front of the trucks."

The canteen was full of hungry students, the smell of cooking fat and the sound of hundreds of people talking inside a small and confined space. We swapped experiences of confronting the army.

"I should never have told Mama about it. She freaked out," my sister went on, "but she did not know that I had also gone to stop trains. Imagine how she would have reacted!"

"You did what?"

"One day we were told that troops were on a train bound for Beijing. So we rushed to the station and sat on the track."

"And then?"

"The mayor came and personally assured us that there were no troops on that train. So we left after three hours."

The line in front of us shrank rapidly, as if there were a line-eating monster inside the serving window. Soon it was our turn. I asked for two plain ones and four with meat and vegetable.

"Are you terribly upset that our parents forced you to come home?" I asked my sister.

"I was, at first. But then I found out that many of my friends had come to Beijing. They are in Tiananmen Square. I have been going there to visit them. But please don't tell Mama and Baba."

Over dinner, I told my parents and Xiao Jie what I had seen in the western mountains. I told them that students were sleeping in front of tanks to stop them from moving, and that local peasants brought water and food for the soldiers and begged them not to open fire on students. I also told them that I had climbed up onto one of the tanks and passed around newspapers.

"I was on top of a real tank. I even touched the gun," I said enthusiastically.

Mama listened with great interest and agreed with me on a number of points, but my father was not amused. In fact, he was rather angry with me and thought that I was being too naïve.

"What do you think this is? You young people. Fun and games? You could all get hurt!"

"Don't worry. The entire country, including the soldiers, is with the students. Just today in Xi Dan, a platoon withdrew after being confronted by students. They don't want to harm the students."

"You are stupid to think like this." Baba's face reddened as it usually did when he was getting into a rage.

"More rice, anyone?" Mama intervened promptly.

It was a particularly warm and sticky day, that day, 2 June 1989, and when I cycled back to Beijing University after lunch, the voice of my father had disappeared completely. It was true that the situation had become more dangerous. In addition to the tanks arriving on the outskirts of Beijing, there had been news of large military maneuvers and more sightings of soldiers inside the city. Many people feared that a crackdown was imminent. But it still seemed that the determination of the students and citizens of Beijing was strong enough to stop the threat. And every story of students triumphing over seemingly sympathetic soldiers raised our spirits higher.

The campus was buzzing with confidence. As soon as I rode past the tranquil stream winding through the Chinese garden near the west gate, I immediately ran into students carrying brushes and paints. At one point, I had to stop and give way to a large banner that read "Freedom China." A long-haired young man, wearing a white headband, and holding a folded flag in one hand, cycled pass me speedily, the two ends of his headband, tied at the back of his head, flying up like the wings of a white butterfly. More students, some holding hands in silence, some talking loudly, were going toward the Triangle.

As I walked around the Triangle, I noticed several new wall posters, questioning the general strategy of the Movement and of the student leaders. These so-called "thought pieces" had appeared more frequently in recent days. One of the wall posters questioned the confrontational style of the student leaders and argued that it might escalate the tension and lead to tragic consequences. A few days before, fearing imminent bloodshed, the Alliance to Protect the Constitution, a liaison group between workers, students and citizens, had called for the students to give up the Square, but the Tiananmen Square Student Command Center, led by Chai Ling, rejected that call. Another wall poster raised the issue of political factions within the top ranks of the government, saying that some of them might be using the Student Movement to weed out reformers. "Be aware, my dear fellow students, of the cunning foxes. Do not let us be used by them. We need not only to be courageous, but also politically wise. So far it looks as if the hard-liners have won."

Back in my new home—Eimin's small room in the Young Faculty Building—he was waiting for me to go to the south gate. We were scheduled for night duty in the Square. Eimin urged me to take a sweater for the night, but I refused. "It's OK. I have been there before. It doesn't get too cold for the first half of the night. And we'll be back before midnight, won't we?"

We walked downstairs and toward the south gate. I told my new husband about the provocative pieces I had seen at the Triangle. "Do you think the students should leave the Square?" I asked.

"Personally I think it was wrong for the Student Command Center to reject the idea—I heard that it had actually got a majority vote in the ASS. The further the conflict escalates, the bigger the stake. One side needs to back down. But I am afraid it's not going to be the government."

"Why not?"

"Because the troops and tanks are already here. Mao Zedong has always said, quite rightly, 'Whoever has the guns has the power,'" said Eimin.

"But we have stopped the tanks. They can't come in. What the government's doing is just *Zhi Louhu*—Paper Tiger, scary only in appearance."

"Why do you suppose that no student movement acting on its own has ever succeeded in Chinese history, including the May Fourth Movement? College students are too elite a group in China. Only one person in every thousand." It was rather strange, the way he talked, as if he were not on the side of the students. I supposed that he was aware of his age, as well as his position as a faculty member.

"But this time it's different. This is not just a student movement anymore, factory workers have marched to Tiananmen Square, and so have journalists, Party members and office workers. This time it's all inclusive."

"But the army isn't on the students' side, is it?" Eimin interrupted me.

"No. Not yet. But it might happen, you never know. Maybe one of the generals will rebel, just like in 1910, when soldiers took part in the uprising that overthrew the Emperor."

"You really think so?" Eimin pushed.

"Well … even if we don't get the army's support, what can happen? All the foreign journalists are here, plenty of TV cameras. The world is watching." I remembered Jerry's words.

Eimin stopped walking. We had reached the south gate. "I suppose this is the one unknown. But would the government care as much about saving face as letting their power be threatened?"

A black truck had just pulled in. It was clear that those on board had returned from a rather long duty in the Square—they looked exhausted and dirty. We cheered for them, but few responded. Some of them seemed to be having trouble keeping their eyes open. I saw Wu Hong, an old classmate, and waved at him. His trademark long wavy hair was tucked under a white hairband, which was now crooked and the characters, which had been written in red paint, were creased. He smiled back.

We climbed up onto the truck as soon as it had finished unloading the previous group. When the truck turned the corner at Zhongguan-cun, the Village of the Middle Gateway, our leader unfurled the flag and sent it flying.

People on the street waved at us and shouted:

"Support the student demonstrators!"

"We want freedom!"

"Long live the students!"

We replied:

"Thanks for your support!"

"We will fight till victory!"

"Long live freedom and democracy!"

We hung on to the side panels of the truck, waving and shouting enthusiastically, with the wind in our hair and sun on our shoulders. I waved to people on buses and bicycles, grocery-carrying grandmothers and children with red scarves around their necks. I waved to pedestrians walking behind street fences and those who lived in high-rise apartment buildings. On this day, as I rode by in the open truck, I was in high spirits, as was everyone in Beijing. I could not wait to be there, in Tiananmen Square. I felt that I was making my contribution, however small, to a better future for China, that I might even be helping to make history.

We arrived at Tiananmen Square in the open truck around dinnertime. As on previous days, tens of thousands of students filled the massive forty-nine-hectare Square. Some, having traveled as much as 500 miles by train, were demonstrating in the traditional Chinese way—sitting in silence. Sitting in silence in defiance of martial law and the government.

Tents donated by supporters in Hong Kong and other southeast Asian countries had arrived. The demonstrators, grouped by university, sat near their tents, below their flags and banners. At the southern end of the Square, near the Zheyang Gate, the Gate of the Sincere Sun, a large half-stretched-out banner read "Democracy, Freedom, Human Rights."

At the center of the Square stood the Monument to the People's Heroes. Lit up by warm sunshine, the obelisk looked like a giant sword piercing the blue sky. At the foot of the Monument the Tiananmen Square Student Command Center—an organization set up on 21 May, one day after martial law was declared in Beijing—had established its base. Loudspeakers continuously broadcast news and speeches from the student leaders.

"Fellow students, I am Chai Ling, the commander in chief of the Square . . ."

Between the Monument and the Gate of Heavenly Peace to the north rose the ten-meter-high white statue of a young Chinese woman holding the torch of freedom—the Goddess of Democracy, modeled after the famous Statue of Liberty in New York City harbor. The statue was made of Styrofoam by a group of art students and had been erected on the Square two days before.

From the outskirts of the Square, the noisy world poured in. Trucks, buses, small vans, cars, scooters and *Sanlun Che*—three-wheeled wooden carts, delivering everything from water, food, blankets and medical supplies to fresh student reinforcements like us. Student monitors wearing red armbands waved traffic to go this way or that. "Move, move," they shouted, "you, not you! Over there!"

The front entrance to the Museum of Chinese History, to the east of the Square, had been turned into a parking lot. In the open space surrounded by thick trees, fresh groups of students were bussed or trucked in to replace those who had been at the Square since early morning. In order to support the thousands of demonstrators in the Square, thousands more were needed every day to help and protect them: medical school students continuously checked on the condition of the demonstrators, supplies were organized and brought in. Several lines of people, forming human chains, circled the enormous Square to defend it, and to make sure that there was order, and also safety, for those who were inside—apparently there had been attempts by the secret police to infiltrate the Square. The number of defense lines had been added to and security had been tightened as the student occupation of the Square went on, and these lines needed constant reinforcement.

Defense was my job on that day. Our leader, a swimming champion from the university, proudly waved the university flag. This flag symbolized the soul and spirit of democracy in this and other moments in China's modern history, such as the May Fourth Movement.

A bus full of students pulled into the parking lot right behind us, and the flag of Beijing University for Trade and Commerce led the way for the students from that bus. A dark-skinned twenty-year-old woman shouted into a megaphone, "Four people a row. Four people a row."

Some of the students brought aluminium water bottles, others straw sunhats. Some brought jackets or sweaters for the night. Once all the students were lined up, their group leader spoke: "Students, many of our fellow students have been in the Square for more than fifteen hours. They are very tired. You will need to take over and look after the demonstrators tonight. The university bus will pick you up once the next group is assembled and ready to replace you. Fight till the end! Never give up!"

With their university flag held high, bright-eyed young men and women, some holding hands, marched toward the south side of the Square. Looking at their faces, you might think that they were a group of students who were on their way to a public exam for which they had been chosen and at which they knew that they would excel.

"Fellow students from Beijing University!" our leader shouted at the top of his lungs. "Follow me to our position! Stay together . . ." Noise from newly arrived trucks and buses that were leaving immediately drowned out the last part of his sentence. As we crossed the belt-way to the Square, student traffic controllers waved the traffic to stop. They clapped their hands and shouted, "Welcome the students from Beijing University!" Drivers waiting on either side of the road joined in with their horns. Our leader waved the flag proudly and shouted back "*Da Jia Xin Ku*—Everyone has been working hard!" Our spirits were lifted, and we followed our leader proudly into Tiananmen Square.

We moved north into the Square and paced ourselves within an arm's length of each other. The sun was now going down. As it did, the western sky turned dark red, and the sweet smell of a summer's evening started slowly to penetrate through the heat. To my left stood my husband, the thirty-five-year-old professor; to my right, a young man of about nineteen, thin and pale, with permed hair. Beyond him, another young man of about the same age, darker, with the typical deep eyes of someone from southern China. Next to him was his girl-friend. I looked down the line and saw more people I did not know, nor did they know me. But for this night, and for this brief time in our lives, we were comrades-in-arms.

The evening of 2 June came as I wish to remember it; sitting on a warm stone tile in the center of the Square that symbolizes China's heart, watching the sunset ignite the sky with its glorious colors, washing down a sausage sandwich with a sparkling drink called *Chi Sui*, or Gas Water. I was among tens of thousands of strangers, and yet I had never felt so connected with people in my whole life.

Darkness soon fell. Behind us, two hundred yards away, scattered sparsely among the trees that lined the beltway, streetlamps came on, giving us a little light but mostly abundant dark and sinister shadows. In front of us the sea of flags, banners, tents and people had disap-peared in the darkness. A few floodlights at the base of the Monument to the People's Heroes provided the only light in the Square. Loud-speakers continued to broadcast.

"Fellow students. Fellow students. I am Chai Ling, the commander in chief of the Square." The high-pitched voice of my former room-mate came through the speakers again. She announced to the crowd that they had just received news that the tanks stationed outside the western suburbs had turned around and withdrawn.

We cheered the news. We did not know at that time, however, that about a thousand miles away another unit of the People's Liberation Army, the 27th Group Army commanded by the brother of Marshal Yang Shangkun, the President of China, had been mobilized. In the darkness, heavily armed soldiers in combat gear, armored personnel carriers, tanks and trucks in camouflage were moving rapidly toward Beijing. It turned out that the soldiers, such as those I had encountered at the western mountains, belonged to a PLA unit stationed not far from Beijing. Some of them were from cities or towns, while the majority of PLA soldiers were peasants. Their close proximity to the city and the interactions they had so far had with the students had apparently made them an ineffective choice for a crackdown, so they were being replaced.

The news of tanks moving out became our main point of conversation for some time. "It just goes to show that, as long as we bind together, students can defeat the army," said my neighbor.

"The tanks are leaving, fine, but what about the soldiers who are already in the city? Where are they now?"

We looked at each other and fell silent. The night was turning cooler. I ran my hands up and down my bare arms and wished that I had listened to Eimin and brought something thicker than just the cotton dress I was wearing. I looked into the darkness. I could see nothing. It seemed that the city had gone to bed for the night. The loudspeakers had ceased broadcasting.

"There are a lot of places in the city that can hide a few thousand soldiers," the thin student with permed hair said. "For example, the Forbidden City." The Forbidden City is where the Emperors used to reside and is now a park roughly half the size of London's Hyde Park.

"You can put a lot more than a few thousand in the Forbidden City," echoed Eimin.

"But it wouldn't be possible. The Forbidden City is open to the public, and no one has seen anything."

"But there are parts of it that aren't open to the public," Eimin countered.

Similar conversations were going on, softly, among our neighbors on the defense line, whispers along the grapevine.

"I heard that there is a system of secret underground tunnels beneath the Great Hall of the People over there." The Southern student pointed toward the darkness in the west. "They were built especially for Party leaders to escape through, if they were surrounded. Soldiers could have moved in there without anyone knowing."

As he talked, I started to imagine the giant doors between the imposing columns of the building swinging open, and thousands of soldiers waving rifles and shining batons charging into the Square.

They could just as well come from the Museum of Chinese History, I thought. I looked behind me, but all was darkness and shadows. I began to wonder what each sound was. I tried harder to listen, but I could hear nothing more than the words and whispers of my fellow students.

I stood up, moved my feet around, tried to conceal my fear—I did not want anyone to know that I was afraid.

Then I heard Eimin's tense voice: "I just talked to our leader. He said our replacements are not here yet and he does not know when they will come. It's already past midnight . . . this is not good. If they attack, the early morning hours are always the best time. Look at the moon. Moonlight is perfect for an attack—they can see us clearly."

I knew then that he was afraid too.

And, as it turned out, our fears were justified. Unknown to us at the time, Li Peng had called a special meeting of the Standing Committee of the Politburo in the morning of 2 June 1989: Party elders, including Deng Xiaoping and his close comrade Yang Shangkun, also attended. At the meeting, Yang Shangkun reported to the Committee that troops had indeed moved into the Great Hall of the People, as well as Zhongshan Park, the Working People's Cultural Palaces and the Public Security Ministry compound. All the officers and soldiers had been thoroughly prepared to clear Tiananmen Square.

Li Peng told the meeting that the Square had become the center of the Student Movement. Following the declaration of martial law, events such as "putting together a dare-to-die corps to block the martial-law troops, gathering thugs to storm the Beijing Public Security Bureau, holding press conferences, and recruiting the Flying Tiger Group to pass messages around," were all plotted in and commanded from the Square. Or so he said.

In addition, the Square housed the headquarters of a number of illegal organizations such as the Autonomous Student Association, the Autonomous Federation of Workers and the Tiananmen Square Student Command Center. Much of the world's media was also focused on the Square, and material aid was being sent there. Therefore, Li Peng stated that in order to restore stability in Beijing and China, the Square had to be cleared.

So as the meeting drew to a close, the Standing Committee voted to forcefully clear the Square. With that decision, Deng Xiaoping gave the order to Yang Shangkun for the Central Military Commission to execute the plan.

While at the time we knew little of the extent of the danger to come, the prospect of being trapped in the Square still sent chills down the defense line. When the silence became too much to bear, we talked about where we were from and what we planned to do in the future. These normally significant conversations for people of our age seemed so lightweight that night that I suspect no one who was there has remembered what they said. But we talked because the silence, and our imaginations, scared us. Many of us, I am sure, thought about death.

For years afterward, I remembered that night with strange sensations. It seemed surreal to have thought of death at the age of twenty-two. But as time went by, my memory faded and so did the fear I had felt in my heart. But I still find myself remembering the night itself, sometimes at the oddest moments, such as when I'm driving through the streets of Paris or walking down Fifth Avenue in New York City, or sitting on the Spanish Steps in Rome. Just as I am saying to myself, "What a beautiful night," I remember that particular night. I suppose fear of death and love of life are like Siamese twins, inseparable. And I still find myself wondering what kind of life the others now lead, and whether their memories of those nights in Tiananmen Square also have a habit of creeping on them, as mine do.

That night, after what seemed like an eternity, my legs started to become numb. Then, sharp as a gunshot, came the rumble of trucks; our replacements had arrived. It was about 2:30 A.M. Immediately everyone jumped up, abandoning their positions and running madly toward the parking lot.

Eimin and I followed the crowd and found the two trucks that had come for us. The groups became completely mixed up; people close to the trucks pushed their way to get on and those still some distance away stepped over each other to get nearer. By the time we got there the first truck was already full. Everyone rushed toward the second one. A tall and strong student stood at the back, controlling the crowd as much as he could. Just as we were about ten people away from the truck, he started pushing people back. "The truck is full! No more."

People were angry. "What about us? Is there another one coming?"

"No. We only have these two trucks tonight. You will have to wait here until we come back for you."

"What? It's two hours from here to Beijing U. It will be daylight when you come back."

"Couldn't you make an exception?" asked Eimin.

The security guy looked at him for a second, "Xu Eimin, Psychology?"

"Yes."

"I took a class with you last year. Come on."

He winked at Eimin and then helped us both onto the truck. The truck drove around the beltway and made a left turn onto the Boulevard of Eternal Peace. As we drove farther and farther away from Tiananmen Square, I could feel my heartbeat slowing down. The longest night of my life was over.

Less than twenty-four hours later, tanks rolled down the same Boulevard and soldiers opened fire.

Blood flowed from heaven.

Fifteen

Blood Flowing from Heaven

Blood tinted the wild grass red;
wolves were in high positions.

—*Li Bai, eighth century*

We slept till half-past three in the afternoon, and by the time we woke up the room was too hot and the sun too bright. We realized that we had not eaten anything since the sausage and steamed buns at Tiananmen Square the evening before, so I shared some cold milk and half a brick of chocolate with Eimin and felt better.

We walked out of the south gate and turned right along Haidian Road. The air was boiling. A few women came down the street, burying their faces under umbrellas. The small noodle and wonton soup shop was open, but had few customers. It used to be a computer shop but it had outgrown the space. A few months before, the computers were moved to Zhongguancun—the Village of the Middle Gateway, the new high-tech district set up by the government.

The daughter of the owner brought us large bowls of wonton soup and then went around mopping the tables. Behind the counter, her parents were talking in their rustic accents, which sounded as if they were singing from the back of their throats. Eimin and I quickly downed the hot soup, saying nothing to each other. Despite hours of sleep, I felt exhausted. I thought of the people who served as student monitors at the Square night after night and wondered what they were made of, that they could stay up all night again and again.

After the soup, we bought ice cream, went back to campus and walked leisurely along its leafy paths. Many students were also coming out for an after-dinner stroll, sharing the shade with us. It was just past six o'clock. Suddenly the university public address system came on, blaring out an official announcement. Eimin and I quickly approached one of the loudspeakers to catch more clearly what the announcer was saying.

> Today, 3 June 1989, the Beijing Municipal Government and the Martial Law Command Center jointly issued the following urgent announcement: . . . [with immediate effect] . . . Beijing citizens must be on high alert. Please stay off the streets and away from Tiananmen Square. All workers should remain at their posts. To ensure their own safety, all citizens should stay at home.

"Something bad is about to happen," said Eimin.

A few minutes later, the announcement was repeated, and then it was broadcast again. Eimin and I hurried home and turned on the television. The same announcement was being broadcast there on all the stations.

"In the early hours of this morning, a small group of counter-revolutionary elements overturned army vehicles, punctured tires and attacked PLA soldiers. Their aim was to stir up counterrevolutionary riots. The Beijing Municipal Government and Martial Law Command Center thus issued the following emergency announcement: . . . [with immediate effect], Beijing citizens must be on high alert . . ."

On the TV screen, we saw an army car on fire. Some buses were also burned and lying on their sides, blocking major intersections along the Boulevard of Eternal Peace. Groups of students could be seen running, and it looked as if it was around dawn.

Eimin and I rushed downstairs to the Triangle. Hundreds of people had gathered there, and more were on their way.

"Large contingents of troops have entered the city and are moving toward the Square. Some of them are armed with rifles and accompanied by tanks and armored vehicles. Some are traveling in plain clothes, on foot or in civilian vehicles, carrying knives and metal clubs," said the announcer on the student radio station.

"Fellow students, we need to defend Tiananmen Square," said a male student, who seemed to be in charge. "We ask every available student to go to Tiananmen Square. The more people we can gather, the safer the Square will be."

At that point, he was interrupted by another young man who added, "Bring wet towels to protect yourselves from tear gas. If you have anything that can be used as a weapon, clubs or batons, bring them too."

"Representatives from each department, please go and find as many people as you can," said the man who'd spoken first. "Start off toward Tiananmen Square as quickly as you can, on your bicycles or on foot. Don't wait for the trucks from the university. We need to get people out there as soon as we can."

Within half an hour, the crowd at the Triangle had grown to thousands strong. I could see flags from some twenty departments. The radio station continued to broadcast news of confrontations between students and troops; and it seemed that Beijing citizens had come out in force to protect the students.

"It's getting too crowded here. Let's move to the other side," Wang Jing, a motherly graduate student, shouted to the undergraduate who was holding the flag from the Psychology Department.

We followed them through the gap between two buildings to the courtyard in front of the Young Faculty Building. Near the flag, I saw my old classmate Wu Hong, tying on his worn-out headband. It was no longer white and the red writing had faded.

"The first group is ready to go," said Wu Hong. Behind him was a group of seven or eight men.

"What about wet towels or weapons? Shouldn't they wait?" asked Li.

"No, we can't. We need to get to Tiananmen Square as quickly as we can." Wu Hong spoke urgently.

"Wu Hong is in charge of this group. Try to get to Tiananmen Square. But if you are needed somewhere else on the way, it'll be up to you what you do," said Wang Jing.

I was still tired from last night, but I wanted to go.

"I won't let you." Eimin pulled me to the side. "Don't be stupid. This is it—the crackdown will be tonight."

"Tear gas and rubber bullets, big deal."

"There may be death tonight." I had never seen Eimin so intense. Without another word, he pulled me away and up the stairs.

As the evening went on, more and more groups headed off toward the center of the city. I stayed on campus, as Eimin had insisted. Later that evening, I lay awake, staring into the dark, wondering what would happen. The images I had seen the night before, of soldiers charging toward student protestors in the Square, resurfaced in my mind. The night before, I had thought I was going to die, and those thoughts returned, but this time I was frightened for friends and classmates who had gone to Tiananmen Square. Perhaps I would have gone with them if Eimin hadn't stopped me, I thought. But I was also afraid of dying.

I didn't want anyone to die. I hoped that Eimin would be proved wrong and that the students would win. But I was torn because I was not with my classmates and, at the same time, I was afraid to be with them. Eventually, I decided that I would join them the next day in the Square and, with that thought, gradually, I relaxed and fell asleep.

We were woken up in the dark hours by a commotion in the hallway. Eimin got up to have a look.

"What time is it?" I was half asleep.

"Three in the morning. You go back to sleep."

He opened the door, the light from the hall shone on my face. I shut my eyes and turned to face the wall.

"What's going on?" I heard someone ask. The noises quietened.

"Xiao Chen has not come back yet. Mrs. Chen is worried."

"What am I going to do?" Mrs. Chen was crying.

"Where is Xiao Chen?"

"He went to the Square."

"Oh dear, that's no good. I heard the soldiers had opened fire," said an older man.

Mrs. Chen cried louder.

I jumped up, tossed a robe over me and stepped outside. I saw Mrs. Chen, the wife of a law lecturer, standing next to another neighbor, Lao Liu, in his T-shirt and oversized boxer shorts. His wife was beside him.

"Lao Liu, where did you hear this?" I asked.

"Downstairs. Everyone was talking about it."

"Any deaths?"

"A lot. People say that the Boulevard has become a river of blood."

Another door down the corridor opened. Another neighbor came out, and walked toward us.

"Mrs. Chen, please calm down. Maybe Xiao Chen is on his way home," said Mrs. Liu. But Mrs. Chen did not look at her, or stop sobbing.

Eimin told Mrs. Chen to be positive.

"Yes, Mrs. Chen, please don't let your imagination scare you. We'll go down and check the latest news," I told her. "We will come back and let you know what's happening."

Eimin and I went out into the courtyard. Under the moonlight were a few ghost-like groups of people. We walked toward them.

"What about the students in the Square?" I heard someone asking.

"They have been surrounded by troops and tanks," a tall man said with gloomy certainty.

"They are done for, dead for sure," a balding middle-aged man in his underwear sighed. "Done for, I tell you."

"Sin!" cried a thirty-something woman whose arms circled her half-asleep young daughter standing in front of her, like a mother hen.

"How many are in Tiananmen Square tonight?" I asked.

"Tens of thousands," answered the tall man.

Suddenly funeral music came from the Triangle. The student radio station came on, and we knew right away that what we had heard was true. There had been death and bloodshed. A black hole opened in my world and my heart sank.

The crowd moved swiftly to the Triangle.

"The truth about the Beijing Massacre," said the news announcer, her voice shaking,

[is that at] around 10:00 P.M. last night, tens of thousands [of] troops armed with automatic machine guns and rifles, supported by thousands of tanks and armored cars began pushing

east on the Boulevard of Eternal Peace toward Tiananmen
Square. When the brave students and citizens stopped their
advance, the soldiers opened fire into the crowd, shooting
wildly. The Beijing Red Cross estimated 2,400 were dead. Fellow students, blood flowed like a river on the Boulevard of
Eternal Peace.

The crowd stood in silence, many of the men still in their undershirts
and boxers. Some fixed their eyes on the small but bright window that
was the student radio broadcasting room, others looked down. The
crowd was silent, dead silent.

The funeral music came on again, and suddenly I cried. After a
while, I calmed down. More news came in.

"This fellow student has just returned from the city center. Let
him tell you what happened."

"Fellow students, I am a third-year student from the Chinese Literature Department. I was at the Muxudi Bridge when [the] troops
came in. First they used tanks to push aside buses that we'd used as
roadblocks. Then the infantry pressed ahead. Hundreds of local citizens and students tried to stop them, throwing bricks and Coke cans.
The soldiers responded with their rifles, firing into the crowd. Sparks
flew where the bullets hit the road. People dropped like flies, blood
was everywhere. Once the shooting stopped, the citizens and students
would charge again, only for the troops to fire again. Bodies of the
dead and wounded littered . . . the boulevard."

Then, another eyewitness came to the microphone. This student
had been at an intersection near Tiananmen Square. "The troops were
in such a hurry to get to Tiananmen Square that they shot anyone who
was in their way. When people came back charging with bricks and
stones, they drove the tanks at the crowd, running [people] down . . .
Everywhere people were panicking and screaming."

I stood in the crowd, under the streetlamp. People around me had
dark shadows on their faces. I wondered what time it was. My body
shivered in the cold.

"Let's go and get you changed." Eimin put his arm around my
shoulder. I realized that I was still in my robe.

We walked to the Young Faculty Building. The courtyard was now
empty. Most windows in the three surrounding buildings were lit. I

wondered about those dark ones. Where were the occupants? Would they come home alive?

We went upstairs and heard Mrs. Chen screaming, "Where have you been?"

Then we saw her grabbing her husband's jacket and shaking him with the weight of her whole body.

"It's OK. It's OK now. I am back." Her husband held her in his arms, trying to stop her from acting so violently.

"I have been worried to death," she cried, letting her head drop onto his shoulder. She looked exhausted.

"See, I told you he'd be all right," said Mrs. Liu, smiling.

"What happened? Were you in Tiananmen Square?" Lao Liu asked impatiently.

Lecturer Chen told us that he wasn't in the Square but on the Boulevard of Eternal Peace, setting up the roadblock. Then the tanks came. It was dark, but you could still see the soldiers sitting on top of the tanks, pointing their rifles in all directions, as if the enemy were all around them.

"How many of you?"

"About fifty." He said they all had wet towels over their mouths, expecting tear gas, but instead the soldiers fired at them. At first everyone thought they were rubber bullets, then they saw sparks where the bullets hit the road, and knew right away that they were real.

"Did you see anyone get killed?" I asked him.

Lecturer Chen was visibly shaken, and in a choking voice told us that two were wounded: one hit on his left leg, the other, a girl, had a shrapnel wound on her shoulder.

"Then? What happened then?" asked Lao Liu.

"Several students took the wounded on bicycles to Fuxing Hospital. We pushed the buses back onto the road and torched them." Lecturer Chen then turned to look at his wife. "I thought of you and knew that you'd be worried, so I left."

"Let them go home," Mrs. Liu said to her husband. "Let Xiao Chen rest. Mrs. Chen must rest too."

"Yes. You go. You go." Lao Liu smiled.

Mrs. Chen opened the door, and her husband followed.

"Xiao Chen," Lao Liu called out. Lecturer Chen turned around.

"You are a brave young man." Lao Liu spoke like a father.

Lecturer Chen nodded with appreciation and then went in after his wife.

At around five o'clock, the first eyewitness report came in from Tiananmen Square.

"At about midnight, troops took up their positions to the east at the Chinese History Museum and to the west, by the Great Hall of the People. Rows of tanks and army trucks lined up at the north end of the Square, near the Golden River Bridges."

Many local citizens had heard about the massacre and come to stand side by side with the students, so that there was a crowd of thousands listening to the stories from the students.

"At the northwest corner, an armored car stalled and a group of students turned it over and tossed Molotov cocktails inside after the soldiers had all got out. The car burst into flames. The troops went crazy, firing several rounds into the students. When the ambulance from the Beijing Emergency Center came to pick up the wounded, the soldiers opened fire on the doctors!"

"Animals!" and "Barbaric!" people shouted.

At five-thirty, the student radio station announced that the estimate from the Beijing Red Cross had risen to 4,000 dead and many more wounded.

"At 4:00 a.m. this morning, the lights in the Square were turned off. Martial law troops, armored cars and tanks started to move into Tiananmen Square from its north edge. The troops, numbered in tens of thousands, advanced in rows, swinging batons, firing assault rifles as they pressed toward the students. The students were being pushed back onto the steps of the Monument to the People's Heroes. Facing death, they loudly sang 'The Internationale.'"

At that moment, we were told that not one of the protestors had left the Square alive.

Several students began to hand out black armbands. The dead must be remembered and grieved for. I took one and put it on my left arm, but there was no time to mourn our dead at that moment.

"Troops are now moving toward the university district. Fellow students, the time has come to defend our campus!" came the call over the radio station.

"With our lives!" the crowd shouted. "Like our fellow students who died in Tiananmen Square."

Streetlamps were being turned off, dawn was breaking.

"Bring as many bottles as you can find, sauce bottles, cola bottles, beer bottles . . . and bring them to all the gates. We will need them for making Molotov cocktails. Fellow students defend our campus, defend freedom!"

I ran back up to our room. There were four unopened Coke bottles in the refrigerator. I opened all of them, dumping the dark liquid in the sink in the washroom. Eimin followed me there as I busied myself with the bottles.

"Don't go. It's too dangerous."

Several neighbors were in the water room. They stared at us. I said nothing.

"Have you gone crazy? Do you want to die?" Eimin raised his voice higher.

I still said nothing. Instead I began to run toward the stairs, carrying the empty bottles. Maybe I had gone crazy. But the world had gone crazy.

"You think you are brave, don't you? It's all an illusion. You are simply naïve. You will regret it, soon," Eimin shouted after me as I ran away.

I did not stop. I hated myself for being a coward the night before. This was going to be my chance at redemption.

On the path that led up to the south gate, I joined the others who were also running toward it, with bottles in their arms. No one looked back.

At 1:00 A.M. on 4 June, martial law troops entered the Square as ordered. Loudspeakers broadcast for three-and-a-half hours nonstop. The emergency announcement from the Beijing Municipal Government and the Martial Law Command Center, urged: "Citizens and students must evacuate the Square immediately so that martial law troops can successfully carry out their mission. We cannot guarantee the safety of violators, who will be solely responsible for any consequences."

As the broadcast continued, helmeted soldiers with assault rifles packed the steps of the Museum of Chinese History on the east side of the Square. To the north of the Square army trucks and tanks were parked in front of the Golden Water Bridges, and soldiers waited on the ground. To the south, armed soldiers appeared north of Qianmen and on the north side of the Mao Mausoleum. To the west, soldiers were waiting for their orders inside the Great Hall of the People. At 2:00 A.M., the soldiers stationed in front of the north gate of the Museum of Chinese History ran onto the Boulevard of Eternal Peace wielding batons and assault rifles and sealed off the avenue.

At 4:00 A.M., all the lights in the Square went out. The loudspeakers then broadcast a "Notice to Clear the Square," saying: "We will now begin clearing the Square and we accept your appeal to evacuate." Martial law troops advanced toward the Monument to the People's Heroes from north to south in columns, pointing rifles alternately into the air and at the students. Tanks and armored vehicles also began to advance from north to south, crushing the students' tents, and the Styrofoam Goddess of Democracy along the way.

At 4:30 A.M., the lights came back on. The students found themselves standing thirty meters away from tens of thousands of armed soldiers, tanks and armored cars. As the troops pressed on, the thousands of students began retreating from the Square.

At 5:30 A.M., dawn broke.

The Square had been cleared.

Sixteen

Morning After

Turn around and look, you will see blood and tears
flowing together.

—*Bai Juyi, eighth century*

The morning mist was lifting when we took up our places. Outside the gate, Haidian Road was empty, while inside the south gate fifty or so students stood guard. No one said anything. I held one Molotov cocktail, four more lined up at my feet, certain that I could feel death approaching us. I stared at the white space in front of me; nothing, not even one of the five million bicycles in the city was visible. I listened but heard no sound coming from any direction. You could not see farther than the courtyard houses across the street, but you knew where the city center was.

I don't know how long we waited; it seemed a long time. On the other hand, time seemed to have stopped. I did not care. Time mattered very little, if at all.

Then we heard the sound of a truck engine. I picked up another bottle. Others standing next to me also tensed their bodies. My heart began to race.

The truck was getting closer, the engine roared loudly, until it appeared in front of us.

It was a military truck.

Immediately, I tossed my bottles as fast as I could toward the truck, though they landed many yards short of the target. People around me hurled stones, bricks and Molotov cocktails toward the truck, shouting as they did so, but very few hit their target. The truck stopped. The noise of the engine disappeared. We stepped out and saw the truck standing alone on the empty street.

The crowd rushed over.

Several students climbed up to the truck and stoned the windows. Shards of glass flew. They opened the door and dragged out the driver. He was a young man of about eighteen or nineteen years old, wearing faded green military clothes.

He tried to protect his head with his arms. His face was bleeding.

"Animal! Bastard!" the crowd shouted, punching and kicking him.

He tried to run, but was soon caught. People at the outer edge pushed themselves in, waving bricks.

"Let me in! Let me get my hands on him!"

The news of the lone truck must have reached the others inside the campus, and a large number of people came running, and shouting, "Beat them! Beat them!"

"You've got to stop! You will kill him!" I screamed.

But the large crowd, having grown to several hundred, surged ahead. Fists and bricks rose in the air. I could no longer see the soldier, or hear his cry. He must have been knocked down.

Some people searched the truck. They did not seem to find anything. In anger, they threw stones at the already broken windows. People tried to flip the truck over, but it was too big and heavy.

"Burn it!"

Several students hurled Molotov cocktails into the driver's cabin. It caught fire.

A group of student monitors wearing red armbands arrived. "Stop! Fellow students! Calm down!"

Three of them were big guys. They pushed their way through.

"Inside the guard's hut, quickly!" some people shouted.

The student monitors half carried, half dragged the soldier toward the hut. The crowd did not let up. One student managed to slam a piece of brick onto the back of the soldier's head. He screamed, his hand reaching up to cover the wound. He fell sideways to the ground, blood pouring down his face. The student monitors again picked him up and pushed ahead.

The student monitors finally managed to take the soldier inside the hut and pushed everyone else out and locked the door. The crowd was still shouting, screaming and waving stones and bricks. Through the windows, I could see the student monitors sitting the soldier on a chair. One of them tore a large strip from his shirt, and they tried to bandage the soldier's wounds as best as they could. The young soldier was crying like a child.

"We understand that you are all very sad and angry about what has happened to your friends and to Beijing," the leader of the student monitors said into the microphone inside the guard hut. "But we need to be clearheaded, especially at this crucial and confusing time. The last thing we want to do is to give the government and the army the excuse to raid our campus."

The ugly mood of the crowd began to subside. Inside the hut, the student monitors were talking to the soldier, who was still crying.

About ten minutes later, the leader said again through the microphone, "This soldier is from the army base in the western suburb of Beijing. He has no idea about what happened last night in Tiananmen Square. He was going to the city center on his day off."

At that time, in China, Sunday was the only day off in the week and 4 June was a Sunday, the weekend, the time to be with family, friends and to go shopping. But that Sunday, we had all forgotten about such things.

Gradually the crowd began to disperse. The students offered to take the soldier to a hospital, but he said he'd rather go back to his base. He got into his truck, helped by a few students. The fire inside the truck had been put out. He started the engine, turned around and drove off.

I looked at my watch. It was 8:20 A.M., but it felt as if hours, even days, had passed. I stood there, not moving; it was the first moment that I had had to myself. I turned around and saw Dong Yi's dorm building a few yards away. Suddenly I feared for Dong Yi. I'd forgotten him in the chaos of the night, and in the hotheadedness of the crowd. Now, nothing else mattered; all I wanted was to see Dong Yi and to know that he was safe.

I ran to the entrance and up the stairs. The hallway was empty. I began to bang on his door and screamed, "Dong Yi!" I banged on the adjoining doors and those across the hall. But no one came out. The building seemed to have been deserted.

After about ten minutes, I stopped. The building was so quiet that I could hear myself breathing. I laid my head against the door, my arms dropping to my sides, and sobbed gently, partly in fear for Dong Yi, partly as the adrenaline that had been pumping through my body in the emotion of the morning ebbed away.

Slowly I walked out of the building. The sunshine was dazzling and the day was dry. I stepped onto the pavement and then I stopped. I felt very tired.

I looked up. Through the white sunlight I saw an open truck come through the south gate. The truck was going at a slow pace, and behind it a massive crowd followed.

The truck passed close by me. I could see a man in a bloodstained white coat, his head dropping onto his chest. He was sitting next to several students, one of them with head wounds. They looked exhausted. I realized they must have been at Tiananmen Square.

I joined the crowd following the truck. While we walked behind, I noticed there was another person, lying in the truck, perhaps too wounded or tired to sit up. The truck turned left at the theater and stopped in front of the number three canteen.

"Dear fellow students." One of the students stood up and began to speak into a megaphone. "We have come from the city center where the army have committed the bloodiest crime—killing innocent people. Many of our fellow students and local citizens have also been wounded. Doctor Fang is from the Beijing Emergency Services. He was at Tiananmen Square last night."

The man in the white coat rose. He was in his early thirties. He carried another white coat in his hands. The student held up the megaphone for him. He cleared his throat and began, "I went with the ambulance and my colleague Doctor Liang to the Square at around one o'clock. When we got to the Square, we turned off the siren. We saw immediately that something was burning in the northwest corner." He again cleared his throat.

"Against the flames we saw a few dozen students throwing stones, bricks and cans of gasoline. Many of the gas cans hit the ground not far from them and burst into flames. Fire lit up the rows of trucks and tanks parked a couple of hundred yards away. We heard gunshots and saw people going down on the ground."

The doctor paused, his voice breaking again.

"When the ambulance stopped near the fire, we jumped out. I heard people shouting, 'Two wounded over there.' We ran toward the wounded, ducking our heads. We all wore our white coats with Red Cross armbands, but the shooting didn't stop. Bullets whistled by. We kept on going. Dr Liang shouted, 'Don't shoot. We are doctors.'"

Suddenly he stopped. The crowd stared at him in dead silence. The doctor opened the white coat he was carrying. The coat was stained with blood.

"But they shot him." His voice trembled. The doctor could not go on. He lifted up the coat for the crowd to see and to hide the tears streaming down his face.

I cried. I heard sobbing around me.

After a while, the doctor regained his voice. "Doctor Liang died trying to save others, for doing his duty as a doctor. He was . . ." The doctor's voice faded away. A *pinbanche*—a wooden cart hitched to a bicycle—stopped beside the truck. A student stood in the cart holding the red Beijing University flag. The crowd made way for the cart.

The doctor sat down, his hands covering his head, weeping. Two of the students jumped down from the truck. The student with the flag handed it over to the cart-driver and joined the other two students. They began to move the person from the back of the truck.

He was dead, not wounded, or just tired, as I had thought.

It was hard to judge his age. His face was white and tinged with blue, but he was definitely a student. He looked like what the peasants called "a reading book man" even in death. His hands, which had probably never held anything but pens and pencils, hung lifelessly. It was hard to tell exactly where he had been wounded or how he had died. He had blood on his head, matted in his hair and on his gray Mao jacket, which was unbuttoned. What had been a white undershirt was now red.

Carefully they laid the body on the *pinbanche*.

"Our dear fellow student died on the Boulevard of Eternal Peace," said the student with the megaphone. "He died defending the freedom we so dearly fought for. He is our hero. He is the most loyal son of our motherland. He will not die in vain. The day will come when the murderers will be punished."

Among the crowd, tears were freely flowing and the sound of sobbing soon became the only sound.

The wooden cart started to move. The two students sat on either side of the body like guards, as the third student opened up the flag. They were going to take the body right through the narrow paths of the campus. People needed to see the dead man for themselves, and to honor him.

Someone began to sing "The Internationale." The students standing on the truck joined in. The doctor stood up and sang. More and more people in the crowd sang.

Stand up the cold and poor slaves of the world!
Stand up the suffering people!
Our blood is already at boiling point,
We will fight for tomorrow.

I pushed my way out of the crowd, I couldn't bear it any longer. Tears streamed down my face. As soon as I left the crowd, I began to run, as if I could run away from blood, death and fear.

When I knocked on Dong Yi's door again, his roommate came to open it. He was just on his way out. That day, everyone on campus was going somewhere, doing something.

"Do you know where Dong Yi is?" I asked.

"I have not seen him since he left last night," he answered, locking the door.

"Where did he go?"

"Tiananmen Square." He turned to look at me, his face full of sadness, like so many I had seen on that day. We stood there for a few seconds, looking at each other.

"I am leaving now," he said and then he disappeared down the stairs. For Chinese people, this is the way you bid someone good-bye when you do not know what else to say.

I did not move. I could not think. Then I walked out into the sunshine once more and up the tree-lined path to the Triangle.

The truck was no longer there. People were collecting and burning their Party membership cards. New wall posters appeared calling on people to resign from the Party and the Party's Youth League. The radio station announced that the students who had safely left Tiananmen Square were now reaching the campus.

The crowd started to move to the south gate. We lined up and waited eagerly for the return of our fellow students. At noon, they came. Chai Ling walked at the front of the column, waving to the crowd. The crowd cheered. My old roommate had changed. She looked darker and thinner, but more confident.

The students looked very tired from the events of the night before, and the long walk back. People walked up and down trying to find the faces of their friends and loved ones. People waved and shouted at those they recognized. I stared carefully at every face in the marching column but I did not see Dong Yi.

Twenty minutes later, we all gathered at the Triangle. Chai Ling spoke to us from the student radio station.

She said that the students had retreated from Tiananmen Square so that there would be no loss of life. But this was not the end of our struggle. On the contrary, our new struggle had just begun. The students would now take our struggle to the people, underground. She urged us not to stop until there was freedom and democracy in our motherland.

Then the students dispersed, back to their dorm rooms to rest. The crowd at the Triangle thinned. It felt like the end of a dream.

I went upstairs to see Eimin and found only a note on the desk, "Gone to the department." I went downstairs and had lunch at the canteen by myself.

Sometime in the afternoon, between my fourth or fifth trip up to Dong Yi's room, hope draining away from me, I ran into two of my old classmates, Wei Hua and Li Xiao Dong, at the south gate. They had come, with others, to collect the Molotov cocktails piled near the gate.

"What if the troops come?" I asked.

"They won't come today. They are busy. Haven't you heard, Beijing citizens are 'rioting' in the city center?" answered Li Xiao Dong.

"We need to take the bottles somewhere safe," said Wei Hua.

"I'll give you a hand." I picked up two bottles, carrying one under each arm.

"Isn't that Cao Gu Ran?" asked Wei Hua suddenly, pointing to the street outside.

"Oh dear, yes." I saw Cao Gu Ran getting off a *pinbanche*. He had thick bandages on his head.

We put the bottles down and rushed to greet him. He looked at us with misty eyes, tried to walk, but only managed to sway from side to side. We caught him before he fell and helped him to the steps of Dong Yi's dorm building.

"Where have you come from?" I asked.

"What happened to your head?" asked Li Xiao Dong.

"From the city center, I think." He touched the bandage and looked shocked by the pain.

"That must hurt," I said.

"Yes, it feels like a huge headache. But I don't remember how I got it."

"Did you get hit by a bullet? Was it at Tiananmen Square?"

"The doctor said it was either a club or a bat. I don't remember where I was. Just that it was dark. I was running. A lot of people were running. Then I saw soldiers charging at us. Don't remember how I got this." He carefully touched the top of his head. "Am I still bleeding?"

"No. What else do you remember?"

"Waking up in the hospital. I will never forget that. I was on a straw mat in the hallway and with all this stuff on my head. Everywhere people were crying and screaming in pain. People in white coats were running around. People were being carried in on stretchers, or doors or just carried in. There was blood everywhere."

"Which hospital was that?" I asked.

"I don't know."

"How come they let you out? You need to be in the hospital. You look terrible," said Wei Hua.

"Has the bleeding started again?" Cao Gu Ran was confused.

"No. You are not bleeding."

"I slipped out. I saw an official-looking guy writing down names and affiliations of the wounded. I got scared. I slipped out."

"Where did you go? You couldn't have gone far with your wound," said Li Xiao Dong.

"Didn't think of that. Just left the hospital and started walking west. Just walked in the opposite direction from the gunshots. Hadn't gone far when this guy driving a *pinbanche* came by."

Cao Gu Ran looked at the street outside. "He brought me all the way here. Didn't say much, but rode like wind."

"You must go to the university hospital. You need to see a doctor," I said.

"I just want to go back to my room and sleep."

"No," we refused. "We must take you to see the doctor."

Li Xiao Dong said, "Wait here. I will get my bicycle."

"You know what depressed me the most in the hospital?" Cao Gu Ran asked.

"No." Wei Hua and I looked at him.

"People were coming in to look for their family members, relatives and loved ones. How wonderful it was to be loved, even in death. But I knew that no one would come to look for me."

Wei Hua and I looked at each other. We did not know what to say.

"I am almost twenty-four and I don't even have a girlfriend. I don't want to die like this." Suddenly Cao Gu Ran started to cry.

"You are not going to die." I looked at Wei Hua, who shrugged her shoulders.

"Keep calm, please. I think your wound is opening again," I said.

"I am not afraid of death, you know that. But I don't want to die alone," sobbed our friend.

It took some time for us to take Cao Gu Ran to the university hospital. The nurse gave him a shot. After he went to sleep, the three of us left quietly and went our separate ways.

Evening had come. But I was not hungry. I had made up my mind. Walking away from the university hospital, I thought that if I could not find Dong Yi on campus, I would go to the hospitals in the city center. I would go and look for him, wherever the search might take me. I would find Dong Yi, alive or not.

It was with just such resolve that I knocked on his door again. The lock clicked, and I saw Dong Yi standing in front of me, his shirt filthy. He must have just arrived and yet he seemed as if he was on the point of going out again.

I wanted to shout at him, for going to Tiananmen Square the night before, for making me worry. I also wanted to run to him, to hug him, to tell him how happy I was to see him back safely. But all I could do was to stand at the door.

For all the worries, anxiety, love, regret, hate and happiness of see-ing him right there and then, I could only say, "I have been looking for you all day."

"I know. My roommate told me."

"Where have you been?"

"I spent all day riding through small alleys trying to get back here. I did not dare use the main roads."

"Has the army sealed off the main roads?"

"I don't know. But the troops traveled on the main roads. All the time I heard gunfire ringing out somewhere. Sometimes I passed main intersections and saw army trucks burning and rubble strewn all over the streets."

"Where were you last night? Your roommate said you had gone to the Square."

"I was going to go to the Square, but I went to Muxudi instead." Muxudi is a stop on the western extension of the Boulevard of Eternal Peace, three miles west of Tiananmen Square.

We sat down on his bed, side by side. Dong Yi reached into his trouser pocket. When he opened his palm, I saw a bullet shell.

"Wei, I don't think I will ever be the same again, not after what I saw."

He lifted his hand and let the bullet shell slide into my palm.

"Tell me," I said gently.

Dong Yi then told me that it was probably ten o'clock when he got to Muxudi subway station. A few hundred people were already there, mostly local citizens and students from the provinces. Then they heard the tanks and armored cars coming; they'd crossed the Muxudi Bridge. Soon they saw the soldiers, with their rifles.

The crowd began to throw stones and bricks from behind the roadblocks. They knew that whatever they could do probably would not stop the army from advancing, but might delay them getting to the Square.

The soldiers charged, protected by their armored cars and tanks, pushing the buses and other roadblocks aside. The crowd shouted "Bandits!" from behind the shrubs in the grass strip in the middle of the road. Some hurled bricks from the pavements.

He paused for a second before continuing, "Then we heard gunshots. At first, many people did not duck because no one believed they were real bullets."

The crowd only started to run when they saw people falling to the ground in pools of blood. Dong Yi was about two hundred yards from the soldiers, not too close. When he saw people falling down and heard someone yelling, "Real bullets!" he started running too. Bullets whistled past him, hitting the ground, and then he heard a girl screaming. He turned around and saw her fall to the ground. Her friends wanted to stop and go back, but the bullets were flying by.

Dong Yi took the bullet shell from me and held it between his thumb and first finger. When he turned the shell, it reflected the light coldly.

The girl was screaming and twisting in agony out there, on the street. Her friends, five of them, all young men, were shouting and crying, wanting to go back to get her. One of the local citizens said it would be too dangerous for all of them to go. So he went on his own, crawling along the road. He got there, picked her up and ran back. He was hit just as he got out, but fortunately not seriously. But the girl had blood pouring out of her stomach. Dong Yi held her while her friends tried to stop the bleeding. She twitched and screeched, the blood was coming out nonstop. Her friends cried and begged her to stay with them. But they all knew that she was going to die.

Dong Yi's voice started to falter.

In her pocket, they found her student ID card and some blood-soaked money. She was a student at Hefei University in Ann Hui province. She came with her classmates on the train the day before. She was only nineteen years old.

I held Dong Yi's hands, as tears ran down our faces.

"I picked up this shell when I left Muxudi. I will keep it forever. This is my witness."

"What are you going to do now?" I asked, wiping the tears from my face.

"Now that I have seen you, I feel much better. I will go and see whether I can get through to Taiyuan. I want to let them know I am safe."

I knew he would say that; and I knew he must do that. Of course he had to call his wife. But still, hearing the words caused me pain and made me sadder still.

"Yes. Yes, you must. You may be able to make the call from the Spoon Garden."

We walked out together and said good-bye.

There was much to be done, people to see, loved ones to inform and plans to discuss. Darkness was falling.

Seventeen

A Promise to Keep

It's difficult to meet again but even more difficult to say
good-bye, the east wind is powerless to stop the death
of hundreds of flowers.

—*Li Shangyen, ninth century*

The army did not raid the campus on 4 June, nor did they come on 5 June. But the rumor was that large numbers of soldiers in plain clothes were making their way toward the university district and knifing those wearing the black armbands that honored the dead. There were also rumors that the 27th Group Army, responsible for the killings at Muxudi and on the Boulevard of Eternal Peace, had got into a fight with the 38th Group Army, which had cleared Tiananmen Square, indicating political struggles among the top ranks in the army. Both rumors later turned out to be false, but at the time they had a tremendous psychological impact on people and on the morale of the city.

Downstairs in the courtyard, Eimin and I saw Li, who was waiting anxiously for her boyfriend, Xiao Zhang.

"Where is he?" I asked her.

"The printing room. They are taking the equipment apart."

"What about the propaganda material and papers?"

"Burned. There should be nothing left for the army," said Li.

"Will the army come in?"

"They will, maybe not today or tomorrow. But they will."

"Too bad the radio station is closed down," said Eimin. "I feel like a blind man, not knowing what is happening."

Xiao Zhang appeared from between the buildings, carrying a large parcel, wrapped in newspapers. Li stopped talking and ran over to help.

"What's this?" said Eimin. "Looks quite heavy. Need a hand?"

"No thanks. We're going to have to hide the parts in people's homes. This is for your room Li, is that OK?"

"Of course. Let's take it up. Wei, why don't you and Eimin move back to your parents'? You'd be safer off campus," said Li. "I'd do the same if my parents lived in Beijing."

After Li and Xiao Zhang left, Eimin and I talked about the idea of moving in with my parents. Across the courtyard, a family was loading sacks onto their bicycles; they seemed to be departing already.

"There are only two bedrooms, and my sister is already there." I thought the idea might be sensible, but not practical.

"At least you can move there. I will stay here," Eimin spoke firmly.

"I can't let you do that. Either we both go or I stay."

In the end, we decided to check with my parents first. It was also time that we told them that we were safe.

As a security measure, the university had closed all but the south gate, local citizens no longer being allowed in. There were no buses running along Haidian Road, only a few cyclists traveling on the usually buzzing thoroughfare.

Eimin and I rode along the quiet road going west, the sun burning on our bare arms.

"Are you students?" The rattle of a *pinbanche* came up from behind us. The driver looked at us.

"No. We are not. I am a teacher and she graduated last year. Why do you ask?" answered Eimin, deliberately avoiding the word "professor."

"Oh, don't worry. I'm just a cart driver, not plainclothes police. I was there that night."

"Where was that?" I asked guardedly.

"On the Boulevard of Eternal Peace. I was hoping to get some work at night. I saw them open fire. I am no idiot, you know."

"No."

"I may be from the countryside but I knew they were real bullets. When the bullets hit the concrete, I said to myself, those are real bullets, all right."

"Did you see any students there?" I asked him.

"Yes, students, locals, many people. City folks don't know, they only started to run when they saw blood spilled. But I knew."

We did not say anything. But he did not seem to mind and continued, as if he had much on his mind that he needed to unload, and quickly. "I tried to go back to the city center today, thinking it would be quieter now and maybe I'd get some work. It was quiet all right. Soldiers were everywhere, the main roads were closed. I rode around near the beltway, but no one wanted to hire a cart. If this goes on, I'll starve. Or I would if I stayed. You don't make much money growing grain, but at least you aren't shot at. I'm going home. Pack up and go home and see the wife. I am no idiot, you know."

We turned off the main road. "Good-bye," we said and wished him luck. The driver went on his way west. A few minutes later, I looked back and saw him chatting to other cyclists.

"Do you think he really is a flatbed cart driver?" I asked Eimin. Rumors had made me wary around strangers. All the time the driver had been talking, I wondered if he was only trying to get us to say something incriminating.

"I believed him," said Eimin, surprisingly relaxed. "He's got a heavy accent and talked like an uneducated man. Don't worry. Even if he were from the secret police, we'd be fine. We didn't say anything that could get us into trouble."

My mother was relieved to see us. My father had gone to work dutifully, as he had, every Monday, for the past thirty years.

"Where is Xiao Jie?" I asked.

"Went to see Lu Yian of course. She is always there." Lu Yian was my sister's childhood friend. She lived in the next building. Her parents were my mother's colleagues.

"I hope that you had the good sense not to go out on Saturday?" My mother handed us two bottles of Coke.

"No. We didn't."

"I was very worried. But your Baba said, 'Wei is naïve, but Eimin will stop her.'"

Eimin smiled.

"You should come home. It's too dangerous staying where you are. Beijing University is the next big target, especially now that the Square has been cleared."

"But how will you manage? Xiao Jie is home and there are two of us."

"Don't you worry about that. Your Baba and I have discussed it. We will sleep in the living room. Remember the folding bed? We will take it out. I can sleep on the sofa."

"But for how long, Mama? A few days may be fine, but it will be hard if we have to stay on long."

"However long it takes. We lived in the labor camp when you were little and then out in the courtyard after the Tangshan earthquake. It will be fine."

So we decided to move in with my parents.

"We'd better go now so that we can pack and be here before it gets dark." Eimin was also relieved to be able to move away from Beijing University campus.

"The telephone is back on. Call if you need to," said my mother.

It was about four o'clock in the afternoon when we got back to Beijing University. I went upstairs to pack while Eimin went to his office to see what he might want to take with him. I opened the door with the key and saw a note lying on the floor. Someone must have slipped it in under the door.

I read the note. It was from Dong Yi, arranging to meet me in the evening. As soon as I read it, I knew that something must have happened: He would never have come here if it were not urgent.

From the time I read Dong Yi's note until eight o'clock in the evening, my mind was in pieces. Eimin came back with some papers and was not pleased to see that I had packed nothing.

"Can we not go today? I'd feel better going in the morning. It'd be safer," I said to Eimin.

"But why? I don't see how. It seems to me that the longer we stay here, the more dangerous it will be."

"Just one night. It won't make much difference."

"If that's what you want. We will go in the morning. But I really don't see why we need to wait till then. Let's go and call your parents."

I ate little at dinner. Eimin became worried about my health, putting his hand on my head to see whether I was running a temperature.

"I am fine." I shook my head. I did not tell him about the note from Dong Yi.

By the time I needed to go, I felt awkward telling him the truth, so instead I told Eimin that I was going for a walk around the lake.

"Want me to come with you?"

"No, it's fine. I won't be long."

"Good. Maybe you just need some fresh air."

I had a habit of going to the lake in the evenings alone, sometimes to write, sometimes to read. Eimin was used to it. He usually spent such time at his desk, writing, or going through departmental paperwork.

Weiming Lake was as peaceful as ever. The branches of the weeping willows had grown since I saw them last, trailing in the water. Lovers were still walking together, holding hands. They never stopped coming, no matter what, even when the world had turned mad. They continued their walks as if no one else existed but them, and nothing else but love.

I waited for Dong Yi on the white stone bridge at the northeast corner, our favorite meeting place at the lake. The evening was getting darker and the clouds that had been building up since the afternoon now covered the sky, making the air sticky and humid. Across the bridge I could see the lonely stone boat sitting next to the island in the middle of the lake.

There was not a single breath of wind, and the water was dark and smooth as silk.

"I wish there was a moon tonight. The lake always looks nice in moonlight."

Dong Yi had come on time.

"Is everything all right? When I read your note, I was really worried."

"Yes, at least for now." Dong Yi smiled at me sadly. We both leaned over the bridge. I remembered the evenings we used to spend here, reading poetry. We were in love and our lives seemed much less complicated. We could have had the world.

"Remember there used to be fish in the lake?" I said.

"I have come to say good-bye. I am leaving Beijing tonight," Dong Yi blurted out.

I looked up. He looked down.

"They will start arresting people soon. Many people have gone underground. More may need to."

"Where will you go?"

"First I want to go back to Taiyuan. I want to check on my family and to let them know that I am safe. The phone lines were down in the Spoon Garden so I could not reach Lan."

"Yes, I know, the main switchboard closed most of the lines yesterday. But will you be safe in Taiyuan? The first place they will check will be your hometown."

"I may have to go somewhere else later, but I don't know where yet."

Streetlamps flickered on as the night closed in.

"How are you going to get out of Beijing?" I asked. I did not think he could simply go to the train station for a ticket out. Besides, the trains might not be running yet.

"Friends will help."

"When will you be back?"

"I don't know. Hopefully, soon." Dong Yi took me by my shoulders and looked deeply into my eyes.

"But I will come back before you leave for America. I promise. I will come to see you. Will you wait for me?"

"Yes, of course. Don't worry about that. Leave quickly. I will wait for you, I promise."

He had to go. His passage had been arranged, it seemed.

The night was moonless, and I felt as if something were falling from my fingertips, lost forever.

Eighteen

Wanted Alive

You do not need to hide your names, today there are so
many just like you.

—*Li She, ninth century*

Eimin and I moved out of Beijing University on the morning
of 6 June. We took with us two small suitcases of clothes,
toothbrushes, towels, an alarm clock and the manuscript
of Eimin's book—a psychology textbook. More people were leaving,
as students from Beijing went home. Lecturers who did not want
their families around when the police came to arrest them sent their
wives and children to the in-laws. Everyone expected that the next
big bloodshedding would happen right there on campus.

In the evening, in my parents' apartment, the five of us crammed
onto the sofa, to watch TV. All three stations, Central One and Two
and Beijing TV, broadcast programs on the "crimes of the rioters."
They reported that twenty-three officers and soldiers had died "during
the riot" on 3 and 4 June. Hundreds of army trucks had been torched
and left burning on the streets of Beijing.

"On the evening of 3 June, en route to Tiananmen Square, a soldier became separated from his platoon and was captured by rioters,"
one reporter said solemnly, standing in front of the Chongwenmen
overpass, two miles southwest of Tiananmen Square. "The rioters carried him up to this overpass behind me, doused him with gasoline

and set him on fire. They then threw him over the side. Afterward, the rioters hung his burned body from the overpass."

There were close-ups of the badly burned body.

An officer of the soldier's unit was interviewed. "We were too far away. We couldn't do anything but watch his body dangling from the bridge."

"How did your platoon react?"

"My soldiers all shouted 'Kill the murderers.' But I told them that, 'We are the people's army, the evil elements are only a small group, and we do not fire on students or residents.'"

The report then switched to the hometown of the fallen soldier. Local officials were filmed visiting his parents, who were peasants. The father said, to the camera, in an obviously coached way, "Our son died a hero. He has brought glory to his family."

The mother cried, and said nothing.

"The people will never forget your son," said the official gravely. But you could tell he relished the attention. He was wearing a newly made Mao jacket. "We promise you the murderers will be captured and punished."

In my parents' home, no one said anything. The horrific images of the dead soldier made me sick in the stomach. No one deserved to die like that. No one deserved to die at all. But on that dark night, so many sons and daughters, too young to even know about death, perished, on both sides. How many mothers and fathers had to go on living with only the memories of their children?

In the days that followed, similar programs became regular features. First the description of the death, then the funeral, then the parents receiving his medal, would-be twentieth birthday remembrances, and finally the renaming of a local elementary school after the dead soldier.

The next day, I decided to go to the city center. I wanted to see it for myself—the bullet holes, the soldiers with machine guns and the strip of road where so many people died. I also wanted to go to the place where Dong Yi stood and witnessed bloodshed and death. The government had sealed off Tiananmen Square and the roads leading into it, but they kept the western extension of the Boulevard of Eternal

Peace open to allow traffic through central Beijing. My sister came with me, and we left right after breakfast.

The streets were filled with commuters traveling to work. Normally the rush hours were extremely noisy, with thousands of cyclists competing with motor traffic on virtually every street. People chatted with their friends; neighbors or colleagues traveled together; children being dropped off at nursery schools screamed on the back of their parents' bicycles. Those who were late rang their bells loudly. But today the crowd was quiet. There was very little chitchat and no cacophony of bells. It felt as if people would rather not be out on the street, unless they had to get somewhere.

When we reached the crossing at the West Second Beltway, a line of army trucks was traveling from west to east. The trucks were covered. We could not see anyone or anything inside, except the rifles that were pointing out from underneath the canvas. A few hundred cyclists had stopped at the crossing. My sister and I were standing in the first row, by our bikes. The trucks hummed loudly as they drove by. I could feel the ground beneath us shaking.

The fear I had felt on my last night in Tiananmen Square returned. Only this time it was several times stronger; now I knew that the guns pointing at us were loaded with real ammunition.

"Please, please, no one shout, or even speak loudly. No one move suddenly," I pleaded silently.

I stared at the dark guns sticking out of the trucks and could not stop praying that no one would be foolish or brave enough to curse the passing troops. We had heard stories of their opening fire whenever they heard people shouting. They had killed and wounded many residents during such outbursts.

I tightly gripped the handlebar of my bicycle, trying to calm the beating of my heart. I looked back. Four or five hundred people had stopped behind me. My nervousness increased, with every minute that passed, dreading shots fired at us because someone shouted, a child cried or even a big package fell down from a bicycle.

The trucks went on, steadily, rumbling past.

Behind me was dead silence.

I could hear my heart beating and feel my feet trembling.

The trucks finally passed, after five minutes. I had been too nervous to count them all but there couldn't have been fewer than fifty.

After they were safely out of our sight, the stalled crowd began to move. People got back onto their bicycles and rode on quietly to wherever they were going.

"Thank heavens no one made a sound. I wouldn't have lasted if we had to wait there for another minute," I said to my sister.

Half an hour later, we arrived at Muxudi. Armed soldiers, within an arm's length of each other, lined both sides of the bridge, their submachine guns pointing at the people crossing.

"Get off your bicycles and walk." A platoon leader, at the head of the bridge, waved his pistol. "Move on quickly. Don't stop. No talking."

My sister and I did as he asked.

"Don't look at them," whispered my sister. "Especially not their eyes. We don't want to get them upset."

We kept our heads down and walked as fast as we could. From the corner of my eye, I could see the dark barrels of the guns and the fingers clutching the triggers tightly. I did not dare look up or look around. We went up and over the other side, walking quickly and quietly. I prayed everyone behind or in front of us would do just the same.

Once the black submachine guns stopped coming into view and the ground beneath had leveled, we knew that we had crossed the Muxudi Bridge. My sister and I got on our bicycles again and rode on. A hundred yards later, we came to the Muxudi subway station, where Dong Yi had been on the evening of 3 June. We looked back. The columns of cyclists walking their bicycles over the bridge seemed endless.

Here pedestrian sidewalks were separated from the street by steel fences. Some distance behind the fences, on both sides, were high residential buildings. Up until this June, this strip was one of the most desirable residential addresses in Beijing. The location was perfect. To the east, the road turned into the beautiful Boulevard of Eternal Peace, cutting through the center of the city. There was the convenience of the subway, nearby were newly developed shopping centers. Many high-ranking government officials and their families lived in the large apartments in these buildings.

On the evening of 3 June, many residents had watched the massacre right beneath their windows. Some cursed and threw bottles, cans and other objects at the soldiers, some simply left their lights on while standing at the window. The troops responded with rounds of machine-gun fire, hosing bullets up and down the buildings, killing several and wounding many residents. Those bullets had left marks on the concrete walls of the building, some as large as a walnut.

My sister and I stopped at the fence on the north side. The street had been washed clean. We saw bullet holes all along the steel bars, some scattered and some in clusters. I touched them, feeling the cold metal and the deadly power of modern warfare. I stared at the size of the bullet holes and wondered whether those were big bullets or if they'd exploded on impact. I thought of the human bodies that other bullets had hit and exploded in, the soft and warm flesh, hot blood gushing out. The young girl dying in Dong Yi's arms, her blood and body turning cold.

"Move on!"

I was startled and turned around. An inch from my face, the barrel of a machine gun was aimed at me. I could almost feel the coldness of the metal.

"Don't you know that you are not allowed to stop?" the soldier said sternly.

I noticed that his finger was on the trigger.

"We are going. Sorry. We are going." My sister pulled and pushed me away.

We got on our bicycles and rode on. But soon we had to stop and turn around. The Boulevard of Eternal Peace had been sealed off in the direction of Tiananmen Square.

"Did you see those burned buses and trucks?" my sister asked. "Why are they still on the sides of the streets?"

"I thought they would have cleared everything away by now."

"There must have been too many."

"Didn't they say five hundred on TV yesterday?" I asked.

"I think so," said my sister.

When we passed Beijing University again, on our way back, heavily armed soldiers and army checkpoints had surrounded the campus. Patrols were on the streets, circling the university.

"Huge news," my mother said as soon as we stepped inside the apartment. "Fang Lizhi and his wife are inside the U.S. Embassy. They're seeking political asylum."

"How did it happen?" I asked, thinking of the secret police outside professor Fang Lizhi's home.

"Oh, how face-losing," my mother laughed. "Whoever was watching them is going to get it!"

"What is going to happen to them?" asked my sister.

"The Chinese government can't do anything to them as long as they are inside the Embassy," said Eimin, who had been waiting with my mother for us to return. "The grounds of the U.S. Embassy are under American, not Chinese, jurisdiction."

"But they can't leave China, can they?" asked my mother.

"No. I am sure they would be arrested as soon as they stepped outside the Embassy."

Surprisingly there was little detail about the incident in the evening news but a strongly worded demand for the American government to hand over Professor Fang and his wife. The U.S. government promptly rejected China's demand. Immediately the two countries went into an intense political standoff, both the U.S. House of Representatives and the Senate voting unanimously in support of President Bush's decision to cease military cooperation with China. The American government announced that the 45,000 Chinese in the U.S. would be allowed to stay after their visas expired.

When, a few days later, the U.S. Embassy reopened, visas to America were granted to the many people who had been waiting in long lines outside. The Chinese government—keen to demonstrate that the crackdown on 4 June was only directed at "a small group of counterrevolutionary elements"—did not stop people who already had passports applying for visas to America. However, the Chinese government did stop issuing new passports. Professor Fang and his wife remained in the U.S. Embassy for some time. They were finally allowed to leave China in 1991.

A few days later I received a letter from Hanna telling me that she and Jerry had married, and were leaving China right away. "Hope you will come out soon too. Give me a call when you are out."

On 9 June, Deng Xiaoping appeared in public for the first time since the massacre, hosting a reception for high-ranking army officers in his compound at Zhongnanhai. A simplified version of his speech was later made public. Deng Xiaoping began the reception by proposing that "we all rise and stand in silent tribute to the martyrs" among the troops. He told the attendees that the 26 April *People's Daily* editorial was correct in labelling the Student Movement as "anarchy." "The word 'anarchy' is appropriate," he went on to say. "What has happened shows that this judgement was correct. It was also inevitable that the situation would further develop into a counterrevolutionary rebellion."

To the ordinary Chinese, Deng Xiaoping's appearance and speech was a clear message. He was telling us who was in charge when the tanks rolled into Beijing, and who was still in charge on that day.

The summer had become even hotter. I did not go out much, partly because of the heat and partly because I had no reason to. Armed soldiers patrolled the streets of Beijing, checkpoints were everywhere. Foreign firms had withdrawn their staff and, in some cases, closed their entire Chinese operation. People who had to go to work did so, but they came straight home as soon as they could. I spent most of my days reading; books, mostly—there was nothing in the official newspapers I wanted to read. All foreign press had been banned and foreign journalists had either left or been expelled.

"Martial law troops were received warmly by Beijing residents," one newspaper article reported. "To combat the unbearable heat, residential groups brought cold water to the soldiers guarding important buildings and streets. Work units also organized food deliveries including watermelons to the troops."

A couple of days later, the same newspaper wrote: "To maintain the highest state of alert and security, the martial law troops have seized water and food from unorganized individuals."

Some pages later, a small article reported that twenty martial law soldiers were poisoned after drinking water delivered by a friendly old lady.

On 12 June, arrest warrants were issued for Fang Lizhi and his wife, Li Shuxian, who were still inside the U.S. embassy. The following evening, the twenty-one "most wanted" list was announced in the evening news on Central One, accompanied by photographs:

Number One: Wang Dan, a first-year student at Beijing University, President of the Autonomous Student Association, medium height . . .

Number Two: Wuerkaixi, a first-year student at Beijing Normal University, leader of the ASA. Tall, large eyes . . .

Number Three: Liu Gang, a graduate of Beijing University . . .

Number Four: Chai Ling, a graduate student at Beijing Normal University, the Commander in Chief of the Tiananmen Square Student Command Center. 1.55 meters tall, round face, short hair, and small eyes.

Number Fourteen: Feng Congde, a graduate student at Beijing University, leader of the ASA . . .

The anchorman continued, "Most of these fugitives have gone on the run. But the army and police will capture them. The government calls on ordinary citizens to show revolutionary spirit and turn in the anarchic elements." I watched the faces of those I knew on the TV screen. I was surprised to see Liu Gang listed so high on the wanted list, even though he was not a leader of the ASA and did not participate in the meeting with Li Peng. Then I thought of his longstanding friendship with professor Fang Lizhi, the group Dong Yi was also involved with, and I understood. At that moment I also realized the level of danger Dong Yi must be in and why he had to leave Beijing hurriedly. Suddenly I feared for his life.

"So many are from Beijing University," said my mother.

"I am glad that we have moved out," Eimin said.

"Where will they go?" I asked.

"It doesn't matter. They will be hunted out. One thing the Communist Party knows how to do is go back to grassroots." Eimin's tone was sure.

"Perhaps they'll go to their hometown," my sister said. "Back to their parents. They will be, probably, the only people who won't give them up."

"Sure, no one else will be reliable," agreed my mother. "People will do anything to save themselves. Look at the Cultural Revolution, aunts turned in nephews, sisters turned in brothers, friends turned each other in."

"But I do hope that they all get away." I had to interrupt, I couldn't bear the thought of someone I knew betraying Dong Yi.

The image of Chai Ling remained with me long into the night. I could not sleep, but tossed and turned, trying to shake her face from my mind. I wondered what the millions of viewers had thought about her. She looked much too young and too fragile, her face too childlike, to be commander in chief. I remembered how, once, Chai Ling had brought rats back from the lab and let them loose in the dormitory. At first we were terrified, but after a while, we were all laughing so hard that we could only fall onto our beds. Where had those innocent days gone? I stared into the dark, wondering where my old roommate and her husband, now fugitives on the run, were tonight.

By the end of June over 1,000 "counterrevolutionary" rioters and "anarchic elements" had been arrested in Beijing, including students, professors, ordinary Beijing citizens and factory workers. Many were hastily sentenced to death in showcase trials, and shot in the back of the head in public executions. Afterward their families were asked to pay for the bullet before they could take away the body.

Many students lived in fear that soon they would be arrested, that their future was, inevitably, ruined. Some of them feared being punished for taking part in the Movement so much that they could no longer sleep at night. One day, when I was at home rearranging my childhood photos, one such student came to see my mother. My father and Eimin had both gone to work and my sister was visiting her friend in the next building.

"Do you remember that rally we had in support of the hunger strike, Professor Kang?"

"Yes," said my mother. "Almost everyone from the university attended."

"I gave a speech at the rally. No, you don't remember? Yes, many people spoke that day. But what if one of the university officials or maybe an undercover policeman remembers me? I have tried not to think about it. But I can't help myself, I am terrified. Sooner or later they will come to arrest me. I haven't slept for days. No, I did not intend to do it. It was a spur of the moment thing. What am I going to do? I am exhausted."

Having lived through the horrors of the Cultural Revolution, when imprisonment and death came so often to those who voiced their objections to Mao's policies, there was little that my mother could honestly say to calm her student. Instead, my mother gave him, as with everyone else who had come before, Chinese herbs to aid sleeping.

Soon people were urged to use a telephone hotline to turn in the "anarchic elements" and "counterrevolutionary rioters" anonymously. They were especially encouraged to report on those with whom they were close—friends, colleagues, neighbors or relatives. The setting up of the hotline sent waves of fear through the entire city. The most evil thing about it was that anyone could call from a public phone and you would be arrested; you couldn't even dispute the accuracy of such information, as the witness had neither name nor face.

Every day I wondered whether I had been reported and when and how the police might show up at my parents" door. Every day that passed without an incident became a bonus gained, a life spared; for I believed that the escape door would shut one day, the net would tighten and I would be caught.

The day before my birthday, near the end of June, I went to Beijing University with Eimin. He went to his office and I went to the bookstore. It was a dry sunny day, and suffocating dust floated everywhere. Along the streets, young willows that had been planted recently, powerless against the heat, had dried out. Even the normally shady chestnut trees folded their leaves in submission to the burning sun.

The Triangle had gone back to its normal state, with university announcements and propaganda material neatly posted inside the glass display windows. One announcement stated that the official number of dead from Beijing University was not hundreds but three. The announcement denounced the ASA for deliberately misleading students.

I read their names, age and departmental affiliations. I did not know any of them. I tried but could not find any statement about where and how they died.

I walked on and read another announcement:

Given the circumstances, the university has authorized the spring semester to end early and summer recess to begin immediately. The university urges the students to use the summer for reflection and for self-criticism. All students are required to report back to their departmental Party officials at the beginning of the autumn term, with accurate accounts of their activities during the anarchy.

I did not read any further. The usual spring term lasts till early July in Chinese universities. At Beijing University, there had not been any classes since April. And so many students had left after 4 June, which meant the summer recess had in effect begun. I supposed the university was simply acknowledging the fact.

Near the bookstore, a wall poster announced the screening of video footage of "the heroic acts of the martial law troops. This footage will tell the truth about what happened on 4 June."

I wondered how many people would show up to watch it. Both my father and mother had received party internal communiqués with more detailed, at times graphic descriptions of the death of the martial law "heroes," some of them burned to death in their armored cars, some bodies mutilated. The communiqué also put the Beijing Municipality's official figures for the civilian dead and wounded on 3 and 4 June at 218 and 2,000 respectively. One report from the Beijing Public Security Bureau said that those killed included university professors, workers, small business owners, high school students and grade school students. The youngest was nine and the oldest a retired worker in her seventies. The numbers of the troops that took part in the crackdown and the extent of their armory were never disclosed, but judging by the number of soldiers wounded (5,000) and military vehicles burned (500), it was not difficult to gauge the overwhelming might of the military force that descended on the unarmed civilians of Beijing over those two days.

Inside the bookstore, the ceiling fan turned slowly. For as long as I could remember, the bookstore had always been busy, frequented by the 20,000 Beijing University students and their friends. The store naturally sold a lot of textbooks. But it also stocked novels, poems and nonfiction, reflecting the taste of the students, the intellectual elite of the young Chinese. I remembered that three years before, we had all come here to buy Charles Dickens" *David Copperfield*, the story of a young man's self-made success, and Goethe's *The Sorrows of Young Werther*, about love and loss in eighteenth-century Germany. Back then everyone wanted to be Copperfield and wished that they could, like the character in the novel, triumph through talent, intelligence and hard work. And then, most of us felt connected to young Werther, for China had just opened up and the young generation was learning to experience the wonders, as well as the pains, of love. But we couldn't get banned books here; for those we had to go to the street market in Haidian village, where the book vendor could pull a copy of *Lady Chatterley's Lover* out of a rice sack from under the table.

The ceiling fan kept the bookstore cool, at least around the display table directly beneath it. I looked through the books. There were plenty of novels about life and death in the Cultural Revolution, which had been popular with the students before the demonstrations. But today, I did not see anyone buying them. Personally I did not feel like reading fictionalized political tragedies anymore.

Finally, I bought a collection of poems by Gou Mourou. Gou was one of the leading writers of the May Fourth Movement in 1919. His writing had been popular with the students both prior to and during the Student Democracy Movement. I thought, if I did manage to go to America, I would like to take this book with me as a memento.

Eimin did not show up at the canteen for lunch as we had agreed, so I went to his office. The administration offices of the Department of Psychology were located just behind the pagoda at Weiming Lake. I parked my bicycle in the middle of the courtyard and noticed a group of people gathered at the administration office. The department chair's office next door was closed, as was Eimin's office, two doors to the right. I walked into the administration office. There, the department chair, Professor Bai, Eimin, my friend Li, the department administrator and two secretaries were talking.

"How awful, what are we going to do?" cried the department administrator.

"There isn't much we can do, is there?" said Li. "The phone lines are open to everyone. He does not even need to say his name."

"I knew he was no good. I knew it from the first time I saw the guy. He's got a sharp nose and his eyes are tiny," said the older secretary, Mrs. Cao.

Professor Bai seemed resigned, and offered to take full responsibility.

I walked quietly over to Eimin and whispered in his ear. "What's going on?"

He whispered back that Ling Huyuan had returned and wanted his job back. He said if he didn't get it back, he would call the police on the hotline "exposing the counterrevolutionary elements" of the department.

I remembered Ling Huyuan, a rude young man who was fond of drinking. He used to be an assistant in the Department.

"Perhaps we could let him come back? Big Sister Cao and I will do his work. We don't mind, do we?" the younger secretary said.

"I've heard that his uncle is a high-ranking official in the Beijing government," added the department administrator.

"He will turn on us all the same," Li disagreed.

"I've got two kids. What will I do?" Mrs. Cao almost cried.

"Let them come and arrest me. If he wants someone ruined, let it be me." Professor Bai was angry now, his face turning red.

"Calm down, Lao Bai," said Eimin. "We'll deal with it when it happens. But at the moment we don't know what kind of things he will say."

"I wish I could leave," sighed the younger secretary. "Wei, what luck that you are going to America!"

"Well, I am not sure," I said, thinking about my fears that someone might call the hotline and turn me in before the border reopened. Maybe I was already on the blacklist. Maybe somewhere, in a small overheated and airless office, photos of me marching or waving newspapers on the tank were stacked on top of a file, my passport application about to be rejected.

I did not know what might happen next; no one knew. Everyone feared the worst.

Amid the anxiety and terror, I celebrated my twenty-third birthday. My parents made their special "long-life" noodles. "It doesn't matter whether you have a cake or not, you must eat long-life noodles," said my mother.

"It's unlucky if you don't," added my sister.

"I know. Remember I was born three years before you?"

"Do you know why they are called long-life noodles?"

"Baba, you ask me the same question every year."

"So, but do you know?"

"Yes—it is one long noodle."

"Eat long-life noodles and live forever," smiled my father.

"It's a bag of nonsense." I dismissed my father's homily immediately. "Everyone eats long-life noodles for their birthday, but not everyone has a long life. Maybe I won't either. Maybe I will die tomorrow."

"Don't you talk like that!" Mama was very upset. "If it doesn't work it is because the noodles were not made right."

"I am sorry, Eimin. Can you believe this? My parents are intellectuals, so how can they believe in such superstitions?"

Nevertheless I ate the noodles, and afterwards Eimin brought out a cake, with twenty-three tiny burning candles. My sister and Eimin sang "Happy Birthday." My parents smiled in the candlelight.

I blew out the candles. My mother turned the lights back on. We all had some of the "Western-style" cake.

That night the armed police took someone away from one of the student dormitories a few hundred yards away, sparking fear of a widespread crackdown. The next day, after a long discussion, my parents decided that Beijing was getting too dangerous.

"Wei could come with me to my hometown," said Eimin. "We'd be safer there."

My parents agreed. Mama said, "I will go to the passport office and read the notice board once it opens. Don't worry. We'll contact you as soon as your name shows up on the 'approved list.'"

Nineteen

Good-bye Love

After we say good-bye here, I shall be a lonely leaf
traveling a ten thousand mile journey.

—*Li Bai, eighth century*

On 5 July came the telegram that changed my life: "Your passport is ready for collection. Come home immediately. Mama."

Eimin and I had been staying with his parents, so the telegram was sent to Eimin's father, Professor Xu of Nanjing University. Professor Xu, who had kindly taken me in when I needed a safe shelter, bought me a soft-bed train ticket. At the time there were four types of train ticket: unseated, hard (wooden) seat, soft (cushioned) seat and soft bed, the equivalent of first class. The soft beds were, up till then, only sold to those with certain Party rankings.

"They will give you less trouble in first class," said Eimin's father. "A former student of mine pulled some strings for me."

The good people of the province cared little about rounding up students, but instead concerned themselves with toys for their children, a good harvest, home cooking, cigarettes, rice wine and being able to do a favor for a beloved teacher.

Eimin decided to spend a few more days with his parents and would return to Beijing later.

The next day, when I arrived at the train station, I was greeted by an aging banner, "Celebrating 1 July, rooting out antirevolutionaries!" hanging above the entrance. The Chinese Communist Party's birthday was 1 July. The station was filled with travelers: people carrying large duffel bags, people sitting or standing in long lines. They were waiting so that they could get on the train early and secure a baggage space, or a strategic place in the aisle to sit or stand. People were on the move. Thousands of farmhands were going to the cities to try their luck.

Arrivals and departures were broadcast through loudspeakers, which worsened the already cacophonous noise level. Parents screamed at their children to stay together. People shouted from one end of the platform to the other, hurrying their neighbors along. Beggars hustled for money. Whenever a uniformed railway employee walked by people would set upon him like eagles attacking prey.

The ticket collector came around soon after the train started, and I showed him my ticket and identity card. After lunch, I settled down to read the newspapers that I had brought with me, a local paper and the *People's Daily*. Most articles reported the activities celebrating the Party's birthday, which seemed to have gained special importance this year. Further on in the newspaper, there was news of further roundups of student leaders and reports of heroic acts by ordinary citizens who had exposed students in hiding. One article talked about "the brave citizens of Beijing rebuilding the city after the destruction from the student-led anarchy."

In one of the editorials, the paper praised the Party's decision to strip reformers, such as the party general secretary, Zhao Ziyang, of their posts. No one was surprised by this. The official announcement about Zhao's resignation only confirmed what we had already known. After all, Zhao Ziyang had brought the divisions within the Politburo into the open for the whole world to see, first at his meeting with the Soviet leader Gorbachev, where he revealed that Deng Xiaoping was behind all important government decisions, including those about the student demonstrations, and then when he visited the hunger strikers in Tiananmen Square. Like his predecessor Hu Yaobang, his sympathy toward the students and pro-reform tendencies had led to his downfall.

I arrived at Beijing Central Station which was, if anything, more crowded and chaotic than the station I'd left. I took the number 325 bus home. As the bus zigzagged west across the city, I looked out and saw that Beijing had changed little in the ten days I'd been away. Martial law was still in force, stalls were still shut along the streets and markets were closed. There were no old men playing Chinese chess under the chestnut trees, and people went about their business on bicycles quietly. People's Liberation Army soldiers patrolled the streets holding submachine guns across their chests. Beijing felt very much like a city under siege.

The next day I had to make the same journey again, this time in reverse, from the western district to the city center. I cycled for two hours to Qianmen Street—the Forward Gate Street—to collect my passport. The passport office was only a few blocks away from Tiananmen Square. Here, there were larger PLA patrols as well as more checkpoints. Outside the passport office I met others who were waiting for it to open after lunch. We chatted about where we were going and what we would study abroad.

The government had announced that no one who had participated in the Movement would be allowed to leave China. The notice posted outside the door stated that passports would only be given to those who could bring evidence of their "revolutionary spirit" during the Student Movement, "such as letters from their employer or the local police chief."

I checked the envelope in my handbag. It was from the head of personnel at my work unit testifying that I was not involved with the Movement. Since my files were "hanging" at my father's office, a friend of his had signed the letter. It might seem as if I were getting around the government's requirements easily, but I knew that I was in fact putting both my father and his friend in danger, because if, later on, even after I had left China, the government found out about my involvement with the Movement, they would be able to punish the author of this letter and those who were connected with it.

I did not believe that everyone had my good fortune, that everyone here had a relative in a position to help. But everyone here today must have carried a similar letter. Who were those authors? They must have known the risks they were taking.

While we waited for our passports and discussed our futures, leaning on our bicycles in the welcome shade, a PLA patrol passed by.

Suddenly, we heard a loud bang.

I dropped my bicycle and fell flat on the ground.

A long silent minute passed.

"Anybody shot?" a voice asked. But no one answered.

Everyone lay on the ground for a few minutes longer. The street seemed calm. On the other side, another fifty or so people were lying down too. After a while, nothing else happened, and gradually people got up, looked around and exchanged words with one another. Bicycles moved again. Traffic floated by.

"It was just a tire blowing out," I heard someone explain.

I pulled up my bicycle, checked it was still working, and waited for my heart to settle and my breathing to calm down. We laughed with relief. We knew that martial law troops had shot people on the streets. When my mother visited a friend a couple of days before, he told her that some students at his university had shouted slogans when a military truck passed by. A few minutes later, the truck came back and the soldiers opened fire. Their shots shattered all the windows in one side of the lecture hall, but fortunately no one was hurt.

"The testifying letter." The woman behind the small window above my head sounded bored.

I handed it up to the window. I could not see the expression on her face.

She seemed to be reading the letter. Then she got up, making a great noise with her chair and went away.

"You are all right," she said when she came back, and handed me my passport. Immediately I tucked what looked like a dark brown booklet into my handbag, and rode home as fast as I could.

Three days later, on a bright summer morning, I received a student visa to the USA. As I walked out of the American embassy, it finally dawned on me that I had, in my hand, the ticket to a brand-new life.

My parents borrowed money to pay for my one-way ticket to America, at the end of August. I spent most of my remaining weeks in China saying good-bye to friends and teachers, and preparing for this strange new world I was going to. One day I met up with my oldest friend, Qing, for ice cream. From the shop window, we could see a fully armed soldier guarding the crossing.

"Should we go and make a face at him?" asked Qing, who was always a daredevil.

"So that we can get shot?" I replied.

"So that you won't leave me and go off to America." She made a face at me then, and I laughed with her.

"I promise to keep in touch." I hugged my dear friend.

Eimin and I moved back to Beijing University for the short time between his return from his hometown and my departure for the USA. The university was now a very different place. The campus had become a fortress, full of ghosts. Most students had either left for their summer break or simply left. Dong Yi had not come back. And as the day for my departure grew closer, I became more anxious about him. I started to go to his dormitory regularly, hoping that he would open the door and say, "I just got back. I haven't had time to come and find you." I started writing letters, which I did not know where to post. I had so much that I wanted to tell him, so much that we had not said because we were busy marching, protesting, stopping tanks and hiding. We'd thought that we would have time; we'd thought that words could wait. But time was now running out. And I started to fear that I would not see Dong Yi again.

I spent a lot of time wandering through the campus, aimlessly, feeling empty. I did not look for anyone in particular because I knew that most of my friends had gone away. I simply walked every path and every corner of the campus, again and again, hoping to store the tiniest details in my memory: the smells, the sounds, the colors, the way things felt, the laughter and the pain. Because my memories were the only things that I could take with me.

One humid afternoon, as I was once again wandering through the campus, I found myself in front of the number forty dormitory. I walked into the dark hallway and climbed up the stairs. All the doors were closed. I knocked on Chen Li's door, without much hope of it opening.

I was surprised to see his roommate still there.

"Is Chen Li in?" I asked, fully expecting him to tell me that Chen Li had gone home.

"He has moved to room one hundred and seventeen. You will find him there."

"Why did he move?"

"You'd better ask him." He seemed uncomfortable.

I hurried downstairs. Without catching my breath I knocked on the dark door of room one hundred and seventeen, on the ground floor.

"Who is it?"

"Is that you, Chen Li? It's Wei."

A long silence, a loud noise, as if something had fallen over or was being kicked, then heavy steps, and the door opened.

Standing in front of me was my dear friend Chen Li, as usual wearing a Beijing University T-shirt and a pair of shorts. He smiled kindly as always. But I was stunned by his appearance.

His tall body was resting on a pair of crutches, one leg cut off at the thigh.

"Nice to see you. Please come in." He closed the door and turned around. He tried to walk quickly, but it was obviously difficult. I stretched out my hands behind him, but I did not touch him. I did not know what I should do to help.

An aluminium mug was on the floor. It must have fallen down when he tried to come to the door. He went to pick it up, but I grabbed it and put it on the table.

We sat down. The window was open, but there was no wind. The campus was dead quiet that afternoon.

"I still have to get used to these things." Chen Li leaned the crutches against the bed. He looked calmly over at me, and then explained, "I was run over by a tank near the Golden Water Bridges when the troops came to clear Tiananmen Square."

He then told me that he was in the Square on the morning of 4 June, throwing gasoline canisters at the troops, with a group of students. There were many different groups coming from different directions. They charged toward the troops and armored cars, then the soldiers charged back, capturing several students.

"Some of us ran back wanting to rescue them. There were troops coming from the west as well. There were fires everywhere, and shouting. It was very chaotic and noisy. I must have lost my bearings, when suddenly I turned around and saw this huge tank coming straight at me."

Chen Li's last memory of that fateful morning was of lying on the ground, staring at the tank and trying to roll out of its way. The next day, when he woke up in the hospital, the doctor told him that he was lucky that the tank only drove over one leg, but they had to amputate it. The bones were all crushed to pieces. They kept him in the hospital until there was nothing more they could do and then gave him the crutches.

"People have been kind. This guy gave me his key before he went home." He patted the bed he was sitting on. "It's just not convenient for me to live on the top floor anymore. I don't go out much. My old roommate gets me food from the canteen and hot water from the boiler room. I am OK. The only difficulty I have is going to the public bathhouse. Summer can be so hot in Beijing! I can't stand people staring. Those who know me pity me when they see me struggling; those who don't curse me because I am slow and block their way. Sometimes I hear them say, 'What's a cripple doing in here?'"

He spoke matter-of-factly, as if he had told the same story so many times that it had stopped hurting. He probably had. But I doubted that it had stopped hurting; my doctor once told me that our tolerance for pain increases if we are exposed to it for long enough. We simply get used to it. But it had only been a few weeks for Chen Li.

"It's surprising to see you. I thought everyone had left but me," said Chen Li.

"I left and then came back. Well, it's long story, I won't bore you with it. But I am leaving again and this time for good. I am going to America."

As soon as I said the word "America," I hated myself. I felt lousy, like the time when I was fourteen, and my neighbor told me that they had bought a TV, the first in the block, but I was not invited to watch it.

"Congratulations, Wei," Chen Li said with a broad smile, "I always knew that you would succeed. You are the kind of person who gets everything you want. You deserve it."

I knew that he meant every word he said. But I wondered whether I really deserved it.

Chen Li had no illusions about his future.

"The special economic zone won't want me now—a cripple and politically undesirable. Remember the wall poster I wrote? I don't particularly care much about the future anymore. But I cannot bear to think how devastated my parents will be when they hear about it."

This is Chen Li, I thought, always thinking of others, never himself. If anyone deserved a bright future, it should have been him. Life is not fair, I thought. Then I recalled the voice of Dong Yi saying, "Nobody ever said it was."

Before I left, I went to the campus store and bought plenty of ice cream and Coca-Cola. I wanted to do something for Chen Li even though it seemed rather trivial or downright stupid.

It rained very hard that evening. Sitting in front of the window, I watched the rain coming down. My mind went back to the carefree days I'd spent with Chen Li, walking along the green paths on campus or sipping coffee in the Spoon Garden Bar. I also thought of the day when we marched shoulder-to-shoulder to Tiananmen Square. Looking at the rain, I heard two voices, one telling me to go to Chen Li and help him, another saying exactly the opposite. Could he bear to see me again and be reminded of the joys of the past, or the loss of his future?

I doubted it. I didn't know, but I doubted it.

Every day news came of further crackdowns, arrests and new programs of rooting out participants in the "anarchic" Movement. Students and faculty were required to reflect on their thoughts and actions and to report on other participants. My mother was named and criticized as a student sympathizer by her university. In addition to having to do selfcriticism over and over again at various faculty meetings that followed, she was no longer allowed to supervise students. My mother was devastated. Teaching had been my mother's lifelong dream. When universities were reinstated in 1977, my mother gave up her well paid and much envied position at the Department of Foreign Affairs to become a lecturer. All her friends had advised against the move. But my mother was tired of the political struggles that had been regular features at work. "Wei, teaching is the best profession," I remembered her telling me. "You don't age as fast as you do at the Department because you are always with the young and purer minds." But the strain of self-criticism and the disappointment of not being able to supervise students led, eventually, to my mother taking early retirement. Her dream job had lost much of its allure.

Some employers, including, but not limited to, the Central Party School, which prepared promising Party members for important government positions, and the Beijing Party Youth League, refused to take graduates from Beijing University even though they had been assigned jobs there. Such a move practically destroyed any sensible future for these young students. There were also reports of Beijing students being beaten up by local thugs in the provinces, and people started to fear that punishments and arrests would spread beyond the key participants of the Movement. Rumors were rampant about who was being picked up: Like the millions who had lived through the Cultural Revolution, my parents knew only too well the horror of political revenge and were very worried about me.

One day, I went to the sales office of Air China to check whether I could take an earlier flight to the USA. Some of my friends had left China earlier than planned and advised me to do the same. I came back and told Eimin that I was to leave for New York the next day. Then I went home to my parents.

That evening in the living room of my parents" apartment we packed for my long trip away. My parents had bought me two new suitcases for the journey. My father did most of the packing as he tried to stack as much as possible into the suitcases: books, clothes for all seasons, towels, blankets, soup bowls, spoons, chopsticks . . . Mama was running around bringing the items, stopping every now and then and saying, "Does she need this?" or "Don't pack so tightly, it'll be too heavy for her to carry."

My sister helped us for the first two hours of packing, and then went to bed.

"I'll see you tomorrow morning," she said as she wished me goodnight.

My parents did not ask me how long I would be gone, though I knew as well as they did that it would be years before I would see them again. We were still sorting through things and packing when the evening turned into night, and when the night turned into early morning. My parents told me to go to bed. "Get a good night's sleep, you have a long journey tomorrow. We will finish packing for you."

Then, with great solemnity, they handed me forty dollars. "Your Baba wrote to your uncle in Hong Kong when you got the scholarship and asked if he could borrow this money. You should have some cash with you when you arrive there. Make sure you put it in a safe place and remember to pay it back as soon as you can." (I had Ning's check for $1,000 but it was not cash and I was not sure whether to use the money.)

I took the money and thanked my parents. At that moment, I realized that they had turned gray in just a short few months. In their eyes, I could see the love they had for each other, and for their children, and the hardship and worry they had endured for me for the last twenty-three years. These feelings were unspoken yet abundant. Now that I was leaving them for a new world that neither they nor I knew much about, which felt as if it were as far away as the edge of the sky, I wondered how much more of a burden I would be to them.

On 2 August 1989, my parents and my sister, Eimin and I arrived at Beijing International Airport. Since only departing passengers were allowed into the check-in area, we said farewell in the departure hall.

Eimin said good-bye first.

"Call me at my office as soon as you get in."

"Of course. I will start the paperwork immediately so that you can come to America."

"Good," said Eimin.

"You take care of yourself and write often," said my father.

"Just write to our parents, they will let me know what has been going on with you," my sister told me. "I can read your letters when I am home for school breaks."

My mother, who had managed to control her emotions so as not to affect mine in the last few days, was now visibly shaking. It seemed as if she'd just realized that there were only a few minutes left for all the things she'd meant to say to me, and that she had a lifetime's love that she wanted to give me. She started to talk about how I was going to cope with a new country and a new way of life.

"Take care, don't walk alone at night. There are a lot of crimes in America . . . If you don't like it there, just come home . . . Xiao Xiao's sister is also studying at the same college. Remember that I gave you her phone number? Give her a call when you get there . . . don't get lost in the airport . . ."

"Don't worry, Mama, everything is going to be fine." I tried to reassure her, though deep down I had no idea what my life would be like from that moment on.

"You'd better go now." Baba nodded at me. I could tell that he was more worried about my mother.

"Good-bye, love." Mama hugged me. She kept her head turned away so that I would not see her tears.

I hugged my sister and Eimin, shook hands with Baba and said good-bye. I walked through the door in the glass partition that separates those who are leaving from those who are staying behind. Once checked in, I took my suitcases through a gate marked "the point of no return" to the conveyor belt. Then I came back to the gate and saw my family still standing in the same place; I waved at them with a big smile and they waved back.

As I turned around, tears streamed down my face. I kept on walking, away from my husband, away from my aging parents, who had raised me through thick and thin, and away from my little sister, whom I loved but felt I did not really know because I had left home for boarding school when she was only nine years old.

I kept on walking, away from the only country that I had ever known and the only life I had ever had. I was about to take the first airplane flight I'd ever taken, and all I could think of was that, from now on, my days would be filled with lonely, homesick dreams.

Twenty

America

Fate comes, it cannot be sought.

—*Zhang Joling, seventh century*

Two days later, I stood on the campus of the College of William and Mary, in Virginia, feeling as if I had just entered somewhere as vast and peaceful as the evening sky on a midsummer night. In front of me, newly cut lawns rolled undisturbed toward a line of delicate two-story redbrick buildings. The lawns had just been watered, and the drops of water glistened in the sunshine on the moist green grass.

The campus had no surrounding walls. There was no one to watch over my shoulders, or eavesdrop on my conversation. There were no deadly whispers in the air. If I had shouted, there would not have been an echo. If I had thrown my hands in the air and danced across the lawn, no eyes would be there to judge me. I was finally free.

I had arrived unexpectedly early for the upcoming academic year, so my department chair, Professor Herbert, and his wife welcomed me into their home while I waited for the graduate student housing to open, two weeks later. The Herberts lived in an old brown house that nestled in deep woods, with wild gooseberry bushes growing along the driveway. Mrs. Herbert was a kind woman in her mid-fifties, who cooked casseroles and, to me, new Western delicacies in her warm kitchen. After dinner, Professor Herbert normally went up to his study to finish whatever work was left from the day. Mrs. Herbert and I would clear away the dishes, load the dishwasher and then sit down at the dining table to talk about our lives. Mrs. Herbert did most of the talking, showing me photos of her children and telling stories of their childhood and her visits to her now grown-up son and daughter. I did not understand most of what she was saying, except for a few words such as "daughter," "work," "Washington, D.C.," "boyfriend" and "sports car." For most of the time, I simply smiled. I showed her the handful of pictures of my family that I'd brought with me, trying, with great difficulty, to explain who they were and what they did for a living. When I couldn't find the right words, I tried gestures.

After our chat, I would go back to their daughter's old room on the first floor, where I slept. The photos of their teenage girl and her friends on the walls showed me the infinite freedom and beauty she'd grown up with, which, though pleasing to see, often made me feel terribly lonely. I was reminded, every moment, and in no uncertain terms, that I was in a foreign land, about which I had no real under-standing—all I'd imagined had proved completely inadequate or mis-taken. But the kindness of Mrs Herbert reminded me of my mother, who was of a similar age and gentleness. In my mind, I could still see my parents" small apartment and feel the love that overflowed in that tiny place. I laid out the photos of my family that I had shown Mrs Herbert and cried. I missed home and wanted to go back. I felt as if I were a newborn baby who wished to return to the warmth, certainty and nurturing of her mother's womb.

I wrote many letters in those days: to my parents saying that I wanted to go home and to my husband Eimin, begging him to come to the U.S. as quickly as he could. In those long evenings, I also thought about Dong Yi, wondering where he was. Sometimes I imagined him in domestic bliss, preparing for the arrival of his first child, while at other times I feared horrible things. I remembered visiting a prison once, two years before, when I was writing an article on criminal psychology for the university newspaper. When we arrived, prisoners lined up in the court-yard and sang revolutionary songs. The inmates we interviewed told us how they had benefited and learned through hard labor. They said that they had repented their crimes against the people and wanted to repay society by working hard. I imagined Dong Yi as one of them, dressed in ill-fitting prison clothing, his head shaved. My thoughts frightened me.

I wrote to him, addressing the envelope to the Physics Department at Beijing University, the only place I could think of to send the letter. I told Dong Yi about my marriage to Eimin, saying that it was the only possible step for me, as we both knew, and the best for everyone.

"In life, so often we can't get what we want, but at least I know that I am loved. Being loved is always better than being alone—much more so now that I am living a lonely existence in America," I told him in the letter. "But I do regret, especially now that I am thousands of miles away and do not know when or whether we will see each other again, that I did not tell you the truth earlier. Time was always ticking by when we needed it to stop, and now it seems to have stopped, and yet you are not here to listen. I feel that I cheated and lied, though neither was my intention. Will you forgive me? I hope you will. There's no use in either of us blaming the other for the things we did and didn't do."

But I did not receive a reply. Two months later, I wrote again. Dong Yi never wrote back. In the meantime, life went by quickly. My class had only eight girls, so we studied together, partied together, traveled to conferences together, like sisters. My English improved rapidly and soon I was able to stop tape-recording the lectures. I went to my first Halloween party at the end of October, dressed in my roommate Ellen's cat outfit, and danced with my many friends. The next month, Ellen invited me to her parents' home in Washington DC for Thanksgiving.

So as the Autumn term drew to an end, and Christmas was just around the corner, I found myself among many kind friends and was lonely no more. Having survived my first six months in America also helped me discover an inner strength that I didn't know I had. I realized that I could fend for myself and that I did not need anyone to rescue or protect me. Such insights opened my eyes and I saw for the first time the truth behind my marriage to Eimin—I had been afraid, as I had always been, of being on my own, especially with the prospect of a dangerous and unfamiliar world abroad. I was also afraid of rejection; I had led an isolated and lonely life for a long time and knew what it felt like. But now I looked again inside my heart and could not find the love I had felt before, for Eimin. Perhaps it had never really been there; perhaps I had confused it with something else, like reliability, always being there and never letting me down. These were Eimin's virtues, which I had thought were the foundations of our love. But now I realized they were simply substitutes.

So when Eimin called one day to say that the paperwork—that I'd sent him during my first month in America—had gone through and that he was coming just in time for Christmas, I panicked. I wanted more time to think things through and make my decision. I was surprised by the way events had suddenly sped up, as if Eimin had realized he must move quickly. I had recently hinted at the change in my feelings toward him in my letters, but knowing how much he wanted to leave China, it didn't feel right to stop him from coming. He deserves at least this much, I told myself. I blamed myself for this marriage that increasingly feels like a big mistake. I was young and confused.

But I did not want to see him, not yet, not before I knew what to say to him. So for the time being I asked Eimin to go to one of his many friends who had come to America via England. Believing that it was not an unreasonable request and with Eimin being such a sensible person, I made no preparations for his arrival and so I was completely caught out when he showed up at the Department with his luggage.

That night, after Ellen had gone to bed, we had a big fight.

"How could you even think of asking me to stay with a friend? What would they say?" exclaimed Eimin.

"I didn't know you cared so much about appearances!" I retorted bitterly.

"What do you want, to get married again? Are you in love with someone here?" Eimin stared at me.

"No." I hadn't the time to think through what I wanted. All I asked for was a little time, but he wasn't going to give me that.

I realized that there was nothing to do now but find a small apartment together, stretching the 600 dollars I received from my scholarship every month. Eimin had come as my dependant; nothing could be done until he found a job.

So I dropped my arguments. I don't know whether Eimin thought the crisis was over or simply chose to ignore it, but he was soon high-spirited as we made arrangements to be in Boston for Christmas. It was my first experience of Christmas. I was mesmerized by the lights that lit up the city, and felt lost in the crowded downtown shopping area. Snow was everywhere and so were people singing Christmas carols. It felt as if I had arrived in a wonderland.

We stayed with his friend Wang Baoyuan, who was at MIT. At

night, other friends, all men around Eimin's age, came to the rent-controlled apartment high above the Charles River.

"Yes, he is here, in America," shouted Wang Baoyuan into the phone. "When can you come? Come straight away, you ought to meet his beautiful young wife too."

They came, drank beer, smoked, laughed, shouted, got hot and opened the windows. They talked about old times, and old friends and acquaintances. They talked a lot about marriage and women, especially to Chinese women living in America. These were the same kind of people as Eimin, who had lived through the harshness of the Cultural Revolution. They had kept to themselves in the UK and America, but were proud of knowing much about Western culture and loved to share their perceptions of their new country with me. They were traditional Chinese men, despite having lived overseas for many years, and they held firmly onto their values from the past. Eimin belonged with these men, and I soon realized that he was much more of a traditional Chinese man than I had ever been a traditional Chinese woman. I became painfully aware of how little I knew the man I had married.

That night, whenever I looked at Eimin, he was beaming with triumph. His friends, many of whom were still single, envied him. I remembered him telling me, on one of the rare occasions he opened up, that when he graduated from the University of Edinburgh he had tried to find a job in the UK or the USA without success. He felt inferior because he had failed, unlike most of his friends, to stay in the West. But now all that had changed.

Watching Eimin, Dong Yi's words surfaced in my mind: "Eimin is not your happiness."

Why had it taken me so long to realize it?

After everyone had left, Eimin and I sat on the floor with our host, watching videotapes of Western news reports of the Tiananmen Massacre.

"You don't get to see any of these in China," said Wang Baoyuan confidently.

In Beijing, I had heard about the killings. My friends, and eyewitnesses, had told me. But I hadn't seen any images of the killings as they actually happened: the crushed bodies and the bloody streets littered with corpses. I saw these images only after I came to America; and they spoke so profoundly of the horror and sorrow that I cried, just as I had the first time I heard about the killings on the cold morning of 4 June, or when I listened to the accounts of the grieving doctor and saw the body of the dead student being lowered from the truck, or when I took the bullet shell from Dong Yi's hand. Since then, I had often seen the famous footage of the young man moving again and again into the path of the tanks. And every time, I thought of Chen Li and what had happened to him.

"Did you take part?" asked Wang Baoyuan.

"Yes, of course," replied Eimin proudly. "We went to the Square a lot."

"Maybe you will see yourself here." Wang Baoyuan seemed impressed.

I fixed my eyes on the TV screen, but my mind had wandered off, to the night Dong Yi had told me about, on Muxudi Street, the dying girl in his arms, the bullet shell in the palm of his hand as he told me, and his voice saying, "I will never forget." I wondered where Dong Yi was now. The year was about to end, and a new year, 1990, was about to arrive. I wondered what he would be doing in the new year and the new decade.

Three days later, we went to the New Year's Eve dance organized by the Boston Association of Chinese Students and Scholars. Eimin sat at the table with his friends, smiling and chatting. I had many invitations and danced nonstop. But although I twirled around the ballroom, my heart and my mind were elsewhere. The only reality for me that night was another night, a moonless night by the side of Weiming Lake when time ticked away and I had not said how I felt when I had the chance.

How young I am, I thought, as I danced. How many years of life with Eimin are there ahead of me? I felt my future like a weight bearing down on me, crushing me. I felt as if I were dying.

As soon as we got back to the College of William and Mary, I began applying for PhD programs elsewhere. Though I still had a year left on my current master's program in psychology, I decided to move. I had to get away. By March 1990, I was accepted at Carnegie Mellon University for a PhD program in business studies, and by May I was moving to Pittsburgh.

Eimin had found a job in Virginia, and he made no objection to my leaving. We were as civil and reasonable as two friends bidding good-bye. On one of my last nights in Virginia, we watched TV in our small apartment. Most of my things had been packed in suitcases and boxes. Suddenly there was a newsflash, reporting the successful escape of Chai Ling to Paris, where she emerged to speak to the media. After the government crackdown on the activists of the Student Democracy Movement, Chai Ling and her husband had gone underground. Over the next year they had managed to evade the Chinese government, moving from province to province, hidden by sympathetic citizens.

Three days later, Chai Ling and her husband arrived in the U.S. A welcome rally was taking place for her in Washington D.C.

I made a stop there on my way to Pittsburgh. In the park, a podium was set up under a huge banner that proclaimed: "Welcome Chai Ling to America!" Over a thousand Chinese students and supporters had gathered to greet her.

While I waited with all the other people for Chai Ling to appear, I breathed in the sweet scent of the grass and the trees. For the past year, I had felt like a small boat pushed out to sea, drifting without anchor or destination. I missed those days when my life had a higher purpose— when I felt part of the struggle for a better tomorrow for China—and I missed sharing such purpose with people I respected, people of my generation. Standing there in the bright sunshine, surrounded by a thousand like-minded Chinese people, I felt again that sense of unity, that sense of purpose. I looked around; everything here—the air, the land and the sky—seemed neat and peaceful, and nothing could ever ruin it. There were no dangers here, nothing anyone need fear. How far we'd all come from those times in China.

Then I saw Chai Ling, a small figure surrounded by a group. She was wearing a floral dress, and her hair, tied at the back, was longer than I'd known her to wear it.

An American lady walked up to the microphone to introduce Chai Ling. "Ladies and gentlemen, supporters of China's Democracy Movement, we have come here today to welcome a brave young lady whose struggle symbolizes the courage of the people of China." For the media gathered at the front, she continued, "Ms. Chai Ling was one of the best-known student leaders of the 1989 Democracy Movement in China. She was the Commander in Chief of Tiananmen Square and one of the Movement's leaders most wanted by the Chinese government. Following the bloody crackdown on 4 June, she was forced into hiding. After a long year underground, Ms. Chai Ling and her husband, Feng Congde, finally escaped from China."

She then gestured across at Chai Ling and said, "Now I am delighted to give you the Nobel Peace Prize nominee, Ms. Chai Ling."

The crowd broke into loud applause. Chai Ling moved slowly to the microphone, visibly fragile. She began to speak in that high-pitched voice that I knew so well, but her voice was so weak that I could hardly hear the end of each of her sentences. Knowing how she used to be, I realized that she was not well. Her skin lacked color and she was much too thin. I could only guess at the conditions and daily pressures she had had to live under for the past year.

"Thank you for coming today. I am touched by your support." Chai Ling talked briefly about 4 June, the Student Movement and her year underground. She thanked those who had risked their lives to help her during the dark underground days. But her speech was short. From where I stood, about 100 yards from the podium, I could see clearly that my friend was exhausted.

Her husband also thanked the audience for their support, but did not give a speech. The blonde lady then came to the microphone again. "Ms. Chai Ling is very tired. She is still recovering from her ordeal in China."

I had hoped to be able to talk to her, or at least to say hello, and was therefore disappointed when she was immediately rushed away. The same year, 1990, Chai Ling was again nominated for the Nobel Peace Prize. In 1992, she and Feng Congde divorced, citing the year underground, and the strains it had put on their relationship, as the reason for the collapse of their marriage.

Pittsburgh fulfilled the promise of a happy new beginning. I loved my new program, and my professors were extremely kind and encouraging. At first I still made trips back to Virginia, trying to work things out with Eimin. But with each meeting, the little tenderness that was left in our relationship slipped away, and it soon became clear to both of us that the marriage was beyond repair. Eimin and I divorced. In 1994 I graduated and became a professor, teaching management at the

University of Minnesota. And all this time, the thought of Dong Yi was never far from my mind. I often wondered where he was and why he never contacted me. But little by little, as my life took a new direction, these thoughts appeared less and less frequently. Gradually, my thoughts of Dong Yi became more abstract, like ideas from a book, or half-remembered conversations about missed chances and the inevitability of things. My life in China drifted further and further into the background, becoming something that had happened long ago in a faraway land. My daily reality was my assimilation into American society, and beginning a successful academic career. A new world was gradually opening up and I found a circle of friends, from all over the world, whose company I enjoyed. Through an Italian friend of mine, I met the man who became my second husband. We were married in 1995.

In the spring of 1996, the dean of the People's University, one of Beijing's major universities, visited the University of Minnesota, where I had been teaching for two years, and invited me to teach their first-ever MBA program. To fit into my teaching schedule in the U.S., my hosts compressed the fourteen-week course into just one month, with frequent lectures. So, in May 1996, I returned to Beijing for the first time since the demonstrations at Tiananmen Square.

Twenty-one

Homecoming

*Where are you now, my old friend? Freezing windows,
lingering dreams, I remember the path we used to
walk together.*

—Zhang Yan, eighth century

As soon as I landed in Beijing, I was reminded of how much I had forgotten about the way of life in China. I had become used to sitting on our back porch in Minnesota and watching birds landing on the marsh. I had taken for granted the reflection of the sunset on my white marble bath while I read a much-talked-about new novel, with a glass of Merlot at my side, and my husband working on his computer in the study. Details of my past life had begun to fade: my parents' expressions, their apartment, the roads to school, the pagoda at Weiming Lake, Dong Yi's shy smile . . .

Every morning of my visit, my father went to the farmer's market and returned with local gourmet specialities. The sweet aroma of steamed buns, fried breadsticks and soybean milk brought back many lost memories of my childhood. I watched my parents working busily around the kitchen, their hair white and their movements fragile, their faces, though, alive with happiness. I felt guilty. They could have had seven years of such happiness, simply being with their child. I had robbed them of that, I had left them alone to their dark apartment and a life of toil. There is an old Chinese saying: "A mother's worries follow her daughter's thousand-mile journey." All those worries had turned into deep wrinkles on my mother's face.

As soon as my jet lag settled down, I called the Psychology Department. I had not been back to China for a long time and didn't know when I would be back again. I felt an urge to plunge back into my old life. I wondered how much I had forgotten.

To my delight I found out that Li was still there, now a senior lecturer. She was surprised to learn that I was in Beijing. "You have not been back since 1989, have you? Come on Friday, I've only a clinic to run. I can't wait to see you. Have you changed much, Wei?"

"Not much. But then you will see for yourself. I may be wrong." Li would be a better judge than me of how much I had changed, I thought.

The taxi dropped me off at the west gate. I paid the driver, and walked into the bright summer sunshine. Hundreds of people were rushing toward the butterfly-roofed gate on their bicycles, ringing bells, the collective din much louder than I remembered. Some got off their bikes when they neared the uniformed guard, but most simply slowed down without stopping.

I was told that university guards only became a formal institution after the Student Democracy Movement in 1989. Restricting the movement of people seemed to have emerged as the key to stability; it did not seem to bother anyone that freedom had been sacrificed in the name of such stability. After living freely for seven years, I found I could not tolerate or pass by a guard without feeling angry. This must have made me more conspicuous.

"Where are you going? Who do you want to see?" Naturally the guard stopped me. When I said that I was going to see a friend, I was led into the guard's house and asked to fill out a form and show my Identity Card. Not having one, I gave him my Minnesota driver's licence, which only made things worse.

"You said your name was Wei. But what is this on the card?"

"My English name." Like many Chinese living in the West, I had taken up an English name after I moved to the U.S., to ease communication. "You said that your friend works in the Psychology Department and that you are a graduate of the same department, but you don't know where the department office is."

"No, I have forgotten. I have been away for seven years. Besides I am not meeting her there. She is at her clinic today."

So they called the university hospital. Li was paged. She confirmed my identity on the phone and said that she was expecting me.

"But you have to come here to pick her up. We need you to sign the entrance book."

A quarter of an hour later, Li appeared. She looked exactly as I remembered her. Her long hair was tied into a ponytail. Her face, without a trace of makeup, showed patches of freckles. She looked twenty-five still. I even recognized the blue-purple floral top she was wearing.

"My dear Wei." She held my hand as we walked out of the guard's house. "It is so nice to see you. But I should have thought of this before. Close to 4 June security gets very tight."

We followed a small stream to the Spoon Garden and then made a turn onto the leafy path outside the English Hall. Bicycles shimmering in the golden sunshine were lined up neatly along rails at the entrance, while the loud chanting of English words and sentences came out of the open windows.

The university hospital was a two-story building of traditional Chinese architecture, its roof curved with the four corners pointing upwards. A wide entrance sat right in the middle of the symmetrical building. Li's office was on the first floor with a view over the building site at the bottom of the small hill across the road.

"You too are a psychologist," said my friend. "I will tell my patients that you are here to observe my sessions. They usually don't object."

I sat while she finished seeing her patients, asking them questions, such as when did they first start to experience delusions or hear voices in their heads. She then prescribed advice and drugs. Her voice was remote and dry. She analyzed without involvement.

Watching Li made me realize that perhaps we could age without adding wrinkles to our face or gaining weight. At one moment I was watching my old friend, but at another, just as she turned her head slightly and spoke monotonously, I saw a tired middle-aged woman who seemed to have become indifferent to life, like the stone statues of gods in a temple.

Seven years before, I had watched her, in tears, running to the student radio station on the morning of 4 June. I had tears in my eyes too, then. But seven years is a long time. I had not cried for a long time. I did not need to feel sad anymore, at least not for me nor for my close friends. I lived a life of comfort and tranquillity in America. But now I had returned, I found the memories of myself as a hot-blooded girl of twenty-two returning. I had left my youth and those momentous days, deep-frozen in China. Now that I had come back I found myself remembering my youthful, passionate and brave self. But was that really me? Was it ever me?

A few times, I caught Li's eyes glancing back in my direction. What did she see? Did I seem as changed to her as she seemed to me?

We had lunch at the number five student canteen and then walked toward the Triangle. The sky was wide and clear, not a trace of clouds. Boys in pressed shorts and girls in floral dresses strolled toward their dormitories for an afternoon nap. Soft winds blew gentle gusts of warm air past us.

"I am married now," Li told me. "You probably remember him, Xiao Zhang. After June 4th he was sent back to his hometown." June 4th is the way the Chinese refer to the Student Democracy Movement of 1989. Li told me that they had married four years before and her husband had since moved to Beijing and was now working in a private company.

I asked whether she had been in any trouble with the authorities after 4 June.

"Not for long. As you know, everyone at Beijing University was considered equally guilty or sympathetic. All I had to do was to attend study sessions." Li told me that they read newspaper articles and Party communiqués at these meetings, and then, under the supervision of the Department Party Secretary, reflected upon the readings and discussed what they had learned.

"But some people, such as the young lecturers who openly supported the hunger strikers, had to write self-criticism," she continued. "Most of them are gone now. Some lost their jobs. Others left after being repeatedly passed over for promotion."

"Worse things happened to the students," Li sighed. "All undergraduate students at Beijing University have to do military training now. So, before they can start their four years of university, they have to do a year at military training camps."

I could not believe what I'd just heard. "But why? They haven't done anything. They weren't even at the university when June 4th happened."

"It's ... 'preventative,'" she said.

I began to get angry, and wondered why some people are so afraid of the power of the mind and of thought. Why did they think that sending the brightest young people in China to military training camps would be good for them, or for the country? How silly, I thought. And I also considered that some people just don't understand that the journey of the mind is never deterred by physical hardship. In fact, probably, just the opposite. The more people suffer, the more they search for answers. My heart felt the weight of a profound sadness. Camps and mass rehabilitations had been the trademark of the Cultural Revolution. Now, twenty-five years after it had ended, people were still being marched to these camps to be "educated."

Li then told me that the year before, the government had reversed the policy, "but not for Beijing University." She continued, "Beijing University is still regarded as a fertile ground for democratic ideas—the most dangerous place in the country." Her voice revealed a trace of pride, which in turn infected me.

Presently we cut across the Triangle and stopped in front of the Young Faculty Building.

"You still live in here?" I was surprised and also startled to have stopped outside my old home with Eimin. Suddenly memories of that tiny room at the corner resurfaced. I looked up to the first-floor corner window and saw floral print curtains draped on both sides. I wondered who lived there now.

"I'm still in the same room. Now instead of a roommate, I have a husband." Li's words pulled my thoughts back. We both laughed.

"You can understand why we are so desperately looking forward to the completion of the new faculty residence." Li spoke earnestly.

I said good-bye to Li outside the building and made my way to Weiming Lake. I took the path behind the Biology building and went up the hill. A light breeze flitted through the bushes along the shady path. As I turned left onto the wide road, the path began to go down steeply and white aspen trees gave way to clear green water. The lake was as tranquil and beautiful as when I had left it. Long willow branches tipped over the water, framing the view of the traditional

Chinese pagoda at the east end. Young girls passed by in colorful long silk skirts, boys carried their bags.

As I got closer, my steps slowed, my breath became heavier and my heartbeat soared. I had to sit down. This was where we used to meet. Though the rocky bank had not changed at all, almost everything else in my life had altered beyond recognition.

Sitting under the weeping willow, I watched the white stone bridge in the distance, thinking about my old life—the leisurely walks around the lake, the starry skies on summer nights, the poems read while the moon was reflected perfectly in the water. A breeze came from the hills behind, sending lazy waves across the lake. At that very moment, my quiet thoughts of the past were disturbed by a startling notion— what if it had worked out for Dong Yi and me? How would my life be now? Would I still be sitting here today, feeling the same nostalgia?

I returned to my parents' apartment just before dinner. The fan was on. My mother was sitting in the corner, in the shade. A few strands of her hair were blowing in the breeze. As soon as I walked in, I knew something was wrong, her face was as white as paper.

"What's the matter?" I asked.

"Yang Tao just left. He came to see you."

Yang Tao was the diplomat I had dated at university.

"How did he find out that I am back in Beijing?"

"I told him. I called him to ask for your diaries back."

"My diaries? What are you talking about?"

"You remember, I told you that he came back, in September 1989, on leave from the embassy, hoping to persuade you not to go to America. But you had already gone. When he left, he took all your diaries."

I did remember. And I remembered how furious I had been when my mother told me. Those diaries were mine. They were private.

"I've never understood why you let him take them," I said, feeling something of my original fury.

"What could we do? How could we stop a strong young man over six feet tall?"

"Is he coming back?" I asked.

"He said that he would come again. He wants to find you."

My mother suddenly started to cry.

"I did not tell you because your Baba and I did not want you to worry, but he has been here many times in the past years, always wanting your address and phone number. He said that as soon as he got a chance, he would go to America to find you. Old Zhang told me that he had just come back a couple of months ago after a long assignment overseas, so I called him at the Department of Foreign Affairs. But how did things get to this point? I always told you to love carefully. Now you understand, don't you?"

I felt sorry for my mother, she had seen too much sadness. I had again unknowingly added more pain to her troubled life.

"If he comes again, tell him I don't ever want to see him again."

I patted my mother on her shoulder and went into my room. Only then did I catch sight of my father, standing silently in the dark kitchen, his face expressionless.

I shut the door behind me. I was angry and sad. I wanted to fly back to the other side of the ocean where my life was free.

It was getting dark outside. Lying with my hands folded beneath my head, I wondered why Yang Tao had come today. For eight years, I had wanted nothing to do with him. Surely he must have known, because my parents told him so every time he came to see them. The gold necklace he brought when he came to ask me to stay in China still sat on the bookcase in the living room.

I thought about my diaries. I had kept a diary from the time I was sixteen to the time I left university. Six years of my life, all my private thoughts and emotions, were detailed in those diaries. The thought of them in the hands of Yang Tao made me sick.

My father knocked on the door to say dinner was ready. I drew the curtain and looked into the small mirror on the desk, my eyes burning with anger and fury. I could see the traces of my tears, so I wiped my face quickly with my hands and swept the loose hair back from my face.

My parents were waiting for me at the dinner table. They were worried and old. I sat down and said to them, "Forget about those diaries. I don't want them back."

I had caused enough trouble for them. What use to them—and what use to me—was my old life?

Twenty-two

Cousin

It's better not to pursue a past that has already been lost.

—*Zhang Liangnang, ninth century*

We ate dinner in silence, except for the occasional "pass me the chilli sauce," or "the teapot, please." I had forgotten about the silent moments like these, so typical of life in China. My coming home was supposed to be a happy occasion; like the ancient saying, "returning home in glorious clothing," it was supposed to bring joy and pride to my aging parents. But I had also brought with me the ghosts of my past.

After dinner, I went straight to my room to prepare for the next day's lecture. Just as I was finishing, my mother came in and laid a piece of paper on my desk.

"Dong Yi's cousin, Hu Anan, is in Beijing," she said. "Here is her phone number if you are interested." My mother spoke quickly and without emotion, as if it were something as simple or insignificant as the phone number of the dry cleaner or the time the taxi would arrive in the morning to take me to the People's University.

I did not hear my mother leave, nor did I see the door close behind her. I was in a space all to myself, cocooned. In front of me, on the desk, lay the key to the way through this space, through the walls of the cocoon to him, and the part of my past that was, once more, vividly resurrected in my memory.

What was my mother's intention? She had called Yang Tao for my diaries and now she had given me the phone number of Dong Yi's cousin. I thought about it for a while and then understood that, for all these years, she had been the guardian of the part of my life that I had left behind here. Perhaps she had waited, every year, for me to come back, so that she could hand me the few loose ends and say, "They are all still here." My old life was all my parents had. They had found the missing pieces and repaired the worn spots. They couldn't do much for me in my new life, so they had taken to repairing the one that I had left behind.

As the anniversary of 4 June approached, the heightening tension became palpable. The guards at Beijing University were stopping and questioning more people at the entrances and, to deter any attempts at commemorating the anniversary, the government began implementing its annual arrests of activists for the duration of the 4 June period. All public gatherings were banned, security was increased in Tiananmen Square and the public were kept away. Articles condemning the 1989 Student Democracy Movement appeared in all the major newspapers such as the *People's Daily*, the *Beijing Daily* and the *Beijing Youth Daily*. In public, people were more careful about what they said. It was therefore not surprising to sense an edginess on the streets when I went to the restaurant to meet Hu Anan.

It turned out that my mother had met her by chance a year before, at the home of a college friend of hers who was a senior editor at the Beijing Press. Hu Anan was his personal assistant. For days I had hesitated about calling her, unsure whether it was a good idea to venture into the past. Perhaps it was better to let it lie, I thought, fearing the pain and anguish it might arouse. But such wavering was dismissed, again and again, by my intense desire to know what had happened to him, all those years before. That telephone number was fate giving me an opportunity, just as fate had taken an opportunity away some years earlier. I couldn't walk away, no matter how much I tried to convince myself that I could. The moonless night at Weiming Lake came back to me again. Again, I heard time ticking away. My stay in China was short; I would soon travel to the other side of the ocean, back to my new life. So I called her.

Hu Anan barely resembled Dong Yi. Short and stocky, she had inherited some of the same family features, but unfortunately those features had been arranged in such a way that her face was completely plain. Although she had been working in Beijing for almost ten years, she seemed ill at ease in her adopted city. Confidence only took control when we stepped into the restaurant that she had picked for our meeting—a small but authentic Cantonese restaurant tucked away in an alley behind a big hotel. It seemed that the restaurant was a meeting place for Cantonese living in Beijing, as most of the customers and staff spoke only Cantonese. Immediately I felt that I had stepped into an alien world. I understood nothing. There are more than forty different dialects in China, most of them, including Cantonese, incomprehensible to someone like me who speaks Mandarin. Luckily, because of the unification of China, we share the same written language and can communicate in writing if necessary.

But sometimes even the written words can be meaningless, as they were on the menu I was given. I could only imagine what might be in some of the dishes which had names like "Pearl in Palm," "Dragon in Phoenix's Cloth," "Oil Cracking Twice," and "Corpse Returned to Life." The list included over a hundred dishes. Seeing me struggling with the menu, the cousin offered to do the ordering.

"By the way, how do you like snakes?"

"I am terrified of them."

"Then don't move. There is one right behind you."

The hairs on the back of my neck stood up. I froze.

Minutes later, the cousin said, "It's OK. The manager is taking it away now."

A man passed our table with a plastic bag. Something rustled inside.

"It's customary for customers to approve the snake before it gets cooked."

I knew that snake was a delicacy in Cantonese cooking, but I did not know that they brought live snakes to the table, just as if they were bottles of wine, for the customer's approval.

For the rest of that meal I had an uneasy feeling, and whenever someone passed by me with a plastic bag, my heart jumped.

I asked the cousin to tell me what she knew of Dong Yi, where he'd been hiding all these years.

"You know, it is so interesting that we are sitting here talking about him, while he is in the U.S. He has lived there for years," she said, picking at a steamed fish.

I was speechless. The shock of this simple statement bit into me. I was surprised and then angry. I had thought about him for so long and wondered what had become of him; I had imagined how he might have lived his life in China. Yet he had been so close to me all these years. We had probably watched the same TV programs, been to the same cities and visited the same landmarks. Why hadn't he tried to contact me?

"Do you know that he had a daughter?"

"No. But I knew that his wife was pregnant."

"She was not yet two when Dong Yi left. It was hard for the little girl."

"His family did not go with him?" I wondered then if he had left everything else behind as he had once intended to do.

"No. It was all terribly difficult. You see, Lan raised the little girl alone in Shanxi. Dong Yi's parents moved back to Guangdong. It had taken my uncle so many years to get permission to go home so, when it came, not moving was out of the question. It must have been difficult for her, given the troubles she had with her parents and her own health. Did you ever meet Lan? She was the kind of woman who looked as if a gust of wind would simply blow her over."

Was she? That wasn't how I remembered her. I wondered why everyone thought of her as being weak.

"Why didn't she go with Dong Yi?" I asked.

"Well, at first her work unit wouldn't let her. Then there was some sort of problem between her and Dong Yi. Then she couldn't get the visa."

"What happened in the end?"

"Eventually they got out. Three years ago Dong Yi moved to Princeton. His new position must have helped—Dong Yi is a scientist in a famous lab there."

So all had ended well. I wasn't surprised. It was just like Dong Yi. I knew he could never hurt the people he loved.

"Is that where he is now?" I asked calmly. The knowledge that he was with Lan and their daughter felt like a relief and a reassurance.

Though, in the past years, I had speculated on many different endings, I was happy to hear that his world was not in fact destroyed.

"Yes. This is the address of his lab, and the phone number. In fact he came back to see his parents last year. But I didn't see him. My father died two years ago; I don't go back to Guangdong anymore."

"I am sorry."

"It's all right. He died of old age. There was little pain at the end."

"And your mother? Does she live with you in Beijing?"

"My mother died in the Cultural Revolution. She drowned herself. I was very young and did not understand. I hated her for a long time. I thought that she must not have loved me. When I was older my father told me that she was tortured badly and couldn't stand the pain anymore."

I didn't know what to say. What do you say to someone when they tell you things like that over lunch?

Instead I said, "Thank you for the information."

"You are welcome. I think it is wonderful that you are still looking for him after so many years. I wish that I had a friend like you— someone who remembered me as much."

I smiled back, thinking of that moonless night, and said, "I am mending a broken promise."

"Would you like me to give him your address and phone number too?" the cousin asked. "I will be writing to him anyway."

"Sure, why not?" I gave her my business card.

And then I paid for lunch.

Twenty-three

Conclusion

Drifting clouds, emotions of a rootless child, sunset, the
love of an old friend.

—*Li Bai, eighth century*

November 1997. New York City.

I looked at my watch again. It was three o'clock
in the afternoon. I flipped through the television
channels. The heating was on high, just the way I liked it. I stood up
and walked over to the window: eighteen floors down, the traffic was
heavy but flowing on Park Avenue.

I walked back, sat down on the bed, flipped through the channels
again. I looked at my watch: five minutes past three.

How ironic, I thought, that I have waited so long to see Dong Yi
and, now that I was about to see him, I couldn't bear to wait another
minute.

It had been more than a year since I'd returned from China. During that time, on many occasions, I'd wanted to call Dong Yi. I had
taken the phone number out of the top drawer of my nightstand, only
to put it back again. For reasons I couldn't explain, I did not call. Many
times I sat on the edge of my bed wondering why he never contacted
me. Perhaps it had to do with my marrying Eimin. Perhaps it had
more to do with his own life, his daughter and his marriage. I wondered whether he would even want me to call now.

I was relieved to know that Dong Yi had left China safely and was working at one of the most famous labs in the world. I was happy for him and wondered whether I should intrude upon his happy life.

And then life became busy. Classes started in September, ended for Christmas and started again in January. When I was not teaching, I went to conferences, traveling to Central America and Europe. In September 1997, my sister, who had been working in Beijing for an American consulting firm, took a job in New York City, moving there with her husband who was just about to begin the MBA program at Columbia University.

A colleague of mine and I had finally, after a year's perseverance, persuaded a large bank in New York City to let us interview their employees for a research project. I was very excited about the opportunity, because it meant that I could then spend the weekend with my sister. When I got to my office the next morning, I called Dong Yi. I now had an excuse, for I would be near him for a few days.

An American picked up the phone. "Just a minute," he said and then I heard him calling, "Dong Yi, it's for you."

"Hello."

"Dong Yi?"

"Yes, that's me," he said with a heavy Chinese accent.

"It's Wei." I said in Chinese.

"How are you?" he exclaimed delightedly.

"Fine. And you?"

"Fine."

"Your cousin gave me your number."

"I know. She told me. But that was last year, wasn't it?"

"I have been busy. You know how things are." I felt embarrassed.

"Yes. I meant to call you too. My cousin sent me your business card. But it's been quite busy here at the lab." His voice was equally uncomfortable.

"Of course," I said. I wondered if he'd looked at my number as often as I'd looked at his—and not called. "So how are you?" I said.

"Well, busy. And you? You are a professor now and you've changed your name."

"Yes, I did that when I got married again. So what are you now? A professor or something?" I asked. I had no idea how physics labs worked.

"I am a senior researcher here," said Dong Yi. He sounded happy. I paused.

"Well, listen, I am coming to New York City for business. I was wondering whether we could meet?"

"When will that be?"

"In three weeks. I am coming in on Tuesday and the work will finish by noon on Thursday."

"Three weeks. Let me check. Yes, Thursday should be fine. I can drive up to Manhattan."

"That will be great. Are you sure it's not too far for you to drive?"

"No problem."

"It will be great to see you. It's been a long time," I said excitedly.

"Yes. It will be great. We will talk then."

"Yes, 'til then."

I gave him my hotel details and said good-bye.

I hung up the phone, smiled and then I went to get some coffee. I skipped down the hall and ran all the way down the stairs.

The phone rang. I reached over.

"Madam, your guest has arrived." The lady on the hotel reception desk had a seductively soft French accent.

"Please let him know I will be right down."

"Yes, madam."

I took my handbag, put on my coat, then stopped in front of the mirror. I ran my fingers through my hair, dusted some powder on my face and put on a new coat of lipstick. I took a final look in the mirror, was satisfied with what I saw and left the room.

It was almost a decade since I'd seen Dong Yi. During those years, he had lived a life among people I didn't know, while I was living with the youthful memory of him. I wondered what he remembered of me. I wondered if we would continue that conversation begun on a moonless night at Weiming Lake and cruelly interrupted. I wondered if there really was anything to continue.

In the lift, I could feel my heart beating as fast as a rabbit runs across a field. Again I looked in the mirror and rearranged my hair. And as I did so I wondered how Dong Yi looked now. And I wondered if he would recognize me right away.

There was no one else in the lobby but him.

First I saw the back of a beige, down parka, then I watched him walking over to the sofa, bending down to look at a copy of a Ming vase on the side table. Then he walked back to the large flower arrangement, and stood in the middle of the lobby.

"Dong Yi," I called out.

He turned around. Behind him the flowers were all the colors of the rainbow.

Dong Yi had aged. His hair was thinning, and had receded. There were bags under his eyes and lines on his face. He was smearing Chapstick on his lips, which had a few visible cracks.

"Wei, you look great." Dong Yi beamed at me, quickly putting away the Chapstick.

We shook hands. I did not know what to say. I suddenly realized that I had been expecting a different person, that the image I had in my mind was one that had been frozen in time, and because I had held onto that image for so long, it had become more real than the flesh and blood I was looking at now.

"Sorry about the delay. Got lost. All these one-way streets. Took a long time to get back." He spoke in the same shy manner I remembered.

"Where is your car? The valet can take it down to the garage."

"It's OK. Didn't know there was a garage here. Parked it in a garage on Sixty-Second Street."

"Are you hungry? I thought we'd have lunch together. Hope you haven't eaten." I felt the effort of trying to put us both at ease.

"No. Lunch is good."

"I don't know the area too well. My colleague and I have been to Vong, a very nice French-Thai place, but it's quite a few blocks away. Or we could go to the Japanese restaurant just across the road. Do you like sushi? If not, they also have noodle soups and a grill."

"Japanese is fine. I like sushi. Don't have it often, it's so expensive," he said, slightly embarrassed. I noticed that the sleeves of his parka were worn. Maybe life had not been easy for him. I knew that researchers were not paid high salaries, even in the most distinguished labs.

"I haven't been there so I don't know whether it's any good. But if you are not picky . . ."

"No. I am not picky," he assured me.

So we walked across the street. It was cold, and the wind was strong.

"It looks like it might snow soon," I said, looking at the gray sky.

The restaurant had large black panels, black tables and chairs and soft lighting. There were two other customers at a table not far from us.

"So, tell me, why didn't you write to me? Didn't you get my letters?" I asked. Dong Yi was looking at the menu.

"I went back to Beijing University in September. I got two letters from you. One was about your marriage and the other . . . I forget."

"They were the only two I wrote."

"I didn't write for a long time, not to you or anyone, I was quite down. But having my daughter was wonderful. She really cheered me up."

I looked at him.

"I did write to you when I arrived in Rochester," he said. "But I never heard back. I suppose you had moved on."

"I left Virginia after a year and, as I told you on the phone, I went to Carnegie Mellon for my PhD."

"I suppose I could have written to your mother for your address, I know I should have," said Dong Yi.

"It doesn't matter now," I said.

"It took the authorities at Beijing University a couple of months to decide that they couldn't really let me continue as a PhD student," said Dong Yi, after a pause. "They said I was too active in the Student Movement, so I went back to Shanxi."

"Did you at least get your master's degree?"

"Yes, I got that. My old professor at Shanxi University registered me as his PhD student, mostly to give me a place to hang my file. I helped with teaching some of his courses. It took almost two years for me to finally leave China."

The waiter brought Japanese green tea. I wrapped my hands around the delicate teacup and took a deep breath of the aroma, as much to give me a break from the awkwardness of our conversation as to enjoy the tea.

"What happened to Eimin and you?"

"We divorced, but the marriage fell apart a long time before that. I should have listened to you. Anyway, it didn't take long for me to realize that I had made a mistake, but it took a long time to correct it. He is married again, still lives in Virginia. I heard that they just had a child."

"Are you ready to order?" asked the waiter.

I looked at Dong Yi. He nodded.

When we'd ordered, Dong Yi leaned over the table toward me. "And your husband, is he American?"

"No. He is European. We met at graduate school."

"Are you happy?" asked Dong Yi abruptly, as if the conversation we'd just had was unimportant nonsense. I could see this was the one question he wanted to ask, the reason he had come to see me today.

Still, his inquiry caught me by surprise, so I just looked at him. He did not look away; he was serious. At that moment all my feelings from the past revived, flooding through my body, drowning me in such sorrow that I wanted to cry. Where were you when I needed you to ask the same question? I thought. What right do you have now to ask me about happiness?

"Yes. Very," I said, eventually. I have finally found someone to love, who loves me back.

And now that he had asked me, I couldn't see why I shouldn't ask him back. "What about you?" I said.

"I have two girls now. The younger one will be two soon. She was born here, so she is an American citizen," he spoke calmly.

"How is work?" I asked. I changed the subject because I did not want to push him. There was no need for that now. We had both endured enough.

"Fine. The pay is not high, but I do enjoy the work."

"How is Lan? What did she say when you told her that you were coming to see me?"

"She stays home for the girls. And no, I didn't tell her. I can't tell her. I can't actually mention your name at all."

"Why? It's been so many years."

"Well, you don't know Lan. I can't look at another woman for too long."

"You're joking."

"No. And it's all because of you. Not that it is your fault, I don't mean that. Whenever we fought about such things, she always brought the conversation back to you. I'd done it once, so why wouldn't I do it again?"

"Did you?"

"No."

Dong Yi seemed sad. I didn't know how to cheer him up. So I was happy when he decided to change the subject and said, "Did you know that Ning lives about thirty minutes from me?"

"No," I said, "I didn't."

I had lost touch with Ning some years earlier. I had just moved to Pittsburgh, and was trying to sort out the mess that was my life when he got married and disappeared into his own domestic world.

"He took a job with Allied Signal last year. He's got a son."

"Do you see him often?"

"No. In fact we don't have much to talk about anymore. He never talks about the past, I don't know why. We can't talk about his work either—he says it's not professional."

"What does he do?"

"He is an engineer."

"Why can't he talk about it, it's not as if he works for the CIA?"

"I feel that I don't understand him anymore," said Dong Yi sadly.

"Since we left China, the past is all that connects us," I said. "Remember the trips we took in the Purple Bamboo Garden? To me, the years we shared at Beijing University were some of the most wonderful in my life."

"I am glad that you still think so. Out where I am, not just Ning, but a lot of people seem to want to cut themselves free from the past. You are supposed to only look forward, and fit in."

We ate the last two California rolls, and shared impressions of our return visits to China, and then Dong Yi said suddenly, "Oh, Liu Gang is also here."

"What do you mean here?"

"He is in New York City, getting a master's degree."

"But I thought he was in prison."

"He was. He was released for medical treatment last year. But he escaped."

"How do you mean, escaped?"

"Through the underground. Apparently it is still operating."

We both smiled.

"How is he?"

"He's recovered all right. He suffered a lot in prison, as you can imagine."

Dong Yi was much more relaxed now. So was I. I was glad that he had asked that question about my happiness. And I was glad that I had answered as I had. And now I felt that we had broken the ice and found, with delight, that beneath it warm water flowed. I looked at this man sitting in front of me, looking years older than he actually was, and in many ways unrecognizable. But I still felt the closest connection with him, his mind and his emotions. I was glad that the bond between us was not broken, that it could still exist in a different form, that we could be friends.

"Let's get out of here," I said. "You don't have to go back right away, do you?"

Dong Yi looked at his watch. "No, I've time."

"Let's go to Central Park," I said.

I waved at the waiter for the bill.

"It's on me. No. Put your money away," I said.

Dong Yi looked embarrassed. "I can afford my own lunch, you know."

"I know you can, but I'd like to pay," I said. "Why don't you get the coffee? We'll stop by Starbucks on our way."

Dong Yi smiled. I paid and we left the restaurant.

Twenty minutes later, we were walking down Fifth Avenue with two Starbucks cups in our hands. I had put on my big faux-fur hat, and the smell of snow lingered in the air. It was about five o'clock in the evening. Outside Bergdorf Goodman, a volunteer was ringing bells, collecting for the Salvation Army. Across the street, FAO Schwarz had already been decorated for Christmas, oversized toys moved in the windows. Streams of shoppers were entering and leaving with large bags. It seemed that Christmas shopping came earlier and earlier every year.

Taxis and limousines were pulling up at the Plaza Hotel. Tourists, businessmen in dark suits and ladies wrapped in Fendi fur and wearing Manolo Blahnik stilettos stepped out.

"Want a carriage ride? Very romantic," asked the driver of one of the horse carriages outside the park.

"No, thank you," I said. It was too late for romance, but fortunately not for a long and lasting friendship.

We entered Central Park. The smell of onions from the hotdog stand was delicious even after the big meal we'd just eaten.

We paid three dollars each and went into the zoo. The zoo was very small and there wasn't much to see, so we came out pretty quickly.

"Do you come here sometimes? I bet the kids would love it."

"No. We don't come up much. If we do, we go to Chinatown."

In the distance, Christmas music was being played. Tiny snow flurries began floating down slowly and gracefully from the sky.

"Did you ever think that one day we'd be walking here?"

"No," answered Dong Yi.

"Neither did I."

We passed the Boathouse, and the Great Lawn and went up the hill. And there it was, the lake looking like a mirror lying at the bottom of a crystal glass as the lights of the skyscrapers shone brilliantly around us, high in the sky.

"Isn't this a beautiful place?" I said, and I turned to Dong Yi, and smiled.

Epilogue

The number of dead and wounded in the Tiananmen Massacre has long been disputed. The Chinese government's official tally put the number of dead at 241, including thirty-six students, among whom only three were from Beijing University. The official tally also stated that over 7,000 people were wounded. The *Associated Press* reported in 1999 that according to foreign journalists who had visited hospitals and residents of Beijing, at least one thousand people died on that day. The same report also cited Chinese Red Cross officials as estimating the death toll to be 3,600. The *Agence France-Presse* filed a report from Taiwan on the tenth anniversary of the massacre stating that newly declassified U.S. information suggested that 2,600 people were killed on 4 June. The sad fact is that we will probably never know the truth—not only because it is difficult to verify official estimates in China, but also because many journalists and foreign independent organizations have been blocked from investigating what really happened. It is becoming more difficult as years go by as the people involved and their families are reluctant to identify themselves.

I keep in touch with Dong Yi and saw him last in 2005 in London. I am glad to have him back in my life. Today Dong Yi is a successful physicist and lives with his family in New Jersey.

Eimin is remarried and lives with his family in Virginia.

Ning is an engineer and lives with his family in New Jersey.

My friend Li is now the Director of Psychiatric and Consoling at Beijing University Hospital. She lives with her family in Beijing.

Chen Li was not given a job when he graduated from Beijing University. The last I heard of him was that he had moved back to live with his parents in Dong Bei, China. In a country where disabled people are frowned upon and millions are unemployed, I can only imagine that Chen Li's life must be difficult.

Chai Ling has become a successful Internet entrepreneur. She lives in Boston.

Liu Gang is a telecom engineer living with his family in Denver.

Professor Fang Lizhi became a professor at University of Arizona after escaping China in 1991. He remains there today.

Hanna and Jerry divorced in 1992. Hanna now lives in San Francisco.

Cao Gu Run is a scholar at the Chinese Academy of Science, and lives with his family in Beijing.

Yang Tao is now a father and successful diplomat. I was told that he had given my name to his daughter. It took him until 1999 finally to return my diaries.

My father is retired. He still lives in the same apartment in Beijing.

My mother died of cancer in April 2005.

My sister, Xiao Jie, is remarried. She and her husband live and work in Beijing.

I am now a full-time writer and live with my family in London.

Acknowledgments

I thank John Saddler and Humphrey Price for their help in shaping the book, and my editors Heather Holden-Brown and Lorraine Jerram at Hodder Headline UK.

I thank Toby Eady, Jennifer Joel and my editor, Marysue Rucci, at Simon & Schuster U.S.

About the Author

Diane Weil Liang was born in Beijing and spent part of her childhood with her parents in a labor camp in a remote region in China. In 1989 she took part in a Student Democracy Movement and prostested in Tiananmen Square. A graduate of Peking University and a former professor in the U.S. and UK, she now lives in London with her husband and their two children. Diane's novels have been translated into over twenty languages.